Web Service Implementation and Composition Techniques

Hye-young Paik · Angel Lagares Lemos
Moshe Chai Barukh · Boualem Benatallah
Aarthi Natarajan

Web Service Implementation and Composition Techniques

Springer

Hye-young Paik
University of New South Wales
Sydney
Australia

Boualem Benatallah
University of New South Wales
Sydney
Australia

Angel Lagares Lemos
University of New South Wales
Sydney
Australia

Aarthi Natarajan
University of New South Wales
Sydney
Australia

Moshe Chai Barukh
University of New South Wales
Sydney
Australia

ISBN 978-3-319-85689-6   ISBN 978-3-319-55542-3   (eBook)
DOI 10.1007/978-3-319-55542-3

Printed on acid-free paper

This Springer imprint is published by Springer Nature
The registered company is Springer International Publishing AG
The registered company address is: Gewerbestrasse 11, 6330 Cham, Switzerland

Preface

Web-accessible services, referred to as Web services, are an integral part of modern information technology, from mobile devices to cloud- and crowd-computing. The Internet of Things (IoT), Big Data, Web 2.0, and social networks all rely on Web-based interfaces to allow connectivity over distributed components, thereby enabling us to deliver innovative and disruptive solutions in every industry in the global market. Long gone are the days when developers had to code each specific service—which often was a highly tedious, manual, and time-consuming task. Instead, Web services are driving the rapid creation of software. Today, with a few lines of code, you can tap into some remarkable resources, whether it is a payment network like MasterCard, a mapping service like ESRI or the machine learning engine that powers IBM's Watson [31].

Web services are created by businesses to empower businesses. This has also been the motivating theme behind some of the major worldwide hackathons, such as *TechCrunch's Disrupt Hackathon*, as well as the joint *NASA-IBM Space App Hackathon*. They all had one endeavor in common: People were not just creating simple applications, but they were stringing together multiple software components and services from which they were pulling data, communicating with the cloud, sending SMS messages, displaying the data on a map, and taking a credit card payment. All of this is made possible by Web services that with a few lines of code enable programmers to tap into a world of services.

At the same time, it is not always simple to make Web services work, and sometimes, developers have to bend the tool to their will [31]. Moreover, maintaining user retention also becomes a major challenge, since 95% of users abandon an app within 30 days, and around 50% within 24 hours [18]. In the mobile industry alone, start-ups often have to face 1.5 million app competitors.

Competing for success will thus strongly involve studying and mastering skills in engineering and utilizing Web services. Accordingly, this book embarks on a mission to dissect, unravel, and demystify the concepts of Web services, including its implementation and composition techniques.

In fact, this will mean different things to different stakeholders. We believe modern Web success will depend on stakeholders, such as business owners and service providers who will need to think carefully about methodological Web services design; the applicability, accuracy, and accessibility of their data; and how this ties back to their business value. Amazon.com is prime example of enduring success, arguably unmatched in any industry [22]. In particular, the fundamental lesson to learn is "creating services that expose business value to other developers who may create the remainder of the solution" [22], while on the other side of the spectrum, other stakeholders such as businesses and developers will focus primarily on reusing existing Web services to create value. Tools such as *IFTTT* [19] have been at the forefront to enable this, and similarly, *StamPlay* [29] does the same for backend development via the browsing of its visual interface to select and configure the right modules.

Accordingly, we have written this book with a broad range of stakeholders in mind. This book provides an overview of the fundamentals of Web services implementation standards and strategies (the former half of this book), while also presenting composition techniques for leveraging existing services to build larger services (the latter half). In addition, its unique value to readers is in its presentation of topics with a sound *overview* of concepts at the onset, followed by a well-targeted technical discussion that is subsequently linked to practical exercises for hands-on learning. We deviate from existing literature in the field, much of which is seemingly disjointed; or focused on a particular context or technology such as a specific implementation language; or highly academic, conceptual, or abstract in nature.

Online Material: Github Site

Complementary to each chapter are practical exercises uploaded and arranged by laboratory section in Github. The address for the website is:

https://github.com/SOA-Book

The software packages used in the exercises are commonly used in many Web development projects; we therefore trust that most readers who are already familiar with basic Web application development would find it easy to load and get started. However, should any issues arise in following the provided instructions when setting up on their own computer, we encourage readers to refer to the included FAQs.

Chapters Overview

In Chap. 1, we begin by understanding the *service-oriented architecture (SOA)* paradigm—the key values and goals SOA endows upon modern and evolving business ecosystems. We present the fundamental notion of a "service" and describe the *SOA architectural stack* in reference to software application integration layers. We then present a prelude to the main realization techniques for SOA. This is followed by an introduction to service composition and data flow techniques, including end-user mashups. This chapter also presents the overall goals, structure, and organization of the rest of this book. Preliminary practical exercise is also provided, mostly related to environment setup, which is required to fulfill the other hands-on exercises found in this book.

In Chap. 2, SOAP and WSDL are explained as important standards that lay the foundation for standardized descriptions of messages and operations of a Web service. We will first describe the core elements of SOAP and WSDL standards with examples and then present how the two standards are fit together to form the common message communication styles, namely RPC and Document. This chapter concludes with a practical exercise covering activities that build a simple Web service and its client application.

In Chap. 3, an alternate view of Web service implementation technique named REST is introduced. Unlike SOAP and WSDL which clearly define standardized protocols and communication formats between services, REST contains a set of generic Web service design principles and guidelines that can be interpreted and implemented differently. In this chapter, we present the fundamentals of the said principles, explaining the core properties that make a service "RESTful." We also discuss how to design a REST Web service and a few basic steps to follow to create a good REST API. As an exercise, we include activities to build a full REST-based service with all READ/UPDATE operations and its client application.

In Chap. 4, we explore the concept of data services, where the main purpose of the service implementation is to provide uniform access to heterogeneous data. This view of a Web service is different from that of SOAP or REST-based services in that the focus is not necessarily on the functional or application logic of remote software. After clarifications of the main concepts, we introduce key enabling technologies for building data services, namely XSLT and XQuery. These two XML-based languages are used to transform and query potentially heterogeneous data into a well-understood standard XML. The laboratory exercises included at the end of this chapter will guide you to learn the basic syntax and usage scenarios of XSLT and XQuery.

In Chap. 5, we introduce the motivation behind Web service composition technologies—going from an atomic to a composite service. In doing so, we discuss the two main paradigms of multiple service interactions: Web service orchestration and Web service choreography. In the rest of the book, we will focus on Web service orchestration as the main paradigm behind Web service composition techniques.

In Chap. 6, we present BPEL and BPMN as two main languages of Web service composition. Both BPEL and BPMN allow the codification of control flow logic of a composite service. We will introduce the core syntax elements of the two languages and their usage examples. The laboratory activities will show how to build a simple BPEL service by composing other services to implement a home loan processing scenario.

In Chap. 7, we examine the data flow aspects of Web service composition. The data flow of a service composition specifies how data are exchanged between services. The data flow description encapsulates the data movement from one service to another and the transformations applied on this data. We introduce two different paradigms based on the message passing style, namely blackboard and explicit data flow. We conclude the chapter with a discussion of mashup applications as a way to implement data flow-oriented service composition.

In Chap. 8, we introduce a framework known as Service Component Architecture (SCA) that provides a technology-agnostic capability for composing applications from distributed services. Building a successful SOA solution in practice can be complex. This is due to the significant lack of standards and specifications, as well as the fact that typical business computing environments contain many different technologies and integrating these technologies is complex. This chapter explores techniques for adopting a consensus on how to describe an assembly of services, as well as on how to implement and access them—regardless of the technology.

Finally, in Chap. 9, we provide concluding remarks offering readers our perspective for continued exploration in the field of service-oriented computing.

Who is This Book for?

In writing this book, we have considered a wide range of audience interested in the space of Web services implementation and composition techniques. We have tried to cover topics of interest relevant to academics (professors, researchers, and research students), professionals (managers, full-stack developers, and software engineers), and practitioners with regard to understanding and employing service-oriented methods and strategies, to both gain insight into the field and apply this knowledge to real-world endeavors. This book is a comprehensive textbook on Web services implementation and composition and therefore could be a useful reference for academics, professionals, and practitioners.

To Professors. You will find this book useful for a variety of courses, from an undergraduate course in Web services foundational technology up through a graduate course in complex Web services composition. We have provided considerably more material than can fit in a typical one-term course; therefore, you can think of the book as a comprehensive guide from which you can pick and choose the material that best supports the course you wish to teach. Moreover, we hope the practical components of the book and the accompanying Web site will be used as a springboard for creating a suite of various online materials (which could be customized for specific courses) and in turn for helping to further support the learning activities on the topics.

To Research Students and Researchers. We hope that this textbook provides you with an enjoyable introduction to the field of Web services and composition. We have attempted to provide a top-down approach, whereby we begin by presenting an overview of the broad concepts, and then systematically present the requisite technical details. In particular, we have combined the technical content found in each chapter with practical exercises. These exercises are designed to be self-guided and provide a good starting point for many Web service building projects.

To Professionals and Practitioners. We believe professional practitioners are often left overwhelmed by the plethora of online resources available about many of the topics presented in this book. We have noticed that much of the information available is disjointed or focused on a particular context or technology, such as a specific implementation language. Other material is highly academic and therefore conceptual or abstract. In this book, we believe we have developed a well-informed view on how to synthesize the concepts in the conventional Web services and "newer" breeds of Web services—to understand the differences and commonalities, and where the concepts should be placed in modern software systems. We trust our book will be used by practitioners as a handbook for revising foundational concepts, while also serving as a practical utility.

Sydney, Australia   Hye-young Paik
                                                                                   Angel Lagares Lemos
                                                                                   Moshe Chai Barukh
                                                                                   Boualem Benatallah
                                                                                   Aarthi Natarajan

Contents

Chapter 1
Introduction to Service Oriented Architecture

Service Oriented Architecture (SOA) is an architectural approach to viewing and creating a business solution as a network of modular components, each component implementing a discrete business function. These components are called *services* and can be distributed across geography, enterprises, and disparate IT systems and can be reconfigured into new business processes as needed. These services are built on open standards and loosely coupled, allowing them to be easily combined both within and across enterprises to create new business processes

1.1 The Service Oriented Architecture Paradigm

Modern IT infrastructures are inherently heterogeneous across application infrastructures. The push toward business automation and the requirement for more reliable executions has generated the need for *integrating* various available applications. However, enterprises are challenged with integrating silos of information and products from multiple vendors and across different platforms. This proves very difficult but enterprises cannot afford to simply take a single-vendor approach to IT, as application suites and supporting infrastructure would be very inflexible for the purpose of organization-specific customizations.

Business organizations need to think about interoperability. They are under increasing pressure to respond to business changes with agility, align business processes with the current market and respond quickly to competitive pressures. Globalization, for instance, is an important factor, as it leads to fierce competition. In turn, this enforces shortened product cycles, as companies look to gain advantage over their competition. Customer needs and requirements change more quickly driven by competitive offerings and the wealth of product information available over the Internet, [14]. Inevitably, the cycle of competition and ongoing improvements in products and services further accelerates. An enterprise must thus rapidly adapt to survive, let alone to succeed in today's dynamic competitive environment, and the IT infrastructure must enable businesses' ability to adapt, [14].

© Springer International Publishing AG 2017
H.-y. Paik et al., *Web Service Implementation and Composition Techniques*,
DOI 10.1007/978-3-319-55542-3_1

As a result, business organizations have evolved from the vertical, isolated business divisions to the horizontal business-process-focused structures - and more recently, towards an "ecosystem" paradigm. We illustrate this in Fig. 1.1. Business services now need to be managed and available as distributed components, with a focus on the extended supply chain, in order to enable customer and partner access to business services.

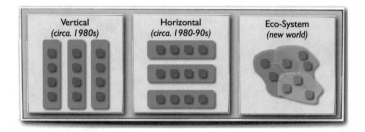

Fig. 1.1 The evolution of typical business architectures

To achieve these goals, organizations need to make their business processes automated, more open and interoperable. SOA is a business-centric, IT architectural approach proposed to address the above goals, through designing business solutions as linked services based on open standards.

1.1.1 Goals of Service Orientation

Service Orientation has brought a fundamental shift in the way in which distributed applications are implemented. Yet, enterprises have been very keen to adopt a service oriented platform and embrace all the changes that accompany this transition. It is important to understand why organisations are ready to make this change. This is because of its ambitious goals and the resulting benefits that service orientation promises to deliver to these enterprises. Thomas Erl has aptly identified seven strategic goals of service orientation, illustrated in Fig. 1.2, which can be further grouped into two categories: seven strategic goals and a subset of them constituted by three resulting strategic benefits.

Increased Intrinsic Interoperability

Interoperability refers to the seamless exchange of information between disparate services. SOA enables application silos to be manifested as reusable services that collaborate using a common technology foundation, and thereby to be easily composed

Fig. 1.2 Goals of SOA. *Source* [15]

into new business solutions. Realization of interoperability will break down the exist-ing application and technology barriers in IT systems.

Increased Federation

An important goal of SOA is to increase a federative perspective of an enterprise where resources and applications are united while maintaining their individual auton-omy. To accomplish this, there must be a wider adoption of standards across business unit boundaries, across department-specific service domains. This will result in an enterprise-wide deployment of consistent and composable services. Ultimately, this leads to an environment where enterprise-wide solution logic becomes naturally harmonized, regardless of the underlying implementation.

Increased Vendor Diversification

Vendor diversification refers to the flexibility with which an enterprise can pick the *best-of-breed* vendor products for its solution implementations. It is not necessarily beneficial to have diverse products, but it is vital that an enterprise be in a state in which it can easily replace solution implementations and technology resources without disrupting the overall federated service architecture. SOA helps to preserve this state, and thereby assists in prolonging the life span of automation solutions, enabling consistent inter-service communication and provide an overall increased return on investment.

Increased Business and Technology Domain Alignment

Traditionally, applications have been designed to fulfill immediate functional requirements. However, SOA promotes a business-centric architecture where each IT investment is viewed as a strategic business decision. Services encapsulate business functions and business process models drive the composition of services. Furthermore, as services are designed to be intrinsically interoperable, as new business processes evolve, services can be reconfigured into new compositions to reflect the changed business conditions. Both business and technology specialists work together effectively in the service analysis phase, so that services are aligned to specific business concepts.

Fig. 1.3   Traditional IT vs SOA. *Source* [30]

Increased Return On Investment (ROI)

Measuring the ROI of automated solutions is a critical factor in determining how cost-effective a given solution or system actually is. The ROI in SOA is measured in years rather than months. The return on up-front initial investment in people, processes, resources and training is realized when newer business processes that capitalize on market opportunities are realized through reuse of existing services. SOA advocates building reusable, composable agnostic services, and as more services are delivered with these characteristics, increasing ROI is achieved, as each IT asset is positioned as a reusable asset that finds itself being repurposed multiple times to automate new business processes.

Increased Organization Agility

Organization agility means adapting rapidly and cost efficiently in response to changes in the market and business environment. SOA is geared towards promoting agility, allowing organizations to deliver value without building completely new systems from scratch. SOA moves away from the traditional application-centric approach to a service-centric state. It does this through enterprise-wide provisioning of service oriented business solutions, composed from highly standardized, reusable services that are agnostic to any particular business process.

1.1.2   What Is a Service?

The fundamental unit of a Service Oriented solution is a *service*. A service is a self-contained, self-describing and modular piece of software that performs a specific business function such as validating a credit card or generating an invoice. The term self-contained implies services include all that is needed to get them working. Self-describing means they have *interfaces* that describe their business functionalities. Modular means services can be aggregated to form more complex applications.

Services are defined to be standards-based, and platform- and protocol-independent in order to address interactions in heterogeneous environments, [2, 26]. A single service provides a collection of capabilities, often grouped together within a functional context as established by business requirements. For example, the functional context of the service below is *account*. Therefore, this service provides the set of operations associated with a customer's account.

Account
•   Balance
•   Withdraw
•   Deposit

Fig. 1.4 Account service

More generally, services in SOA may take one or more of the following three roles: (i) service-provider, (ii) service-requester, and (iii) service-broker, (refer to Fig. 1.5a). The service-provider publishes a description of the service using a service-broker. The service-requester can then find a provider via the broker. The service-provider then binds to the requester to begin an interaction. However, service-requesters and providers can also be made known to each other by other means, such as via human referral. Services may be combined to build coarser-grained services, referred to as composite services as mentioned earlier, (refer to Fig. 1.5b). In this case, such a service plays two roles at the same time: it acts as a service-requester for the services that it consumes, and also as a service-provider offering the aggregated functionalities of other component services.

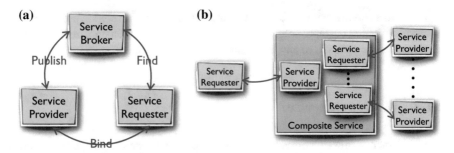

Fig. 1.5 Service roles and interaction in the Service Oriented Architecture (SOA)

Service Interface

Services are expected to express their functional capabilities, service-level agreements (SLAs) and policy constraints through contracts. Service capabilities are invoked by sending requests to service endpoints that conform to a specific contract. A service endpoint is an address, a URI or a specific place where the service can be found and consumed. Services could be implemented with different technologies such as Java, C++, and BPEL, but the service interface helps to decouple the underlying service implementation from the interface definition and hides the implementation of the service from the service consumer.

1.1.3   The SOA Architectural Stack

Software Application Integration

Software application integration is important in two typical types of scenarios: Firstly, when integrating internal systems of each enterprise (referred to as *"Enterprise Application Integration" (EAI)*); and secondly, in the integration with external entities (referred to as *"Business-to-Business integration" (B2Bi)*), [32, 33]. More specifically, in the case of the former, we may need to integrate data and applications related to various systems. For example, if a particular system implements the procurement and sales of a supermarket chain, the business may need to maintain a database for storing procurement data and a database for storing inventory and sales data. It may also need a data-warehouse for storing historical sales transactions that collects and integrates data from these two data sources. In the case of the latter, each of the businesses may also implement an overall business process for fulfilling its business objectives, and sometimes it becomes relevant (or desired for enhancing productivity and reducing duplication) to connect two or more systems together.

However, achieving the above poses significant challenges; often best understood with respect to the various "integration layers" inherent in an application, [2, 3]. Typically, the structuring of these layers goes from lower-level layers (which are needed by most or all interactions) to higher layers (which build on top of the lower layers and may or may not be needed depending on the application). We identify the following relevant layers (as illustrated in Fig. 1.6):

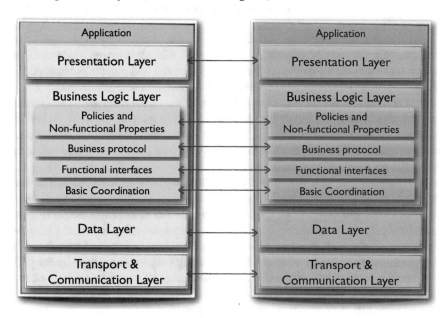

Fig. 1.6 Software application integration layers

Transport and Communication Layer. The first step for any application is to be able to interact with others by exchanging information; *transport* thus refers to the sending and receiving of request and response messages between one application (the producer) and another (the consumer). This is mainly achieved through the definition of an agreed-upon *communication protocol*, which is the mechanism by which the provider and consumer communicate the request and response messages, irrespective of the syntax and semantic of the information content. Other than HTTP, other examples include *IIOP in CORBA* and *VAN in EDI* standards, [23].

Data Layer. At this layer, integration should involve seamlessly understanding the content of data (documents and messages) that are exchanged. The challenges at this layer occur in the syntax, structure and semantics of the data elements in the exchanged information, [3]. The general method to overcome the challenges is via mediators and languages (e.g., ETL) for transformation and mapping in order to convert data from one format to another, albeit, in general, this area still requires further advancement, as while there has been some progress to help facilitate data-level interoperation, users still play a major role in identifying the mismatches and developing their mappings and transformations, [36].

Business Logic Layer. Integration at this layer refers to connecting and combing the "logic" of one or more applications in order for them to work together. Applications define interfaces (i.e. APIs) as well as behavioral and non-functional constraints. Integration at this layer can be divided into the following sub-layers, [3]:

(i) Basic coordination is concerned with the requirements and properties related to the exchange of a set of messages amongst two or more partners, for example, two applications coordinating to provide atomicity based on two-phase commit; federated security management specifications; etc.;

(ii) Functional interfaces are in relation to the interface that the application declares (e.g., the set of operations or messages that are supported). Integration at this layer may thus involve finding correspondences and mappings between the signatures of operations of two different applications to be integrated;

(iii) Business protocol gives the definition of the allowed operation invocation (or message exchange) sequences. For instance, this may be relevant as heterogeneities between applications can arise due to different message ordering constraints, or due to messages that one service expects (or sends) but that the interacting partner is not prepared to send (or receive);

(iv) Policies and non-functional properties may also be included in the definition of an application. This includes policies (e.g., privacy policies) and other non-functional properties (e.g., QoS descriptions such as response times) that are useful for partners for deciding whether or not they are willing to interact with the application. From an integration perspective, the challenges involve two categories: the syntax, semantics and structure for expressing policies (e.g., two similar policies could be interpreted differently), and differences between the policies of two applications (e.g., offered/expected quality of service, response time, etc.). Resolution of mismatches of this type may require negotiation and agreements between applications.

Presentation Layer. At this layer, integration refers to constructing applications by combining components at the graphical user interface (GUI) level. GUI-level integration often fosters a higher level of abstraction, where graphical representations of components are composed to build a new application. The integration-related challenges at this layer include the definition of a language and model for representation of components so that the integration may be facilitated, [11].

SOA Interoperability Layers: The *"Services-stack"*

Prior to the service-oriented paradigm, as we mentioned earlier, the various different methods and technologies for performing software application integration inevitably led to loosely coupled, potentially heterogeneous, and autonomous systems, [2, 7, 26]. SOA was therefore introduced in order to provide a platform- and protocol-independent approach to meet integration challenges. It achieved this by enabling "software applications" to be packaged as "services" that can be described, discovered and reused, [2, 26].

A service may thus be considered *"an executable unit of code that provides physical black-box encapsulation"* [1]; however services also need to *"be connected ... [and] communicate with each other"* [12], as well as ideally be "accessed from any platform using any technology and programming knowledge", [13, 25]. By intent, therefore, service-based technologies are not implemented in a monolithic manner, but rather represent a collection of several related technologies - generally referred to as the "services-stack" [14, 25], as illustrated in Fig. 1.7. Moreover, since "services" essentially resemble a "software application", it comes as no surprise that the layers in the services-stack very closely mimic the software "integration layers" that we identified earlier.

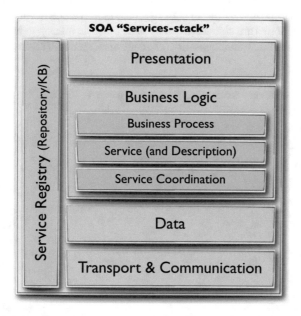

Fig. 1.7   SOA Interoperability Layers – The *"services-stack"*

SOA Realization Technologies

There are currently at least three prominent Web-based service-implementation categories that realize the SOA paradigm. We briefly delineate this below, and also illustrate the various techniques (including popular technologies and tools implemented) in Fig. 1.8.

- **WS-* family.** The WS in *WS-* family* stands for "Web Services", and is often considered the "first-generation" implementation technology to realise SOA. The goal was to introduce various open-standard specifications and protocols for all relevant layers of interoperability. The "WS-* specifications" thus refer to a group of standards proposed by industrial software vendors that develop specifications in an incremental and modular manner: specifications are introduced in a bottom-up

fashion where the basic building blocks are simple, horizontal specifications, [3].
The stack is gradually extended, with specifications at higher levels of abstraction
built on top of more foundational ones. We therefore generally find well-accepted
standards for (almost) all layers of the services-stack.

- **RESTful services.** REST is an architectural style that identifies how resources
  in a network, and specially the Web, are defined, addressed and accessed. It
  also defines a set of architectural *constraints*, such as: stateful resources, stateless interactions, global identification of unique resources, uniform interfaces and
  multiple resource representations. In this manner, REST aims to guarantee the
  scalability of the interaction between architectural components, the uniformity
  of the interfaces between such components, and its independent evolution, [17].
  It thereby also promotes the design of *"resource"*-oriented architectures, [34].
  These architectures are characterized by their intrinsic interoperability, loose coupling, high scalability and flexibility. The central element, therefore, in REST is the

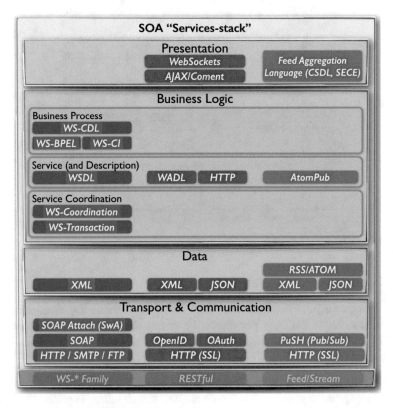

Fig. 1.8 Comparison of SOA realization technologies

"resource", consisting of server-side conceptual entities that can be globally addressed and referenced through URIs and whose state is passed to clients through representations encoded in various media types, [27].

- *Feed/Stream Services.* With the increasing number of data sources available as services, *Feed (or Stream) Services* represent a specialized breed of services, proposed as an extension to RESTful services. Feeds initially started as a way of representing machine-readable updates on websites, often for news sites or blogs. However, more recently, as Internet users spend billions of minutes per month on Web 2.0 and other user-contributed and social websites, [28], extremely challenging data-management challenges have emerged for coping with the large volumes of users and content. For example, at present *Facebook* claims over 1.3 billion active users per month (as of January 2014), each with an average of 130 friends, [6]. *Yahoo!* has over 650 million unique users, and allows users to import their Facebook connections and to follow this extended collection of connections. These sites thus generate extremely high volumes of feeds, whilst also needing to cope with high feed query rates across their consumers, [28].

Additionally, feed-based technology has also been identified as ideal for highly scalable[1] event-driven architectures, [34]. Moreover, specialized events such as time-, calendar-, location-, and device-based events can be encoded as feeds, thus allowing us to combine communication, calendaring, location as well as devices in the physical world [5] in order to build more powerful systems, with also the potential for system-to-system interactions, [34].

1.2   Service Composition and Data-Flow

The power to *compose* independent services into coarser-grain services presents immense value that further promotes productivity and reusability. Independently, services are used to wrap existing applications as well as to develop new applications. As illustrated in Fig. 1.9, these services are called *component services* (e.g., Loan Approval), which in turn, may then be composed to form *composite services* (e.g., Customer Banking Management), [4, 13]. These types of services (both, single and component) coexist along with other systems in the *resource layer* to implement the business process.

Services are therefore expected to be effective composition members, part of a richer, complex composite service. However, a service does not present much reuse potential if it is unable to be effectively assembled into a composition in an effective fashion. An important prerequisite to any composition approach is *data-flow*.

---

[1]However, feed-based solutions (like any Web-based system) trade scalability for latency, not making it appropriate for very low-latency notifications. Although, if these latency requirements could be relaxed to where seconds, or, better still, minutes or hours pass between events being produced and consumed, this solution could work very well.

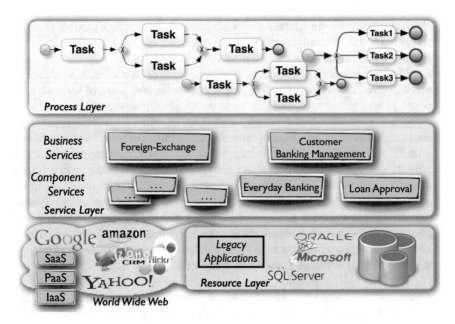

Fig. 1.9 Typical service- and process-oriented enterprise stack: Web services play a core role in application development and integration

Accordingly, we preface our discussion with a discussion of data-flow techniques followed by a summarization of various composition approaches.

1.2.1   Data-Flow Paradigms

Data-flow in service composition specifies how data is exchanged between services. More specifically, it describes the actions performed on an output message, or data element of a previously consumed service that is then transferred to the input of a later executed service. The data-flow description encapsulates the data movement from one service to another and the transformations applied on this data. Broadly, there are two different paradigms based on the message passing style, namely, *blackboard* and *explicit* data-flow [15, 20].

Blackboard

The blackboard paradigm is based on storing data centrally: every process instance has a set of variables, which are used as sources and targets of each Web-service activity and are commonly shared by all the services; hence the use of the term blackboard. The blackboard is the imaginary place where all services read their inputs from and write their outputs to. The main implication of using the blackboard paradigm is value overwriting: if a service generates a value of a variable different from the value previously generated by another service, the value will be overwritten and the last one will be the only one active and stored. The concept is similar to how conventional programming languages such as Java or C handle data. Several Web service composition languages also follow this paradigm, among them Web Service Business Process Execution Language (WS-BPEL).

Explicit Data-Flow

The explicit data-flow paradigm makes data flow a fully and clearly defined part of the composition. It does this by specifying the data flow between different services by means of data connectors. A data connector describes how data is manipulated and routed to or from Web services. Unlike the blackboard paradigm, data is not overwritten: two services can generate the same variable as an output, and a third service can be designed to gather the value from one or the other by using a data connector. This paradigm is commonly used by data-centric systems which require simple control flow. Due to the data-centric approach of Web 2.0 (intensified in the Semantic Web), the Web composition languages designed for that environment (i.e., Mashup tools) principally follow the explicit data-flow paradigm [35].

1.2.2   Composition Techniques

The basic ingredients of any composite application are the software components. These encapsulate functionality or a user interface (UI) which can be reused, and provide a set of operations, which allow one to programmatically interact with the encapsulated functionality or UI. In the context of services, typical examples may be SOAP and RESTful Web services (e.g., for credit card payments), although they may also include RSS and Atom feeds (as provided by most online newspapers today), and even W3C widgets (e.g., to plot a map on a Web page).

Composition includes a number of dimensions, such as: language (e.g., notation: textual, visual or hybrid); degree of automation (e.g., for data-flow and transformation); tool support; execution platform; and target users.

At present, BPEL is the most widely accepted service composition language, although, more recently lighter-weight alternatives have been produced, such as Bite [9], specifically designed for RESTful environments. Similarly, IBM's Sharable Code platform [21] follows a different strategy for the composition of REST or SOAP services: a domain-specific programming language from which Ruby on Rails application code is generated, also comprising user interfaces for the Web.

1.2.3 End-User Mashups

However, all these approaches focus on the application and data layers; they do not focus on UI or simplification techniques. Moreover, most conventional service composition languages are targeted at skilled IT professionals as opposed to end-users and less technical domain experts.

To enable more rapid and light development of new services, *Mashup* technology has typically provided easy-to-use graphical user interfaces and extensible sets of components to develop composite applications. For instance, Yahoo! Pipes[2] focuses on data services integration via RSS or Atom feeds, based on simple data-flow composition language. JackBe Presto[3] adopts a Pipes-like approach for data mashups and allows a portal-like aggregation of UI widgets (mashlets) visualizing the output of such mashups. IBM QEDWiki[4] provides a wiki-based (collaborative) mechanism to glue together JavaScript- or PHP-based widgets. Nonetheless, mashup development overall is still an adhoc and time-consuming process, requiring advanced programming skills (e.g., wrapping Web services, extracting contents from websites, interpreting third-party JavaScript code, etc).

1.3 Goals, Structure and Organization

Service Orientation is a design paradigm characterized by a distinct set of design principles. A *Service Oriented Architecture* (SOA) is an architectural style governed by these principles, and *Service Oriented Computing* revolves around applying a Service Oriented Architecture (SOA) to design and deliver a Service Oriented solution. Figure 1.10 summarizes and clearly shows the relationship between the various elements of a service-oriented platform.

The goal of this book is to: introduce the various different approaches to implementing Web services. Throughout the chapters of this book we also blend our technical discussion with practical hands-on exercises to enable potential readers to consolidate their understanding. In particular, this book is organized as follows: In Chap. 2, SOAP and WSDL are explained as important standards that lay the foundation for standardized descriptions of messages and operations of a Web service. In Chap. 3 WSDL is presented as an alternate view of Web service implementation technique named REST. In Chap. 4, we then explore the concept of data services, where the main purpose of the service implementation is to provide uniform access to heterogeneous data. In the later chapters, we then learn how to compose Web services to build bigger, complicated services. In Chap. 5, we introduce the motivation behind Web service composition technologies – going from an atomic to a composite service. In Chapter 6, we present BPEL and BPMN as two main languages of Web

---

[2]http://pipes.yahoo.com.

[3]http://www.jackbe.com.

[4]http://services.alphaworks.ibm.com/qedwiki.

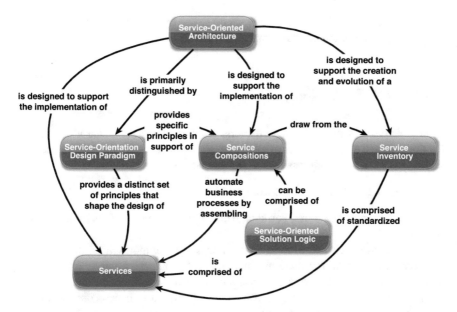

Fig. 1.10 Conceptual landscape of elements in SOC. *Source* [15]

service composition; and in Chap. 7 we examine the data flow aspects of Web service composition. In Chap. 8, we introduces a framework known as Service Component Architecture (SCA) that provides a technology-agnostic capability for composing applications from distributed services. Finally, in Chap. 9 we provide concluding remarks, offering readers our perspective for continued exploration in the field of Service Oriented Computing.

Setup for the Practical Exercises

1.4 Lab Exercise 00 – Practical Exercise Environment Setup

In this lab, we will set up the computing environment necessary for the programming exercises in the upcoming chapters. This exercise will guide you through the necessary preparations and installation setups for some software packages used in the exercises.

Ideally, we would need to consider setting up several different environments depending on the purpose: e.g., development, testing and deployment. In this exercise, we will assume that it is primarily for our own practice and development, so we will provide the guideline suited for your own personal computers running Mac OS, Linux or Windows. In all practical exercises from here on, we assume that your exercise environment is correctly set up to use the software packages and their configurations per instructions shown in this exercise.

1.4.1 SOA-Book Github Site

In the exercises in the following chapters, we will refer to exercise files required for the practical activities. All exercise files are uploaded and arranged by each lab section in Github. The address for the website is:

- `https://github.com/SOA-Book`

For each practical exercise, you should download the relevant files from the above address.

The software packages used in the exercises are commonly used in many Web development projects and there are plenty of information available about how to obtain and install them to your own computing environment.

Hence, we are not going to give you detailed instructions here as our assumption is that you are already familiar with basic Web application development. However, if you have any problem following these instructions in your own computer, refer to the above Github site for updates and FAQ.

1.4.2 Preliminaries

To make the instructions more readable, the $\sim$ character will be used to denote your "*home*" directory. Consider it as your main working directory where you are going to create and modify all exercise files. It is up to you to decide where this should be.

When you are asked to issue commands, you should do so from a terminal window session available in your computer. The $ symbol will be used to mean the prompt in the terminal windows.

We expect that these instructions should be applicable to different computing environments. All instructions we provide here are easily translated to Windows, Mac OS or Linux. All the instructions are tested with the versions and configurations of the software packages explained in this exercise. The basic three software packages you need to have are:

- Java SE Development Kit,
- Eclipse IDE,
- and Apache Tomcat Web Application Server.

Java SE Development Kit.

In the exercises in this book, we use JDK version 1.7. If there are multiple versions of Java installed on your machine, make sure that the environment variable JAVA_HOME is correctly set to Java 1.7 distribution for the exercises. Although you may experience no problem with the versions higher than 1.7, the exercises are only tested with this version.

Eclipse IDE.

For the coding, compiling, testing activities, we use J2EE developer package of Eclipse. The version we will use is called Kepler (Eclipse Kepler). Eclipse regularly releases updates, the latest release at the time of writing this book being Eclipse Luna. Any stable release of Eclipse after Kepler should be suitable for the exercises. But the practical exercises are written and tested with Kepler. If you need to upgrade or download Eclipse Kepler, you can find the link for Eclipse Kepler Download page here:

- https://eclipse.org/downloads/packages/release/Kepler/SR2

On the page, look for *Eclipse IDE for Java EE Developers* and suitable distribution file for your own environment.

One configuration setup that might be useful to do is to configure Eclipse to start with Java 1.7. For this, edit the eclipse.ini file. The file can be found in the same directory as the Eclipse binary file. Once the file is located, do the following:

- Make a copy of the eclipse.ini file. This way, you can get back to the original if you make a mistake.
- Name the copy eclipse.ini.original
- Open the eclipse.ini file and add a -vm entry to the file before any -vmargs entry. The -vm entry should point to the path to the bin directory of your JDK 1.7.

When it is done, the eclipse.ini file should look similar to the following. That is, there are two lines added before -vmargs to specify the path to the Java 1.7 installation location).

```
/// snip ...
-product
org.eclipse.epp.package.jee.product
--launcher.defaultAction
openFile
--launcher.XXMaxPermSize
256M
-showsplash
org.eclipse.platform
/// snip ...
-vm
C:/Program Files/Java/jdk1.7.0_67/bin
```

```
-vmargs
-Dosgi.requiredJavaVersion=1.5
-Xms40m
-Xmx512m
```

Note for Windows users: the `eclipse.ini` *file requires that the slashes ('/') are reversed from back-to-forward slashes ('\').*

Once Eclipse is started, also update the installation path in `Installed JREs` settings under the menu `Preferences` → Java.

Tomcat Server.

For the Web container, we use Tomcat 7.0.42. If there is a Tomcat server installed and configured in your computer already, you can leave the setup as is. Just make sure that you have the following two important environment variables set as expected: `CATALINA_BASE` and `CATALINA_HOME`. For example, the values are typically set to:

- `CATALINA_BASE=/home/YOUR_USER_NAME/apache-tomcat-7.0.42`
- `CATALINA_HOME=/home/YOUR_USER_NAME/apache-tomcat-7.0.42`

where `/home/YOUR_USER_NAME` are replaced with the actual path from your own computer environment. If you need to download Tomcat 7.0.42, you can find the binary distributions suitable for your own environment from the following links:

- `http://archive.apache.org/dist/tomcat/tomcat-7/v7.0.42/bin/`

Once installed, make sure that the server can be started and stopped without any problem.

1.4.3   Installing Apache Maven and Eclipse Maven Plug-in

For the Web service development exercises, we will use Apache Maven and Apache CXF as main software tools. We will first setup Maven, as Apache CXF uses it heavily.

1.4.3.1   Installing and setting up Maven

We use a popular build management tool called Maven to (i) generate project templates, (ii) manage class dependencies, class paths, and (iii) compile and package project artifacts. We do not need to understand the functionality of Maven comprehensively to start using it. We can start with the parts that are relevant and, of course, learn more about the tool as needed.

If you are already familiar with Maven, you can skip this part. Just double check that the environment variable MAVEN_HOME is set correctly.

1. Download a Maven binary distribution from the *Maven Download Page*[5]. Look for Maven 3.2.5 (current stable version at the time of writing). Choose either tar.gz or zip binary distributions to download.

2. Extract the downloaded package (e.g., apache-maven-3.2.5-bin.tar.gz) to the directory of your choosing. For the sake of illustration, we will assume that the installation directory is /usr/dev/. In a terminal window, do the following:

```
$ cd /usr/dev
$ tar -zxvf apache-maven-3.2.5-bin.tar.gz
$ rm apache-maven-3.2.5-bin.tar.gz
```

This will extract the contents to a new directory called apache-maven-3.2.5 and delete the downloaded file to save disk space. The all important directory here is apache-maven-3.2.5/*bin* and you want the directory to be in your PATH for convenient access.

3. Now configure the values for the following two environment variables:

   - MAVEN_HOME: this should point to the root directory of the installation, e.g., /usr/dev/apache-maven-3.2.5,
   - PATH: this environment variable should now include the Maven bin directory (e.g., /usr/dev/apache-maven-3.2.5/*bin*). This will make sure that the Maven commands can run from any location in your computer.

   Depending on your environment, how this is done would be different. In Mac OSX, for example, you could edit the .profile file located in your home directory and add the following lines:

```
export MAVEN_HOME=/usr/dev/apache-maven-3.2.5
export PATH="$PATH:/usr/dev/apache-maven-3.2.5/bin"
```

4. After setting up the environment variables, run the following Maven command to make sure that it is setup correctly. In a terminal window, enter:

```
$ mvn –version
```

   You should see Maven reporting back the version of Maven and JDK.

1.4.3.2 Integrating Maven with Eclipse IDE

We will use Maven both from the command line through a terminal window as well as the Eclipse IDE. From Eclipse, we can access Maven through a plug-in designed to integrate the tool with Eclipse. You can install the plug-in from Eclipse by the following steps:

---

[5]http://maven.apache.org/download.cgi.

1. Open the Eclipse IDE
2. Click Help → Install New Software...
3. Click the Add button at top right corner
4. At the pop-up window, fill in:

   - Name as M2Eclipse
   - Location as http://download.eclipse.org/technology/m2e/releases

5. In the following step, there should be a dialog window looking similar to Fig. 1.11.

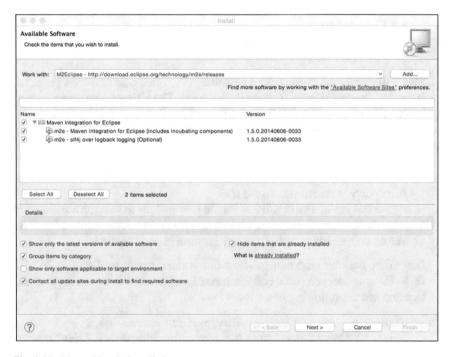

Fig. 1.11 Maven Plug-in Installation

6. Make sure to tick 'Maven Integration for Eclipse' and follow through with the installation process. After the installation, you may be asked to re-start Eclipse.

Now we want the Maven plug-in to point to the locally installed version of Maven, rather than the internal/embedded version in Eclipse. To configure this:

1. Go to Preference → Maven → Installation.
2. Click the 'Add' button. Add the location of the locally installed Maven (i.e., your MAVEN_HOME). For illustration purpose, Fig. 1.12 shows the location to be '/usr/dev/apache-maven-3.2.3' (3.2.5 in our case).
3. Click OK.

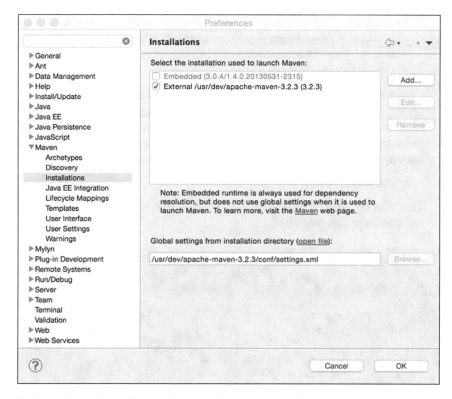

Fig. 1.12 Maven Plug-in Setup and Configuration

1.4.3.3 A Little Exercise with Maven

To check that the Maven installation and Eclipse plug-in are configured correctly to work together, let us do a little 'HelloWorld' exercise.

1. Open a terminal window, and change your working directory into Eclipse's workspace. It is normally

    '/home/YOUR_USER_NAME/workspace',

    where /home/YOUR_USER_NAME is replaced with your own home directory. For example, in the author's machine, it is '/Users/hpaik/workspace'. Since the exact path will be different for everyone, let's call this YOUR_WORKSPACE from now on.
2. Now under YOUR_WORKSPACE, type in the following (all in one line).

```
$ mvn archetype:generate -DgroupId = com.mycompany.app
-DartifactId=my-app
-DarchetypeArtifactId=maven-archetype-quickstart
-DinteractiveMode=false
```

Do not be alarmed if this takes a while. During the execution of this command, Maven is downloading necessary libraries to your local repository. This is normally located in a directory called '.m2' under your own home directory. Eventually, you should see the '*Build Success*' message. Spot the INFO lines in the output. It should tell you that a project is created under the directory:

YOUR_WORKSPACE//my-app

This matches '-DartifactId' parameter. Think of it as the name of your application/project (see Fig. 1.13).

```
●  ●  ●                 workspace — cs9322@williams .../00 — bash — 80×24

[INFO] Generating project in Batch mode
[INFO] ------------------------------------------------------------------------
---
[INFO] Using following parameters for creating project from Old (1.x) Archetype:
 maven-archetype-quickstart:1.0
[INFO] ------------------------------------------------------------------------
---
[INFO] Parameter: groupId, Value: com.mycompany.app
[INFO] Parameter: packageName, Value: com.mycompany.app
[INFO] Parameter: package, Value: com.mycompany.app
[INFO] Parameter: artifactId, Value: my-app
[INFO] Parameter: basedir, Value: /Users/hpaik/workspace
[INFO] Parameter: version, Value: 1.0-SNAPSHOT
[INFO] project created from Old (1.x) Archetype in dir: /Users/hpaik/workspace/m
y-app
[INFO] ------------------------------------------------------------------------
[INFO] BUILD SUCCESS
[INFO] ------------------------------------------------------------------------
[INFO] Total time: 15.954 s
[INFO] Finished at: 2015-03-08T20:55:31+11:00
[INFO] Final Memory: 12M/156M
[INFO] ------------------------------------------------------------------------
hpaik@vana.BigPond: []
```

Fig. 1.13 Maven Project Template Generation

3. Open Eclipse. Go to File → Import → Maven → Existing Maven Projects.
4. Navigate to YOUR_WORKSPACE/my-app and click 'Finish'.
5. Open the '/my-app' project and briefly examine the files and the project directory structure generated by Maven (e.g., App.java). It should look something similar to Fig. 1.14.
6. Note the pom.xml file. It is the configuration file for Maven. We will not do much with the file here, but from the following lab exercises, we will be working with this file closely. As mentioned earlier, we will learn the elements of Maven POM as we go.

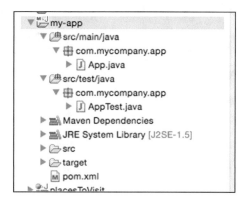

Fig. 1.14 Maven Project Structure (in Eclipse)

7. Now, do right click on the project name '/my-app' → Run As → maven install.
8. By Maven convention, running 'mvn install' will prompt Maven to perform the following tasks:

   - compile all Java files under src/main/java, include all dependent libraries in the classpath,
   - package the classes into a jar file, and place it into the '/target' directory,
   - install the jar file in the local Maven repository. This repository is normally .m2 under your own home directory.

9. As a result, you will find my-app-1.0-SNAPSHOT.jar in the target directory.
10. Now from a command line, try the following:

```
$ cd YOUR_WORKSPACE/my-app
$ java -cp target/my-app-1.0-SNAPSHOT.jar com.mycompany. app.App
```

11. You should see 'Hello World!' in return.

We have run through the setup process of the software packages we will be using in the rest of the practical exercises. At the end of the setup process, see if you can tick the following boxes before you move on to the next exercises.

- I know where my Java 1.7 installation is, and JAVA_HOME is set accordingly.
- I have Eclipse IDE running and I have configured eclipse.ini for JDK 1.7.
- I know where my Tomcat 7 installation is. The environment variables CATALINA_BASE and CATALINA_HOME are set, and I can start/shutdown Tomcat successfully.
- I know where my Maven installation is, and MAVEN_HOME, PATH are set. I can run the mvn command from a command line in my terminal window.
- I have integrated Eclipse IDE and Maven with a plug-in. I have completed the little 'HelloWorld' exercise to verify it.

Chapter 2
Web Services – SOAP and WSDL

Web services as a concept is broad and abstract. This is because the discussions about Web services are meant to be widely applicable to any situation that requires communications between remote software components without our having to worry about the platforms or the programming languages of the components involved. However, Web services also define how such a generic and abstract concept can be practically realised and implemented in many different ways. In the following two chapters, we will explore two of the most popular ways to implement Web services, namely SOAP/WSDL services and RESTful services.

In this chapter, we start with SOAP/WSDL-based services. In doing so, we briefly introduce two of the most important Web services standards that underpin the implementation aspects of Web services. Figure 2.1 shows a logical structure of

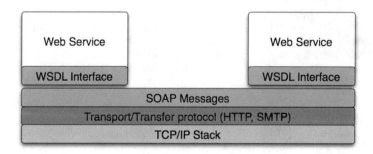

Fig. 2.1 Web services: communication stack

the communication stack for Web services. In this picture, at the top, we see a Web service which has its interface declared using a standard interface language called WSDL. At the bottom, we see the common Internet protocol layer TCP/IP.

What we see between the Web service interface and the TCP/IP layer are the message protocol SOAP and the message transport protocol (most commonly HTTP

© Springer International Publishing AG 2017

H.-y. Paik et al., *Web Service Implementation and Composition Techniques*,

DOI 10.1007/978-3-319-55542-3_2

or SMTP). For a Web service to send and receive the messages to/from its client, it first needs SOAP. SOAP governs the format of the messages sent and received by Web services. The message (formatted according to the SOAP standard) is then transported by HTTP or SMTP. That is, Web services use the good old Internet application protocol HTTP as the carrier of their messages. By utilising the widely supported message transport protocol and having an agreed-upon message format, we are able to simplify the communication issues in Web services significantly.

In the following sections, we will introduce an overview of SOAP and WSDL standards.

2.1 Simple Object Access Protocol (SOAP)

SOAP is a protocol used by Web services to construct and understand the messages they exchange. SOAP is at the heart of Web services architecture in that it allows the interacting parties in the architecture to communicate with each other using a standard, well-understood message format.

The specification and evolution of SOAP is maintained by W3C.[1] The specification defines an XML-based standard message format, describing how the message metadata and payload should be packaged into an XML document.

Let us look at the basic layout of the message format (Figs. 2.2 and 2.3). SOAP Envelope signals the start of a SOAP message. Each message consists of SOAP Header and Body sections. The payload is included in the body section. The additional processing instruction details, such as the transaction protocol or security policies, go into the header section of the message.

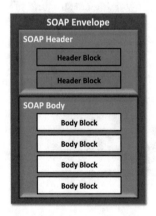

```
<?xml version="1.0"?>
<soap:Envelope
  xmlns:soap="http://
  www.w3.org/2003/05/soap-envelope/"
  soap:encodingStyle="http://
  schemas.xmlsoap.org/soap/encoding/">
  <soap:Body xmlns:m="http://
                    www.test.org/stock">
    <m:GetStockPrice>
      <m:StockName>IBM</m:StockName>
      <m:StockPrice>126</m:StockPrice>
    </m:GetStockPrice>
  </soap:Body>
</soap:Envelope>
```

Fig. 2.2 SOAP message   **Fig. 2.3** An example of a SOAP request

---

[1]http://www.w3.org/TR/soap12-part1/, SOAP Specification.

Figure 2.4 illustrates the round-trip of a Web service request and response communication based on SOAP over the Internet. First, a client application (service requester) constructs a SOAP message (request) and transmits it over the network via HTTP. On the server side, a SOAP server – special software that listens for SOAP messages and acts as a distributor and interpreter of SOAP documents – accepts the message and dispatches it to the intended recipient (service provider). The service is executed per request and its response is generated. The response is again constructed as a SOAP message (response) and transmitted over HTTP back to the client.

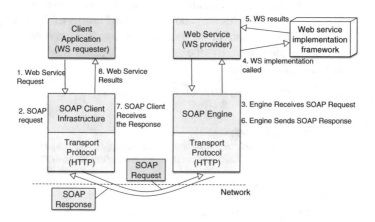

Fig. 2.4 SOAP messages: communication between services. *Source* [24]

Google Web service example: A simple but more complete example of SOAP request and response messages is shown in Google Web service interface.[2]

Here is an example of a SOAP v1.1 request message that sends a search query to the Google Search Engine (available as a Web service) to search for a string "shrdlu winograd maclisp teletype". According to the payload part of the message, besides the actual query string q, the interface accepts other parameters such as the number of maximum results returned, the position of the filter feature (on or off), etc.:

```
<?xml version='1.0' encoding='UTF-8'?>
<soap11:Envelope
  xmlns="urn:GoogleSearch"
  xmlns:soap11="http://schemas.xmlsoap.org/soap/envelope/">
  <soap11:Body>
    <doGoogleSearch>
      <key>00000000000000000000000000000000</key>
      <q>shrdlu winograd maclisp teletype</q>
      <start>0</start>
      <maxResults>10</maxResults>
      <filter>true</filter>
```

---

[2]This is for illustration only. The actual service is now deprecated. http://www.w3.org/ 2004/06/03-google-soap-wsdl.html.

```
      <restrict></restrict>
      <safeSearch>false</safeSearch>
      <lr></lr>
      <ie>latin1</ie>
      <oe>latin1</oe>
    </doGoogleSearch>
  </soap11:Body>
</soap11:Envelope>
```

Here is an example of a SOAP 1.1 response message returned from the Google Web service (snippet). The payload part of the message shows some metadata about the search operation (e.g., search time) and the itemised results of the Web pages matched. This example demonstrates the standard message formats in SOAP-based Web service communication, as well as the nature of XML-based messages that make them easily machine processable.

```
<?xml version='1.0' encoding='UTF-8'?>
<soap11:Envelope
  xmlns="urn:GoogleSearch"
  xmlns:google="urn:GoogleSearch"
  xmlns:soapenc="http://schemas.xmlsoap.org/soap/encoding/"
  xmlns:soap11="http://schemas.xmlsoap.org/soap/envelope/">
  <soap11:Body>
  <doGoogleSearchResponse>
  <return>
  <documentFiltering>false</documentFiltering>
  <estimatedTotalResultsCount>3</estimatedTotalResultsCount>
  <directoryCategories
            soapenc:arrayType="google:DirectoryCategory[0]">
  </directoryCategories>
  <searchTime>0.194871</searchTime>
  <resultElements soapenc:arrayType="google:ResultElement[3]">
  <item>
  <cachedSize>12k</cachedSize>
  <hostName></hostName>
  <snippet> <b>...</b> on a simple dialog (via <b>teletype</b>)
  <b>...</b></snippet>
  <directoryCategory>
    <specialEncoding></specialEncoding>
    <fullViewableName></fullViewableName>
  </directoryCategory>
  <relatedInformationPresent>true</relatedInformationPresent>
  <directoryTitle></directoryTitle>
  <summary></summary>
  <URL>http://hci.stanford.edu/cs147/examples/shrdlu/</URL>
  <title><b>SHRDLU</b></title>
  </item>
  <!-- more items -->
  </resultElements>
  <endIndex>3</endIndex>
  <searchTips></searchTips>
  <searchComments></searchComments>
  <startIndex>1</startIndex>
```

```
<estimateIsExact>true</estimateIsExact>
<searchQuery>shrdlu winograd maclisp teletype</searchQuery>
</return>
</doGoogleSearchResponse>
</soap11:Body>
</soap11:Envelope>
```

SOAP fault messages: When a problem occurs during the processing of a SOAP message, the Web service can return an error or exception message to the client instead of a normal response content. In this case, the body section of a SOAP message will act as a propagating medium for errors and exceptions, providing an extensible mechanism for transporting structured and unstructured information about things that went wrong. The SOAP specification describes a separate element called `Fault` to indicate the message is an error message rather than a normal response content. For example, the following SOAP message shows a SOAP fault response, explaining that the request input value for a date field was wrong.

```
<?xml version='1.0' encoding='UTF-8'?>
<soapenv:Envelope
  xmlns:soapenv="http://schemas.xmlsoap.org/soap/envelope/">
  <soapenv:Body>
    <soapenv:Fault>
      <faultcode>soapenv:Server</faultcode>
      <faultstring>Invalid date value: wrong type</faultstring>
      <detail>Accepted values are of XML DateTime type</detail>
    </soapenv:Fault>
  </soapenv:Body>
</soapenv:Envelope>
```

2.1.1   Binding SOAP Messages to a Transportation Protocol

As seen in the Web service communication stack in Fig. 2.1, a SOAP message is transmitted over the Internet via any application-level transfer protocol such HTTP or SMTP. The term 'SOAP binding' is used to indicate the transportation mechanism by which a SOAP is transmitted. For example, when a SOAP is bound to HTTP, the SOAP message is embedded in the body section of the HTTP request (and response). The following shows an example of a raw HTTP POST request containing a SOAP message in its body section.

```
POST /StockQuote HTTP/1.1
Host: www.stockquoteserver.com
Content-Type: text/xml

<?xml version="1.0"encoding="utf-8"?>
<soap:Envelope xmlns:xsi="http://
           www.w3.org/2001/XMLSchema-instance"
  xmlns:xsd="http://www.w3.org/2001/XMLSchema"
  xmlns:soap="http://schemas.xmlsoap.org/soap/envelope/">
```

```
<soap:Body>
  <ns:GetLastTradePrice xmlns:ns="http://stock.sample">
    <ns:symbol>DIS</ns:symbol>
  </ns:GetLastTradePrice>
</soap:Body>
</soap:Envelope>
```

Naturally, the HTTP POST request is then matched by an HTTP response, as shown below. The HTTP response carries in its body a SOAP message which is the response of the previous SOAP message sent.

```
HTTP/1.1 200 OK
Server: Apache-Coyote/1.1
Content-Type: text/xml;charset=UTF-8
Transfer-Encoding: chunked
Date: Tue, 22 Jul 2014 03:23:23 GMT

<?xml version='1.0' encoding='UTF-8'?>
<soapenv:Envelope
  xmlns:soapenv="http://schemas.xmlsoap.org/soap/envelope/">
  <soapenv:Body>
    <ns:GetLastTradePriceResponse xmlns:ns="http://stock.sample">
        <ns:Price>34.5</ns:Price>
    </ns:GetLastTradePriceResponse>
  </soapenv:Body>
</soapenv:Envelope>
```

Just to complete the illustration of SOAP message transportation, the following example shows a raw SMTP message carrying the same SOAP message as above. Note the SMTP headers such as To, From and Reply-To. The SOAP response to this request will be sent to either the From or the Reply-To address.

```
To: <soap-node@soapexample.org>
From: <soap-client@soapclient.com>
Reply-To: <soap-client@soapclient.com>
Date: Tue, 22 July 2014 23:27:00 -0700
Message-Id: <1f75d4D515-C3EC3F34FEAB5CGE89PA@soapclient.com>
MIME-Version: 1.0
Content-Type: text/xml; charset=utf-8

<?xml version="1.0" encoding="utf-8"?>
<soap:Envelope xmlns:xsi="http://
          www.w3.org/2001/XMLSchema-instance"
  xmlns:xsd="http://www.w3.org/2001/XMLSchema"
  xmlns:soap="http://schemas.xmlsoap.org/soap/envelope/">
  <soap:Body>
    <ns:GetLastTradePrice xmlns:ns="http://stock.sample">
      <ns:symbol>DIS</ns:symbol>
    </ns:GetLastTradePrice>
  </soap:Body>
</soap:Envelope>
```

2.1.2 SOAP Extension Using SOAP Headers

The message processing model for SOAP is designed in a way that adding extra information to the header sections of the message is easy. SOAP servers provide a message processing model that assumes the following: A SOAP message originates at an initial SOAP sender and is sent to an ultimate SOAP receiver via zero or more SOAP intermediaries. That is, the messages pass through a number of intermediate nodes between the sender and the receiver.

Each intermediary is assigned to process a particular header section. For example, the following snippet in a SOAP header section shows the WS-Security standard being used to add a login/authentication function to the message processing logic. By adding the WS-Security header, the intermediary nodes delegated to check for the WS-Security header will intercept the message, invoke security checking logic and pass the message along to the next processing node if the details are correct. If not (e.g., wrong password), a SOAP fault is generated. It is noted that the following is a simplified example, and completely understanding and implementing WS-Security would require a more complicated explanation.

```xml
<?xml version="1.0"encoding="iso-8859-1"?>
<soap:Envelope xmlns:soap="http://
                            schemas.xmlsoap.org/soap/envelope/">
 <soap:Header>
  <wsse:Security xmlns:wsse="http://
                         schemas.xmlsoap.org/ws/2003/06/secext">
   <wsse:UsernameToken wsu:Id="soasample"
      xmlns:wsu="http://schemas.xmlsoap.org/ws/2003/06/utility">
    <wsse:Username>soasample</wsse:Username>
    <wsse:Password Type="wsse:PasswordText">tada</wsse:Password>
    <wsu:Created>2015-09-19T08:44:51Z</wsu:Created>
   </wsse:UsernameToken>
  </wsse:Security>
 </soap:Header>
 <soap:Body>
    <ns:GetLastTradePrice xmlns:ns="http://stock.sample">
      <ns:symbol>DIS</ns:symbol>
    </ns:GetLastTradePrice>
  </soap:Body>
</soap:Envelope>
```

Many SOAP server providers provide their own processing model based on these basics. Apache CXF, the SOAP server used in this book for practical activities, allows for creating user-defined headers and their processing nodes using its *Interceptors and Phases* architecture, where the message processing logic is broken into several phases (e.g., before reading a message, after writing the response message) and an interceptor with some custom processing logic can be invoked before or/and after each phase.

Some of the common examples of intermediaries would be logging messages, and data encrypting/decrypting or auditing messages (e.g., for billing or compliance purposes).

Regardless of the actual implementation of the processing model, the main idea behind it is to allow the Web services to extend the basic SOAP standards to support the various needs arising from complicated enterprise applications such as security.

2.2 Web Services Description Language (WSDL)

As we know, a Web service interaction typically involves two roles: a client of the service, who initiates an interaction by sending a request message, and a provider of the service, who follows up with a reply to the request. In the previous section, we have explained SOAP as the message format standard to be used during this interaction. Now that we know how to format a message to communicate, let us look at what determines the content of the communication.

WSDL – pronounced "Whiz Dull", is a machine-processable specification of the Web service's interface.[3] That is, it is a document that the service provider would write to inform the clients what kinds of services are offered by the provider and how to use the services. Typically, in a WSDL document, you will find a list of operations (i.e., the service functionality offered by the service). For each operation, details of the input data expected and the output it produces are described.

Like SOAP, it is also XML-based in that the syntax is described by a set of XML elements. It describes a service in terms of the operations that make up the service, the messages that each operation requires, and the parts from which each message is composed.

Importantly, it is used by the client to generate a proxy (client stub) to the Web service. The proxy then acts as a go-between between the Web service and the client. This activity is usually supported by a tool and is almost fully automated. We will go through some of the details about generating stub code in the practical lab exercises later in the chapter.

A WSDL document broadly contains two parts: abstract and concrete. The abstract part defines operations and messages exchanged through them (i.e., conceptual design of the service in terms of what it offers functionally). The concrete part contains information about network deployment specifics and data format bindings. The split between abstract and concrete parts is useful for separating Web service design and Web service deployment environment details. That is, the same message definitions designed in the abstract parts can be bound to an HTTP transportation or SMTP transportation depending on the details of the concrete parts in its WSDL (Fig. 2.5).

---

[3]Specification: http://www.w3.org/TR/wsdl.

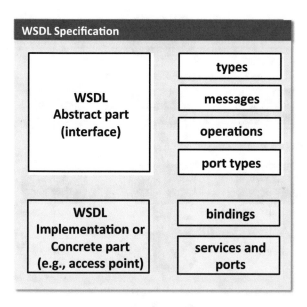

Fig. 2.5 WSDL: Two parts, concrete and abstract

2.3 WSDL Main Elements

Unlike the SOAP messages, where the construction and consumption of the messages are automatically handled by a Web service runtime environment most of the time, WSDL documents are one of the artifacts that a Web service developer may have to deal with manually. For example, to develop a new Web service, one would have to write a WSDL document from scratch. Therefore, although it is not necessary to memorise each WSDL element, it is quite important that we understand the WSDL elements defined in the WSDL specification in reasonable depth. The physical structure of a WSDL document is depicted in Fig. 2.6. It is worth trying to 'read' the overall structure of the WSDL. For example, let us look at the abstract part of the document. The `PortType` element has one or more `Operations`. Each `Operation` could have at most one `Input Message`, at most one `Output Message` and zero or more `Fault Messages`. This, of course, implies that it is possible for an operation to have no input or output. This allows the Web service operations to support various message exchange patterns. More about the message exchange patterns is explained later. Let us continue to read the abstract part.

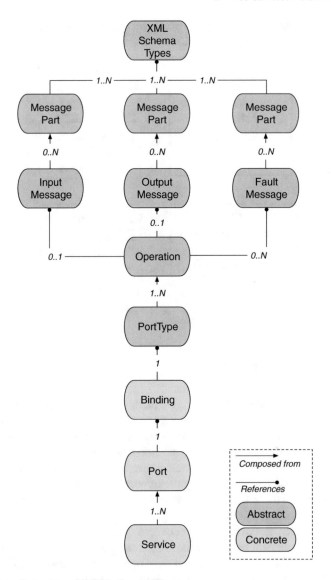

Fig. 2.6 Overall structure of WSDL. *Source* [8]

definitions:

Let us say we want to describe a Web service that offers an operation named
`GetStockQuote()`. It takes `symbol`, a string value representing a stock code,
as input and returns the price of the stock.

```
double GetStockQuote(string symbol);
```

We start writing WSDL with the following WSDL element. The `definitions` element signals the start of a WSDL document (i.e., the parent for all other WSDL elements) and it contains all relevant, globally declared namespaces.

```
<wsdl:definitions targetNamespace="http://stock.example.org/wsdl"
              xmlns:tns="http://stock.example.org/wsdl"
              xmlns:stockQ="http://stock.example.org/schema"
              xmlns:wsdl="http://www.w3.org/2003/02/wsdl">
   <!-- child elements -->
</wsdl:definitions>
```

types:

The `types` element encloses a number of XML types and XML elements used in the interface description (XML Schema types). For the stock quote service, we define the types as follows.

```
<wsdl:definitions ...>
   <wsdl:import namespace="http://stock.example.org/schema"
        location="http://stock.example/org/schema"/>
   <wsdl:types xmlns:xs="http://www.w3.org/2001/XMLSchema">
      <xs:element name="stock_quote">
       <xs:complexType>
        <xs:sequence>
         <xs:element name="symbol" ref="stockQ:symbol"/>
         <xs:element name="lastPrice" ref="stockQ:price"/>
        </xs:sequence>
       </xs:complexType>
      </xs:element>
      <!-- other type/XML elements definitions -->
   </wsdl:types>
</wsdl:definitions>
```

Note: the 'ref' attribute indicates that, in another document, you can find definitions for the `symbol` and `price` elements. For example:

```
<xsd:schema targetNamespace="http://stock.example.org/schema"...>
   <xsd:element name="symbol"type="xsd:string"/>
   <xsd:element name="price"type="xsd:string"/>
</xsd:schema>
```

message:

The `message` element declares the form of a message that the Web service sends and receives. For the stock quote service, we define the following messages.

```
<wsdl:message name="StockPriceRequestMessage">
   <wsdl:part name="symbol"element="stockQ:symbol"/>
</wsdl:message>
<wsdl:message name="StockPriceResponseMessage">
```

```
    <wsdl:part name="price"element="stockQ:stock_quote"/>
</wsdl:message>
<wsdl:message name="StockSymbolNotFoundMessage">
    <wsdl:part name="symbol"element="stockQ:symbol" />
</wsdl:message>
```

The message element defines what kind of message is expected as input, output and fault by this Web service. Each message is constructed from a number of XML Schema-typed `part` elements. A message may contain multiple parts.

portType:

The `portType` element contains a named set of operations. It defines the functionality of the Web service (i.e., what the service does). For our service, there is only one operation in the portType. A portType is a way of grouping operations. Note that WSDL 1.2 changes `portType` to `interface`.

```
<wsdl:portType name="StockBrokerQueryPortType">
    <wsdl:operation name="GetStockPrice">
       <wsdl:input message="tns:StockPriceRequestMessage"/>
       <wsdl:output message="tns:StockPriceResponseMessage"/>
       <wsdl:fault name="UnknownSymbolFault"
                    message="tns:StockSymbolNotFoundMessage"/>
    </wsdl:operation>
</wsdl:portType>
```

operation:

Not all operations will have a single input, output and fault. The `operation` element indicates a message exchange pattern (transmission primitives):

- **Request-response** (i.e., Input–Output): The Web service receives a message, and sends a correlated message (or fault).
- **One-way** (i.e., Input only): The service receives a message. The service consumes the message and does not produce any output or fault message.
- **Solicit-response** (i.e., Output–Input): The service generates a message, and receives a correlated message (or fault) in return.
- **Notification** (i.e., Output only): The service sends a message. It does not expect anything in return.

Synchronous interactions are defined using request-response and solicit-response, while asynchronous interactions are defined using one-way and notification operations.

The following shows how the message exchange patterns can be defined using the operation element.

- One-way Operation:

```
<wsdl:definitions .... >
   <wsdl:portType .... > *
      <wsdl:operation name="nmtoken">
         <wsdl:input name="nmtoken"? message="qname"/>
      </wsdl:operation>
   </wsdl:portType >
</wsdl:definitions>
```

- Notification Operation:

```
<wsdl:definitions .... >
   <wsdl:portType .... > *
      <wsdl:operation name="nmtoken">
         <wsdl:output name="nmtoken"? message="qname"/>
      </wsdl:operation>
   </wsdl:portType >
</wsdl:definitions>
```

- Request-response Operation:

```
<wsdl:portType .... >
   <wsdl:operation name="nmtoken" parameterOrder="nmtokens">
      <wsdl:input name="nmtoken"? message="qname"/>
      <wsdl:output name="nmtoken"? message="qname"/>
      <wsdl:fault name="nmtoken"message="qname"/>
   </wsdl:operation>
</wsdl:portType >
```

- Solicit-response Operation:

```
<wsdl:portType .... >
   <wsdl:operation name="nmtoken" parameterOrder="nmtokens">
      <wsdl:output name="nmtoken"? message="qname"/>
      <wsdl:input name="nmtoken"? message="qname"/>
      <wsdl:fault name="nmtoken"message="qname"/>
   </wsdl:operation>
</wsdl:portType >
```

binding:

A binding defines the *message encoding format* and *protocol details* for operations and messages defined by a particular portType. It is the concrete part of a WSDL document.

```
<wsdl:binding name="StockBrokerServiceSOAPBinding"
                       type="tns:StockBrokerQueryPortType">
 <soap:binding style="document"
   transport="http://www.w3.org/2002/12/soap/bindings/HTTP/"/>
   <wsdl:operation name="GetStockPrice">
     <soap:operation soapAction="http://
                       stock.example.org/getStockPrice"/>
```

```
    <wsdl:input>
       <soap:body use="literal" encodingStyle="http://
                                   stock.example.org/schema"/>
    </wsdl:input>
    <wsdl:output>
       <soap:body use="literal" encodingStyle="http://
                                   stock.example.org/schema"/>
    </wsdl:output>
    <wsdl:fault>
       <soap:fault name="StockSymbolNotFoundMessage"/>
    </wsdl:fault>
   </wsdl:operation>
</wsdl:binding>
```

There are two contexts in which the binding element is used in a WSDL document. The context is disambiguated by 'wsdl' and 'soap' prefixes, respectively. <wsdl:binding> points to the relevant portType to be used. The purpose of the SOAP binding element, <soap:binding>, is to signify that the binding is bound to the SOAP protocol format: *Envelope, Header* and *Body*. This element makes no claims as to the encoding or format of the message. The element contains the following information:

- style attribute: this can be 'rpc' or 'document'. It determines how the SOAP body is constructed (rpc-style or document-style).
- transport attribute: transport protocol to use (e.g., HTTP, SMTP).

The 'binding' element contains two sub-elements named `wsdl:operation` and `soap:operation`. <wsdl:operation> maps each operation in the portType to a binding. For each operation in the portType, the sub-element specifies how the input and output messages are encoded.

<soap:operation> has soapAction attribute which specifies the value of the SOAPAction header for this operation. For the HTTP protocol binding of SOAP, this value is required and it has no default. Finally, the <soap:body> sub-element specifies how the message parts appear inside the SOAP Body element. The encoding could be either literal, that is it literally follows an XML Schema definition, or SOAP-encoded, where it follows SOAP encoding specification.

service:

The `service` element normally appears at the end of the WSDL document and it points to the specific network endpoint for a binding (i.e., access point of the service).

```
<wsdl:service name="StockBrokerService">
  <wsdl:port name="StockBrokerServiceSOAPPort"
       binding="tns:StockBrokerServiceSOAPBinding>
    <soap:address location="http://stock.example.org/"/>
  </wsdl:port>
</wsdl:service>
```

By separating the abstract part of the service from its concrete definitions (i.e., data format binding, network address, etc.), it is possible to expose a single abstract definition to the network via a number of different transportation protocols having different data format bindings or offered on different ports numbers (Fig. 2.7).

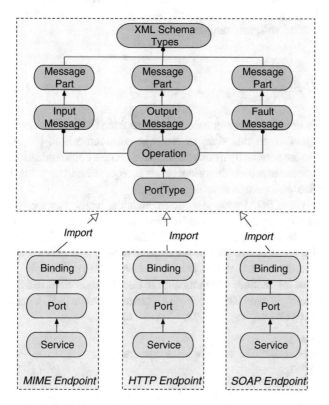

Fig. 2.7 Logical and physical separation of a service. *Source* [8]

2.4 Message Communication Model in SOAP/WSDL

The SOAP encodingStyle attribute conveys information about the serialization rules used in a SOAP message. The encoding style or rules in the SOAP specification are based on a simple type system that is commonly seen in other type systems in programming languages. A type either is a simple/scalar type (e.g., int, string) or is a compound type (e.g., Struct, Array) constructed from several parts where each part is a type, for example, the SOAP message shown in Fig. 2.3.

This attribute may appear on any element, and is scoped to that element's contents and all child elements not themselves containing such an attribute, much as an XML namespace declaration is scoped. There is no default encoding defined for a SOAP message.

SOAP supports two different message communication styles, namely RPC and document. Configuring the message communication style directive in the SOAP binding element within the WSDL binding section will cause the message content (the SOAP Body part) to be structured according to the corresponding style. Let us look at each option with an example.

2.4.1   RPC-Style

The RPC-style of message communication stems from the conventional remote procedure calls (RPCs). In this style of message communication, the client (caller) always refers to the service by its operation name and the communication is expected to be synchronous, in which the client sends a request and waits for the response from the service who returns a result.

The RPC-style of SOAP message communication, hence, is conceptually similar to the existing RPC mechanisms and its message structure reflects that. That is, an RPC-style Web service appears as a remote object to a client. The client expresses its request as a *method call* with a set of *parameters*. The service then returns a response containing a return value. This style supports the well-known synchronous request-response interaction, which means the client and service are tightly coupled.

Here is an example of an RPC-style SOAP communication [24], where the binding is set as "`<soap:binding style='rpc' ...>`".

```
<env:Envelope ...>
      <env:Header> some header </env:Header>
      <env:Body>
         <m:GetProductPrice>
             <product-id> 450R60P </product-id>
         </m:GetProductPrice>
      </env:Body>
</env:Envelope>

<env:Envelope ...>
      <env:Header> some header </env:Header>
      <env:Body>
         <m:GetProductPriceResponse>
             <product-price> 134.32 </product-price>
         </m:GetProductPriceResponse>
      </env:Body>
</env:Envelope>
```

The key point in recognising SOAP RPC-style communication in messages is that the SOAP `Body` must conform to a structure that indicates the method name and contains a set of parameters. The response always has 'Response' appended after the request method name (see GetProductPrice and GetProductPriceResponse).

2.4.2 Document-Style

The Document-style of message communication style is designed to promote loose coupling of the operation that actually processes the message from the message itself. This style is also known as message-oriented style.

First, in this style, WSDL definitions must contain XML schema definitions of request and response messages. The body of each message then is any legal XML fragment as defined in the WSDL document. That is, a SOAP message actually contains a piece of 'XML data'. The client sends an entire XML document (e.g., purchase order) as a request to an endpoint, rather than a discrete set of parameters and a service operation name. The endpoint on the server side is responsible for forwarding and dispatching the request to the right service operation that can process the message. This is often described as a message-driven, asynchronous communication model, which makes the client and server decoupled.

The following shows an example of a Document-style SOAP [24], where the binding is set as "`<soap:binding style='document' ...>`".

```
<env:Envelope ...>
  <env:Header> some header </env:Header>
  <env:Body>
    <po:PurchaseOrder orderDate="2004-12-02">
      <po:from>
       <po:accountName> RightPlastics </po:accountName>
       <po:accountNumber> PSC-0343-02 </po:accountNumber>
      </po:from>
      <po:to>
       <po:supplierName>Plastic Supplies Inc.</po:supplierName>
       <po:supplierAddress>Melbourne</po:supplierAddress>
      </po:to>
      <po:product>
       <po:product-name> injection molder </po:product-name>
       <po:product-model> G-100T </po:product-model>
       <po:quantity> 2 </po:quantity>
      <po:product>
   </po:PurchaseOrder>
  </env:Body>
</env:Envelope>
```

As can be seen in the example, the SOAP actually contains well-formed XML documents and the server-side process decides where and how to dispatch the request. This is very a flexible communication style that provides the best interoperability. In fact, modern SOAP engines use the Document-style as the default message communication style.

Practical Exercise I

2.5   Lab Exercise 01 – Developing Simple Web Services with Apache CXF and Maven

In this lab exercise you will develop a simple Web service using Apache CXF and Maven. Apache CXF is an implementation of the JAX-WS standard (i.e., Java standard for Web services, especially the kind of services that deal with SOAP protocol and WSDL documents). It is normally setup to run within a servlet container such as Apache Tomcat through `CXFServlet`.

This lab assumes you have completed the setup necessary to carry out this exercise. The setup procedure is described in Sect. 1.4.

Exercise Files

The exercise files involved in the lab can be downloaded from the Github site:

- `https://github.com/SOA-Book`

Follow the repository `exercises`, then `lab01`.

2.5.1   Activity 1: HelloWorld with Apache CXF

To become a little bit more familiar with the tools, let's do another little HelloWorld exercise, this time using Apache CXF.

First, we are going to run Maven and ask it to generate a project template for a CXF Web service. Through the Maven Archetype, which is a templating tool that standardises the folder structure and artifacts of a project build, Apache CXF provides a project template called `cxf-jaxws-javafirst`. We will use it to quickly build and test out a Web service.

1. In a terminal window, navigate to `YOUR_WORKSPACE`.
2. Type in the following in the command prompt (mind the ':' at the end) .

   ```
   $ mvn archetype:generate -Dfilter=org.apache.cxf.archetype:
   ```

3. When prompted to 'Choose archetype:', enter number 2. That is, choose the `cxf-jaxws-javafirst` archetype option.
4. Then at the 'Choose a version:' prompt, enter number 95. You may choose the latest version offered from the tool, but this lab exercise has been written and tested with version `v3.0.4`..

5. Then, at the next prompt, 'Define value for property groupId:', enter the following text: `au.edu.unsw.soacourse`.

   NOTE: The groupId property in Maven is similar to that of a Java package name. Think of it as a way to group your applications (e.g., typically this could be by a department in an organisation, or an organisation itself, expressed as reversed domain name). We will use `au.edu.unsw.soacourse` *as our groupId.*

6. At the next prompt, 'Define value for property artifactId:', enter `Hello WorldCXF`. The artifactId property in Maven corresponds to the title of your project/application.
7. The next prompt will be 'Define value for property version:'. The default value here is `1.0-SNAPSHOT` (case-sensitive). Leave the value as is, and hit Enter.
8. Lastly, you will be asked to 'Define value for property package:'. When prompted, enter `au.edu.unsw.soacourse.hello`. This defines the Java package name the tool is going to produce for you.
9. Now Maven will generate the template code. You should see '*Build Success*' in the output messages. Under your workspace, you should also see a new directory called 'HelloWorldCXF'.

Now the project template is ready. Let us import this template into Eclipse IDE as an existing Maven project and examine what has been generated.

1. Open Eclipse, and navigate to File → Import → Maven → Existing Maven Project. Find the `HelloWorldCXF` folder and complete the import process.
2. Open up the folders (as indicated in Fig. 2.8) and note the Java files and WEB-INF/ ∗ .xml files. Of course, note the pom.xml file for the Maven project as well.
3. Open `HelloWorld.java`. You should see that it is an interface with one method called `SayHi()`. Especially, note the package imported, `javax.jws.WebService`, and the Java annotation @WebService.
4. Open `HelloWorldImpl.java`. This implements the `HelloWorld` interface. Pay attention to where the @WebService annotation appears and to the reference to an endpoint `au.edu.unsw.soacourse.hello.HelloWorld`. All this leads to Apache CXF exposing the operation `SayHi()` as a Web service operation at an endpoint.
5. Open web.xml. You see a servlet declaration named CXFServlet, whose implementation is provided by Apache CXF itself and is specified in `org.apache.cxf.transport.servlet.CXFServlet`.
6. In the same file, you also see a servlet mapping declaration which maps all URL patterns for this Web application to the servlet CXFServlet.
7. The configuration for the servlet CXFServlet is loaded from the information specified in beans.xml. Inside beans.xml, you will see an endpoint declaration id="helloWorld". Now you can see that:

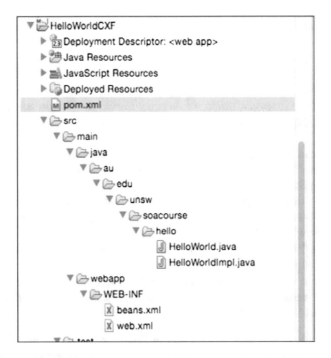

Fig. 2.8 Maven project folders

- The endpoint is *implemented by* HelloWorldImpl, which has the SayHi() operation.
- The endpoint is available at an address called '/HelloWorld'.
- The address is a relative URL from the Web application root. That is, assuming the service it is deployed locally on port 8080, the full path is http://localhost:8080/HelloWorldCXF/HelloWorld.

So far, we have examined what the template code contains and the main elements that are noteworthy. This template code is already complete and functional. Let's compile and deploy it onto Tomcat. First, to compile and package the project:

1. Right click on the project name HelloWorldCXF. Choose Run As → Maven install.
2. You should see in the Console window a message 'Build Success'. Then, refresh the project, and you should see the target directory now populated with compiled code. The final package 'HelloWorldCXF-1.0-SNAPSHOT.war' is produced as well. Refer to Fig. 2.9.
3. Note that you can also do this from a command line by typing in 'mvn install'.

The project is now fully compiled and it is ready for deployment for testing. To deploy the project onto Tomcat and run the service, do the following:

Fig. 2.9 Maven project folders (build complete)

1. If you haven't done so, create a new server configuration in Eclipse to work with your Tomcat 7 installation (see the detailed instructions in Sect. 1.4).
2. Right click on the new server (it is probably named something like 'Tomcat v.7 server at localhost' by default). Choose the 'Add and Remove' option. Add 'HelloWorldCXF' project and click 'Finish'.
3. Start the Tomcat server
4. You should not see any error message on the Console view. We expect you to see something like (roughly):

```
INFO: Loading XML bean definitions ... [/WEB-INF/beans.xml]
INFO: Loading XML bean definitions ... [META-INF/cxf/cxf.xml]
INFO: Creating Service ...HelloWorldImplService from
class au.edu.unsw.soacourse.hello.HelloWorld
INFO: Setting the server's publish address to be /HelloWorld
```

If you are not seeing this message, something has gone wrong. You should try to fix any issue before proceeding with the rest of the exercise. Refer to the Github site for updates and FAQs.

Let us see if the service is actually functional by calling and testing its operation. Eclipse IDE provides what is called '*Web Service Explorer*' for this purpose.

1. Go to Run → Launch the Web Service Explorer. On the Explorer page, click the little icon 'WSDL page'. The icon is located in the top-right corner, next to the yellow star icon.
2. On the Explorer, from the Navigator pane, click 'WSDL Main'.

3. Then, enter the following address for the WSDL, and click 'Go'.

```
http://localhost:8080/HelloWorldCXF/HelloWorld?wsdl
```

4. Click on the operation 'sayHi'.
5. The 'sayHi' operation is expecting one argument. Click 'Add' next to arg0.
6. Type in a string value 'fromApacheCXF' and click 'Go'.

You should see the appropriate response from the Web service operation sayHi in the Status window of the Web Service Explorer. Now in the next section, we will build our own services.

2.5.2 Activity 2: Building Simple Services

First, the user guide documentation from the Apache CXF Web site[4] gives a good overview of how to use the CXF libraries to build Web services. There are two main approaches to Web service development:

- Bottom-up approach (code first): taking your existing (Java) code and exposing it as a Web service.
- Top-down approach (contract first): starting from designing the service interface and writing its WSDL.

In this exercise activity, we will briefly look at both approaches.

2.5.2.1   Bottom-Up (Code First) Web Service Development

In bottom-up development, you build a Web service from an existing Java class. To do this in Apache CXF, you take the following steps:

1. Create a Service Endpoint Interface (SEI) that defines the methods you want to expose as a service.
2. Add the required Java annotations to your code.
3. Generate the WSDL contract for your service (optional).
4. Publish the service as a service provider.

In fact, in HelloWorldCXF, we have seen the results of these steps in the exercise above. In the above exercise, we saw an example of an SEI (i.e., the HelloWorld interface declaring the sayHi() method). HelloWorldImpl.java was the exiting Java class which contains the actual implementation of sayHi(). Because the SEI is a standard Java interface, the class

---

[4]http://cxf.apache.org/docs/developing-a-service.html.

that implements it is a standard Java class. If you start with a Java class you must modify it to implement the interface. If you start with the SEI, the implementation class implements the SEI.

In `HelloWorldCXF`, we published the service using `CXFServlet` as an WAR file to the Tomcat server. We did not explicitly generate the matching WSDL contract, but we know that Apache CXF must have generated one based on the SEI because we could access it via the URL:

```
http://localhost:8080/HelloWorldCXF/HelloWorld?wsdl
```

The automatic code generation part for this bottom-up approach is based on the `@WebService` annotation added to the SEI and its implementation class. Note that, as you have seen from the `HelloWorldCXF` exercise, the `@WebService` annotation should be added to *both* the SEI and the implementation class.

The `@WebService` annotation establishes the metadata used to map the SEI to a fully specified service definition. For example, the SEI corresponds to a `wsdl:portType` element. The methods defined by the SEI correspond to the element `wsdl:operation` in the element `wsdl:portType`.

The complete list of properties associated with `@WebService` can be found in Apache CXF documentation.[5] It is not necessary to give a value to all of them. But you may as well test them out and see the effects.

Expose SimpleServices.java as a Web Service (Code First)

Now, take the exercise file `SimpleServices.java`. Let's consider this Java class as your '*existing*' Java code that you want to expose as a Web service. Using the information given in the `HelloWorldCXF` exercise, create a Web service that exposes two methods (`importMarketData()`, `downloadFile()`) in the `SimpleService` class. Pay particular attentions to the following:

1. You can start with the auto-generated Maven archetype from the `HelloWorldCXF` exercise and replace the source files with your own.
2. Use `groupId=au.edu.unsw.soacourse`, `artifactId=SimpleServices`.
3. You need to declare the SEI for the implementation class `SimpleServices`.
4. `@WebService` annotations appear on both the SEI and implementation class.
5. The Apache CXF relevant libraries for this exercise are already configured with Maven (`pom.xml`), so those will be correctly included in the class path for compiling and packaging.
   In `pom.xml`, the default Java compiler version may be 1.6 in the given file. If that is the case, modify the value to version 1.7 instead. Look for the following XML configuration part:

---

[5]`http://cxf.apache.org/docs/developing-a-service.html#Developinga Service-The@WebServiceannotation.`

```
<plugin>
  <groupId>org.apache.maven.plugins</groupId>
  <artifactId>maven-compiler-plugin</artifactId>
  <configuration>
    <source>1.6</source>
    <target>1.6</target>
  </configuration>
</plugin>
```

Update 1.6 with 1.7. Save pom.xml and run 'Update Project' by right-clicking on the project root folder → Maven → Update Project.

6. In the beans.xml file, configure the jaxws:endpoint element. Set the address of the service and also the implementor class correctly.
7. Run Maven install, and add the project to the Tomcat server to deploy.
8. Test the service operations using the Web Service Explorer in Eclipse.

2.5.2.2   Topdown (Contract First) Web Service Development

Although the bottom-up approach gives you a way to expose an existing Java class as a Web service quickly, the final product is not as flexible as a service you create from scratch. Using the 'contact first' approach, you are required to *think* about what the new service is *going to do* (i.e., what is the client going to get from your service?). In this approach, one defines the functionality of the service in an abstract manner first, then implements it accordingly. In this service development method, we write the service contract in WSDL. That is, the functionality of the service to be created is defined in WSDL.

Now we are going to add a new service to the existing project from the previous exercise 'SimpleServices'. This time, we are going to implement the same service operations using the contract-first approach.

Design and Build SimpleServices.java from WSDL (Contract First).

1. First, you should add new folders under src/main to house the WSDL file. The path should look like src/main/resources/wsdl. You might have to update the project again to make sure that Maven knows about the new project folders (see Fig. 2.10).
2. Use the WSDL editor provided by the Eclipse IDE. Right click on the folder 'src/main/resources/wsdl'. Go to New → Other → Web Services → WSDL. Name the file 'TopDownSimpleService.wsdl'.

   - Set 'http://topdown.soacourse.unsw.edu.au' as the Target Namespace for the WSDL.
   - Leave the following settings as they are: *Protocol* – SOAP, *SOAP binding option* – document/literal.

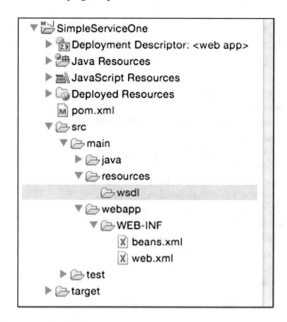

Fig. 2.10 Adding new project folders

3. Now you have a simple skeleton of a WSDL file. We do not recommend the graphical view (i.e., the 'Design' view) of the editor. It is better to edit the XML directly using the 'Source' view.
4. Let us think what we are going to change here. Examine `SimpleServices.java` again. There are two operations, `importMarketData()` and `downloadFile()`.
5. Go to the '`portType`' element in WSDL. This is where we will define the two operations and their input/output messages. First, for the operations, change the skeleton code so that it looks like the code shown in Listing 2.1.

```
1 <wsdl:portType name="TopDownSimpleService">
2    <wsdl:operation name="importMarketData">
3      <wsdl:input message="tns:importMarketDataRequestMsg"/>
4      <wsdl:output message="tns:importMarketDataResponseMsg"/>
5    </wsdl:operation>
6    <wsdl:operation name="downloadFile">
7      <wsdl:input message="tns:downloadFileRequestMsg"/>
8      <wsdl:output message="tns:downloadFileResponseMsg"/>
9    </wsdl:operation>
10   </wsdl:portType>
```

Listing 2.1 portType definitions

6. Now, go to the '`message`' elements. Here, we will detail the messages we named in the operations in the `portType` element. Let us say every message

we use will have one part (i.e., a single XML fragment). Change the skeleton code so that it looks like the code shown in Listing 2.2.

```
1  <wsdl:message name="importMarketDataRequestMsg">
2    <wsdl:part name="parameters"
         element="tns:importMarketDataRequest"/>
3  </wsdl:message>
4  <wsdl:message name="importMarketDataResponseMsg">
5    <wsdl:part name="parameters"
         element="tns:importMarketDataResponse"/>
6  </wsdl:message>
7  <wsdl:message name="downloadFileRequestMsg">
8    <wsdl:part name="parameters"
         element="tns:downloadFileRequest"/>
9  </wsdl:message>
10 <wsdl:message name="downloadFileResponseMsg">
11   <wsdl:part name="parameters"
         element="tns:downloadFileResponse"/>
12 </wsdl:message>
```

Listing 2.2 Message definitions

7. Then we need to describe what each part in the message looks like. That is, we will define the composition of the XML elements:
   `importMarketDataRequest`, `importMarketDataResponse`,
   `downloadFileRequest`, `downloadFileResponse`.
   To do this, go to the 'types' element. Change the skeleton code of the 'schema' section as shown in Listing 2.3.

```
1  <wsdl:types>
2    <xsd:schema
       targetNamespace="http://marketservice.soacourse.unsw.edu.au">
3      <xsd:element name="importMarketDataRequest">
4        <xsd:complexType>
5          <xsd:sequence>
6            <xsd:element name="sec" nillable="false"
         type="xsd:string"/>
7            <xsd:element name="startDate" nillable="false"
         type="xsd:string"/>
8            <xsd:element name="endDate" nillable="false"
         type="xsd:string"/>
9            <xsd:element name="dataSource" nillable="false"
         type="xsd:string"/>
10         </xsd:sequence>
11       </xsd:complexType>
12     </xsd:element>
13     <xsd:element name="importMarketDataResponse">
14       <xsd:complexType>
15         <xsd:sequence>
16           <xsd:element name="returnData" nillable="false"
         type="xsd:string"/>
17         </xsd:sequence>
```

```
18            </xsd:complexType>
19          </xsd:element>
20          <xsd:element name="downloadFileRequest">
21            <xsd:complexType>
22             <xsd:sequence>
23                  <xsd:element name="eventSetID" nillable="false"
        type="xsd:string"/>
24             </xsd:sequence>
25            </xsd:complexType>
26          </xsd:element>
27          <xsd:element name="downloadFileResponse">
28            <xsd:complexType>
29             <xsd:sequence>
30                  <xsd:element name="returnData" nillable="true"
        type="xsd:string"/>
31             </xsd:sequence>
32            </xsd:complexType>
33          </xsd:element>
34       </xsd:schema>
35    </wsdl:types>
```

Listing 2.3 Message type definitions

8. Go to the 'binding' and 'service' elements. Change the skeleton code of the sections as shown in Listing 2.4.

```
1  <wsdl:binding name="TopDownSimpleServiceSOAP"
        type="tns:TopDownSimpleService">
2    <soap:binding style="document"
        transport="http://schemas.xmlsoap.org/soap/http"/>
3    <wsdl:operation name="importMarketData">
4       <soap:operation soapAction=
5  "http://marketservice.soacourse.unsw.edu.au/importMarketData"/>
6       <wsdl:input>
7          <soap:body use="literal"/>
8       </wsdl:input>
9       <wsdl:output>
10         <soap:body use="literal"/>
11      </wsdl:output>
12    </wsdl:operation>
13    <wsdl:operation name="downloadFile">
14       <soap:operation soapAction=
15  "http://marketservice.soacourse.unsw.edu.au/downloadFile"/>
16       <wsdl:input>
17          <soap:body use="literal"/>
18       </wsdl:input>
19       <wsdl:output>
20          <soap:body use="literal"/>
21       </wsdl:output>
22    </wsdl:operation>
23  </wsdl:binding>
```

```
24 <wsdl:service name="TopDownSimpleService">
25   <wsdl:port binding="tns:TopDownSimpleServiceSOAP"
26       name="TopDownSimpleServiceSOAP">
27     <soap:address location=
28 "http://localhost:8080/SimpleServiceOne/TopDownSimpleService"/>
29   </wsdl:port>
30 </wsdl:service>
```

Listing 2.4 Binding and service definitions

9. Now validate the finished WSDL. Right click on the WSDL file → Validate. See if everything is OK. If there is any error, fix the issue before proceeding. Pay particular attention to making sure that every opening tag is properly closed.
10. From the contract (WSDL), the Apache CXF tools will auto-generate some code. First, run the tool and examine the results. Open the pom.xml file. Enter the following into the 'build' element.

```
<plugins>
  <plugin>
    <groupId>org.apache.cxf</groupId>
    <artifactId>cxf-codegen-plugin</artifactId>
    <version>3.0.4</version>
    <executions>
      <execution>
        <id>generate-sources</id>
        <phase>generate-sources</phase>
      <configuration>
        <sourceRoot>src/main/java-generated</sourceRoot>
        <wsdlOptions>
          <wsdlOption>
            <wsdl>${basedir}/src/main/resources/wsdl/
                  TopDownSimpleService.wsdl</wsdl>
          </wsdlOption>
        </wsdlOptions>
      </configuration>
      <goals>
          <goal>wsdl2java</goal>
      </goals>
      </execution>
    </executions>
  </plugin>
</plugins>
```

By doing this, you are adding a Maven plug-in from Apache CXF for code generation (cxf-codegen-plugin). This plug-in runs WSDL2Java, which is the actual tool that generates code from WSDL. This plug-in will run as a new goal, 'generate-sources', which means you can execute it using 'mvn generate-sources' in the command line, or from the context menu in the IDE. Do Run As → Maven → mvn generate-sources.

11. Save `pom.xml` and update the project by right clicking on the project root →
Maven → Update Project.
12. Now run `wsdl2java`. Right click on the project root → Run As → Maven
generate-sources. You should see s 'Build Success' message in the console.
Refresh the project to see the newly generated content. The new source code
should be under `src/main/java-generated`.
13. Examine the Java source files. You will see the classes that represent the
request/response message parts in Java objects (e.g., `ImportMarket`
`Request.java`). Notice the `ObjectFactory.java` file and examine the
content. An `ObjectFactory` allows you to pragmatically create new instances
of the Java representation of the XML message parts we see (e.g., `create`
`ImportMarketDataRequest()` method).
14. The next file to look at is the SEI (service endpoint interface) file for the service
itself (`TopDownSimpleService.java`). WSDL2Java has mapped the definitions available in the WSDL to the interface using annotations. You can get
more information about those extra annotations that you see in the Apache CXF
documentation page.[6]
15. Now your task is to implement the SEI by creating and completing the file
`TopDownSimpleServiceImpl.java`. You may want to look at the sample
exercise file `TopDownSimpleServiceImpl.java` included in the exercise
files. But try to code this yourself as an exercise.
16. After the coding is done, you are ready to configure the service and deploy it.
You may replace `beans.xml` with the new `beans.xml` file provided. Notice
the new configurations added:

- a new endpoint for `TopDownSimpleService`
- Java Spring context 'component-scan' – this will automatically scan the
specified package space to recognise any new beans to be included.

17. Double check that you are comfortable with the endpoint address and the path
to the implementor class.
18. Run Maven Install and deploy it to Tomcat. Test the new service using Web
Service Explorer.

---

[6]`http://cxf.apache.org/docs/developing-a-service.html#Developinga`
`Service-DefiningOperationPropertieswithAnnotations`.

Practical Exercise II

2.6   Lab Exercise 02: Fault Handling in Apache CXF and Web Service Client Development

In this lab, we will look at two more aspects in Web service development with Apache CXF.

- Defining and handling custom (i.e., user-defined) SOAP Faults.
- Writing a Web service client application as a consumer of the Web service.

We assume that you have completed *Lab Exercise 01 – Developing simple Web services with Apache CXF and Maven* already. You may find that detailed instructions are skipped when similar instructions were shown or given in the previous labs.

Exercise Files

The exercise files involved in the lab can be downloaded from the Github site:

- `https://github.com/SOA-Book`

Follow the repository `exercises`, then `lab02`.

2.6.1   Activity 1: Adding SOAP Faults to TopDownSimpleService

Let us start by getting a fresh Maven template by following the steps through the Maven template generation process.

1. Run the following from a terminal under `YOUR_WORKSPACE`:

   `$mvn archetype:generate -Dfilter=org.apache.cxf.archetype:`

2. When the template generation is complete, import it into Eclipse as an existing Maven project as in the previous lab.

   - Use `au.edu.unsw.soacourse` as the groupId,
   - Use `TopDownSimpleService` as the artifactId,
   - Name the package as `au.edu.unsw.soacourse.marketservice`.

3. We are going to start by taking the `TopDownSimpleService.wsdl` file from the previous lab. Put the file under the 'src/resources/wsdl' folder.

4. Examine the file. The WSDL contains definitions of `importMarketData()` and `downloadFile()` operations.

   NOTE: A real implementation of the above operations would involve, roughly, (i) reading a file from a data source (URL) which contains second-by-second data of price changes on a stock, (ii) filtering the relevant lines in the file according to the given date range, (iii) preparing the resulting lines as a separate file so that it can be downloaded (via a `downloadFile()` *operation). However, for the exercise, we do not need to implement the real business logic of these two operations. We will leave the operation implementation as it was in the previous lab (i.e., mainly string concatenation), but add other aspects to the service that we want to practice on, such as SOAP faults.*

   Now, let us assume that we want to create one custom exception for each operation in the WSDL file.

- In `importMarketData()`, we will check if the input element `sec` is in the format expected by the service. If not, we will raise an exception.
- In the `downloadFile()` operation, we will check if the input element `eventSetId` is 'known' to the service. If not, we will raise an exception.

   Of course, these exceptions are going to be sent over to the requester as SOAP faults.

   In the contract-first design approach, we should declare these custom faults in the WSDL file. Open the WSDL file and edit it as instructed below:

1. In `wsdl:portType` and `wsdl:operation`, for each operation add a fault message as a possible output option. Now your operation definitions should look like what is shown in Listing 2.5.

```
1  <wsdl:portType name="TopDownSimpleService">
2      <wsdl:operation name="importMarketData">
3         <wsdl:input message="tns:importMarketDataRequestMsg"/>
4         <wsdl:output message="tns:importMarketDataResponseMsg"/>
5         <wsdl:fault name="secfault"
       message="tns:importMarketFaultMsg"></wsdl:fault>
6      </wsdl:operation>
7      <wsdl:operation name="downloadFile">
8         <wsdl:input message="tns:downloadFileRequestMsg"/>
9         <wsdl:output message="tns:downloadFileResponseMsg"/>
10        <wsdl:fault name="eventfault"
       message="tns:downloadFileFaultMsg"></wsdl:fault>
11     </wsdl:operation>
12  </wsdl:portType>
```

Listing 2.5 Adding faults to operations

2. Now in the `wsdl:message` sections, we need to declare two fault messages for the operations: `importMarketFaultMsg` and `downloadFileFaultMsg`.

In each of the fault messages, we declare that it has elements importMarket
Fault and downloadFileFault. The types of these new elements will be
defined in the next step. The new message definition sections should be like what
is shown in Listing 2.6. Note the new fault messages.

```
 1 <wsdl:message name="importMarketDataRequestMsg">
 2    <wsdl:part name="parameters"
         element="tns:importMarketDataRequest"/>
 3 </wsdl:message>
 4 <wsdl:message name="importMarketDataResponseMsg">
 5    <wsdl:part name="parameters"
         element="tns:importMarketDataResponse"/>
 6 </wsdl:message>
 7 <wsdl:message name="importMarketFaultMsg">
 8    <wsdl:part name="parameters"
         element="tns:importMarketFault"/>
 9 </wsdl:message>
10 <wsdl:message name="downloadFileRequestMsg">
11    <wsdl:part name="parameters"
         element="tns:downloadFileRequest"/>
12 </wsdl:message>
13 <wsdl:message name="downloadFileResponseMsg">
14    <wsdl:part name="parameters"
         element="tns:downloadFileResponse"/>
15 </wsdl:message>
16 <wsdl:message name="downloadFileFaultMsg">
17    <wsdl:part name="parameters"
         element="tns:downloadFileFault"/>
18 </wsdl:message>
```

Listing 2.6 Adding fault message definitions

3. Now in the wsdl:types → xsd:schema section, let's add type definitions for the two fault messages and their elements. We'd like to have the
   errors to have a custom error code and some text. So, for each fault message, declare one common type, called serviceFaultType, which has a
   sequence of two elements: errorcode and errortext. After that, we will
   finally declare elements importMarketFault and downloadFileFault
   of serviceFaultType. The code is shown in Listing 2.7. Note the service
   FaultType definition and the two new fault message elements import
   MarketFault and downloadFileFault.

```
1 <wsdl:types>
2     <xsd:schema
        targetNamespace="http://marketservice.soacourse.unsw.edu.au">
3         <xsd:element name="importMarketDataRequest">
4           <xsd:complexType>
5             <xsd:sequence>
6               <xsd:element name="sec" nillable="false"
        type="xsd:string"/>
```

```
 7              <xsd:element name="startDate" nillable="false"
        type="xsd:string"/>
 8              <xsd:element name="endDate" nillable="false"
        type="xsd:string"/>
 9              <xsd:element name="dataSource" nillable="false"
        type="xsd:string"/>
10          </xsd:sequence>
11         </xsd:complexType>
12        </xsd:element>
13        <xsd:element name="importMarketDataResponse">
14         <xsd:complexType>
15           <xsd:sequence>
16               <xsd:element name="returnData" nillable="false"
        type="xsd:string"/>
17           </xsd:sequence>
18         </xsd:complexType>
19        </xsd:element>
20        <xsd:element name="downloadFileRequest">
21         <xsd:complexType>
22          <xsd:sequence>
23              <xsd:element name="eventSetID" nillable="false"
        type="xsd:string"/>
24          </xsd:sequence>
25         </xsd:complexType>
26        </xsd:element>
27        <xsd:element name="downloadFileResponse">
28         <xsd:complexType>
29          <xsd:sequence>
30              <xsd:element name="returnData" nillable="true"
        type="xsd:string"/>
31          </xsd:sequence>
32         </xsd:complexType>
33        </xsd:element>
34        <xsd:complexType name="serviceFaultType">
35       <xsd:sequence>
36        <xsd:element name="errcode" type="xsd:string"></xsd:element>
37        <xsd:element name="errtext" type="xsd:string"></xsd:element>
38       </xsd:sequence>
39     </xsd:complexType>
40     <xsd:element name="importMarketFault"
         type="tns:serviceFaultType"></xsd:element>
41     <xsd:element name="downloadFileFault"
         type="tns:serviceFaultType"></xsd:element>
42     </xsd:schema>
43   </wsdl:types>
```

Listing 2.7 Adding fault message type definitions

4. Now these new changes have to be reflected in the binding definitions as well. In the `wsdl:binding` section, add a message binding for the faults in each operation so that the fault messages are also recognised here. Note that in `soap:fault`, the name attribute (which refers to the name of the fault message defined) is compulsory. The new binding section should look like the code shown in Listing 2.8. Note the addition of wsdl:fault and soap:fault in each operation.

```
1 <wsdl:binding name="TopDownSimpleServiceSOAP"
       type="tns:TopDownSimpleService">
2   <soap:binding style="document"
       transport="http://schemas.xmlsoap.org/soap/http"/>
3   <wsdl:operation name="importMarketData">
4     <soap:operation soapAction=
5 "http://marketservice.soacourse.unsw.edu.au/importMarketData"/>
6     <wsdl:input>
7       <soap:body use="literal"/>
8     </wsdl:input>
9     <wsdl:output>
10       <soap:body use="literal"/>
11     </wsdl:output>
12     <wsdl:fault name="secfault">
13       <soap:fault name="secfault" use="literal"/>
14     </wsdl:fault>
15   </wsdl:operation>
16   <wsdl:operation name="downloadFile">
17     <soap:operation soapAction=
18 "http://marketservice.soacourse.unsw.edu.au/downloadFile"/>
19     <wsdl:input>
20       <soap:body use="literal"/>
21     </wsdl:input>
22     <wsdl:output>
23       <soap:body use="literal"/>
24     </wsdl:output>
25     <wsdl:fault name="eventfault">
26       <soap:fault name="eventfault" use="literal"/>
27     </wsdl:fault>
28   </wsdl:operation>
29 </wsdl:binding>
```

Listing 2.8 Adding fault message to binding definitions

The above step completes all the information required to declare SOAP faults in WSDL. Now based on this new contract, you want to generate the code and complete the service logic.

1. To generate the code, add the code-gen plugin configuration into `pom.xml`. You may copy from the previous lab. While doing this, make sure that the maven-compiler-plugin part is referencing JDK 1.7. Update the Maven project and make sure that you are seeing no errors.

2. Run 'mvn generate-sources'. Refresh the project content and examine the src/main/java-generated directory. In addition to the usual Request/Response beans, you should notice new SOAP fault message-related beans like ServiceFaultType, ImportMarketFaultMsg, and DownloadFaultMsg.
3. Also, in the SEI TopDownSimpleService, you should see download File() throwing DownloadFileFaultMsg, and also importMarket Data() throwing ImportMarketFaultMsg.

Now let us implement the interface SEI TopDownSimpleService, this time with the SOAP faults.

1. Create a new class TopDownSimpleServiceImpl. To start with, the new class skeleton should be something like in the Listing 2.9.

```
 1 package au.edu.unsw.soacourse.marketservice;
 2
 3 import javax.jws.WebService;
 4
 5 @WebService(endpointInterface
       ="au.edu.unsw.soacourse.marketservice.TopDownSimpleService")
 6 public class TopDownSimpleServiceImpl implements
       TopDownSimpleService {
 7
 8     ObjectFactory factory = new ObjectFactory();
 9
10     public ImportMarketDataResponse
       importMarketData(ImportMarketDataRequest parameters) throws
       ImportMarketFaultMsg {
11
12       return null;
13
14   }
15
16     public DownloadFileResponse downloadFile(DownloadFileRequest
       parameters) throws DownloadFileFaultMsg {
17
18       return null;
19   }
20 }
```

Listing 2.9   New implementation class

That is, the class TopDownSimpleServiceImpl implements the SEI interface. It should also have the @WebService annotation (with the matching endpointInterface correctly defined). The skeletons of the methods in question are ready to be filled in.
2. You may have a look at the sample implementation of the class provided in TopDownSimpleServiceImpl.java. It includes the rough code for

generating SOAP faults for each operation. Complete the necessary sections, but also modify the code as you see fit.

3. Once you are happy that the code is complete, configure the project for compilation and deployment. Go to `src/main/webapp`, and open `beans.xml`. Configure the endpoint as shown in Listing 2.10.

```
1  <?xml version="1.0"encoding="UTF-8"?>
2  <beans xmlns="http://www.springframework.org/schema/beans"
3    xmlns:xsi="http://www.w3.org/2001/XMLSchema-instance"
4    xmlns:jaxws="http://cxf.apache.org/jaxws"
5    xsi:schemaLocation="
6    http://www.springframework.org/schema/beans
       http://www.springframework.org/schema/beans/spring-beans.xsd
7    http://cxf.apache.org/jaxws
       http://cxf.apache.org/schemas/jaxws.xsd">
8
9    <import resource="classpath:META-INF/cxf/cxf.xml"/>
10
11   <jaxws:endpoint
12     id="topdownfault"
13     implementor=
14 "au.edu.unsw.soacourse.marketservice.TopDownSimpleServiceImpl"
15     address="/topdownfault"/>
16 </beans>
```

Listing 2.10 WS endpoint configuration: beans.xml

4. Now save everything, compile and deploy the code to Tomcat.

2.6.1.1 Seeing the SOAP Faults

Once the service is deployed, you may use the Web Service Explorer in Eclipse to quickly check if the SOAP faults are thrown as expected, but the Web Service Explorer may not display the actual SOAP message in XML clearly. We will look at using a popular Web service testing tool named *SoapUI*.

Using SoapUI as a test client

Download a binary distribution of SoapUI from the SourceForge site.[7] After downloading, install it according to their instructions. Run SoapUI, then try the following for quick testing.

1. Go to File → New SOAP Project. On the pop-up window, name the new project (e.g., Lab02 Test) and enter the URL of the WSDL. In this lab, it should be (refer to Fig. 2.11):

---

[7]http://sourceforge.net/projects/soapui/files.

```
http://localhost:8080/TopDownSimpleService/topdownfault?wsdl
```

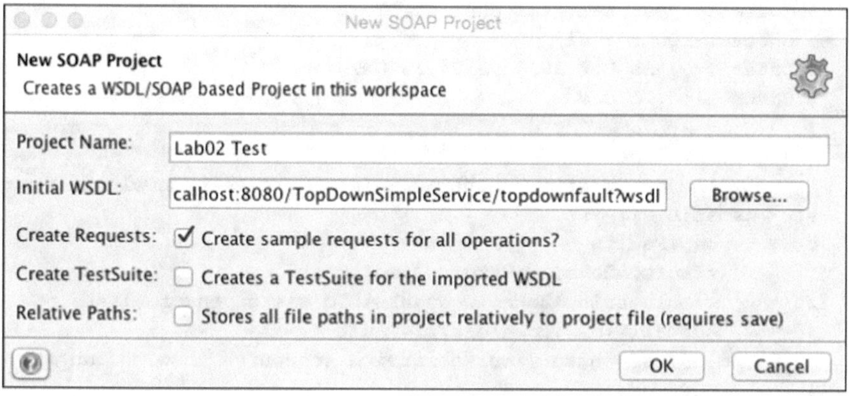

Fig. 2.11 SoapUI – New Project

2. On the navigation pane, of the tool on the left, you should see the new project created. Expand the project to see the service and its operations. When you click on the name of the operation, it should expand to show 'Request 1'. Double click 'Request 1'. Fill in test values (in the SOAP request). Press the green arrow button (at the top left corner). You should see the SOAP response. Send a request that will generate a fault (e.g., 'XXX') and see the structure of the returned SOAP fault. When you examine the raw content of the SOAP messages exchanged through SOAP UI, you should see something like the following. Listing 2.11 shows the SOAP request content, and Listing 2.12 shows the SOAP response content. In this case, the custom SOAP fault we have defined is showing.

```
 1 POST http://localhost:8080/TopDownSimpleService/topdownfault
        HTTP/1.1
 2 Accept-Encoding: gzip,deflate
 3 Content-Type: text/xml;charset=UTF-8
 4 SOAPAction:"http://marketservice.soacourse.unsw.edu.au/downloadFile"
 5 Content-Length: 312
 6 Host: localhost:8080
 7 Connection: Keep-Alive
 8 User-Agent: Apache-HttpClient/4.1.1 (java 1.5)
 9
10 <soapenv:Envelope
        xmlns:soapenv="http://schemas.xmlsoap.org/soap/envelope/"
        xmlns:mar="http://marketservice.soacourse.unsw.edu.au">
11    <soapenv:Header/>
12    <soapenv:Body>
13       <mar:downloadFileRequest>
14          <eventSetID>XXX</eventSetID>
15       </mar:downloadFileRequest>
16    </soapenv:Body>
17 </soapenv:Envelope>
```

Listing 2.11 Showing SOAP request (raw content; the request is wrapped in HTTP request)

```
 1 HTTP/1.1 500 Internal Server Error
 2 Server: Apache-Coyote/1.1
 3 Content-Type: text/xml;charset=UTF-8
 4 Content-Length: 417
 5 Date: Tue, 25 Oct 2016 03:04:33 GMT
 6 Connection: close
 7
 8 <soap:Envelope
      xmlns:soap="http://schemas.xmlsoap.org/soap/envelope/">
 9   <soap:Body>
10    <soap:Fault>
11      <faultcode>soap:Server</faultcode>
12      <faultstring>Unknonw eventSetId was given</faultstring>
13      <detail><ns2:downloadFileFault
      xmlns:ns2="http://marketservice.soacourse.unsw.edu.au">
14      <errcode>ERR_EVENT</errcode>
15      <errtext>Unknonw eventSetId was
      given</errtext></ns2:downloadFileFault>
16      </detail>
17    </soap:Fault>
18   </soap:Body>
19 </soap:Envelope>
```

Listing 2.12 Showing SOAP Fault response (raw content; the response is wrapped in HTTP response)

2.6.2   Activity 2: Developing a Web Service Client Application

In this part of the lab, we will learn how to develop a proper consumer application of a Web service. It is likely that your client application is also a Web application. So, let's look at the option where a Web service is consumed as part of some other Web application. In this exercise, we will use Spring MVC libraries to create a typical MVC-based Web application.

In the following, we will build a Web application (MVC-based) that will access the operations of the TopDownSimpleservice we implemented above.

Project Template Creation, Maven, Spring MVC Configurations, and Setting Up the Basic Structure for the MVC Operation

Let's create a Web application template using a Maven archetype first. Run the following (all in one line):

```
mvn archetype:generate
-DgroupId=au.edu.unsw.soacourse
-DartifactId=TopDownServiceClient
-DarchetypeArtifactId=maven-archetype-webapp
-DinteractiveMode=false
```

If running this for the first time, it may take a while for the tool to complete the command. After running it successfully, you should get a new directory named 'TopDownServiceClient'.

Import the template into Eclipse as 'Existing Maven Project'. After importing the files, examine the template directory. It is quite bare at the moment. Note some generic stuff here, such as the pom.xml file, src/main/webapp and src/main/webapp/WEB-INF.

- Note the basic info in pom.xml such as 'groupId' and 'arfifactId'.
- The webapp directory contains most of the Web application programming files (e.g., JSP), static HTML files, and Web application configuration files (such as web.xml)

We need to add some code to make it more relevant to our task. First, create a directory named 'java' under /src/main. We will create Java files for the project there. Second, create a 'jsp' directory under /src/main/webapp/WEB-INF. We will create JSP files for the project there.

Note on creating new projects in Maven. *At this point, let us think about creating these new templates in Maven. Obviously, you do not want to run Maven's* archetype:generate *every time. Also, the archetypes do not give you the precise structure of the project and artifacts. For example, you may want the directory* /src/main/java *all the time, or you'd like* pom.xml *to have the necessary plugins declared already. Obviously, one easy way to do this is to have your own Maven project directory structure and artifacts. Save it as your own template (in any archive file format will do, such as zip or tar). Whenever you want to create a new project based on the template, you could import the template as an existing Maven project. Another way to do this is to create your own custom Maven archetype using the template. It may take a bit of effort at the start, but if you are going to use the template often, it probably is worth the time spent. More information about how to create your own custom Maven archetype can be found in the Maven user guide.*[8]

---

[8]https://maven.apache.org/guides/mini/guide-creating-archetypes.html.

Now let us start adding some code and configuring the project to work with Apache CXF and Spring MVC.

1. Take the `pom.xml` file provided for this exercise. Replace the existing `pom.xml` with this version. Let us examine the new POM file to see what configuration changes have been added.

   - First, there are the Apache CXF libraries (this is the same as in the server-side project configuration).
   - Second, there are Spring MVC libraries and JSTL libraries, so that we can build a Web application using a simple Spring MVC framework guide.
   - Third, other Maven plug-ins we have been using in the previous labs such as the compiler are already added.

2. Now, we are going to add the `code-generation` plug-in, so that we can generate the client-side code template from the WSDL of `TopDownSimple Service`. To do this, add the following declaration, inserting it just below the `<build>` element, and above the `<pluginManagement>` element:

```
<plugins>
<plugin>
  <groupId>org.apache.cxf</groupId>
  <artifactId>cxf-codegen-plugin</artifactId>
  <version>3.0.4</version>
  <executions>
    <execution>
      <id>generate-sources</id>
      <phase>generate-sources</phase>
      <configuration>
        <sourceRoot>src/main/java-generated</sourceRoot>
        <wsdlOptions>
          <wsdlOption>
          <wsdl>http://localhost:8080/TopDownSimpleService/
                topdownfault?wsdl</wsdl>
          </wsdlOption>
        </wsdlOptions>
      </configuration>
      <goals>
        <goal>wsdl2java</goal>
      </goals>
    </execution>
  </executions>
</plugin>
</plugins>
```

While adding this information, pay particular attention to the address of the WSDL file. It is referring to the already deployed service's location. That is, it is the endpoint of the service to which the client program sends a request.

3. After the configuration update, take the `web.xml` file provided for this exercise and replace the existing one (under `src/main/wcbapp/WEB-INF/`) with this version. You do not have to change anything in this file. The file is commented to explain what the configuration details are for. To summarise the main points to note in the file:

   - `WEB-INF/dispatcher-servlet.xml` is the Spring MVC configuration file for this project.
   - The dispatcher servlet, which is supplied by the Spring MVC itself, is declared and mapped. According to the mapping configuration, all URLs matching the specified URL pattern will be handled by the Spring MVC dispatcher servlet.

4. Now, take the `dispatcher-servlet.xml` file provided for this exercise and place it under `WEB-INF`. You can do this by importing the file into the project. This is the main configuration file as far as Spring MVC and its working with Apache CXF goes. Open the file and examine the following points:

   - Spring MVC `viewResolver` bean is going to use `WEB-INF/jsp/*.jsp` for the 'View' part of the MVC framework.
   - `jaxws:client` is similar to the `jaxws:endpoint` declaration on the server side, except for the fact that it is now for the client application to use. Let us look at the properties.
     - `id="simple"`: identifier for the Web service client bean
     - `address`: The URL to connect to in order to invoke the service
     - `serviceClass`: The fully qualified name of the interface that the bean should implement (typically, same as the service interface used on the server side).

       In our case, the fully qualified SEI points to:

       `au.edu.unsw.soacourse.marketservice.TopDownSimpleService`

5. Now, take the `MarketServiceController.java` file provided for the exercise and import it into `/src/main/java`. Adjust the content so that you have the proper package structure recognised. Let's look inside the code for a moment:

   - The `@Controller` annotation just tells the container that this bean is a designated controller class. If you are interested, the 'component-scan' declared in `dispatcher-servlet.xml` will enable Spring to automatically detect the bean annotated with `@Controller` and recognise it as such.
   - The `@RequestMapping` annotation is used to map a particular HTTP request (URL) to a specific class/method in the controller, which will handle the respective request. The `@RequestMapping` annotation can be applied at both the class and the method levels. The intention here is that a request whose URL ends with "/importMarketData" will be handled by the method named `processImportMarketData()`, and the ones that end with "/downloadFile" will be handled by the `processDownloadFile()` method. There are some TODO lines that we will fill in as we go.

6. According to the controller code above, the methods will return to the views 'processImportMarketData' and 'processDownloadFile' respectively.

   To complete this, let us create some template JSP files for them (note: you could probably do this as a single view, but let's try and create separate views for the sake of the exercise here).

   Take the two JSP files provided for this exercise: processImport MarketData.jsp and processDownloadFile.jsp. Import and place them under the WEB-INF/jsp/ directory. Open the files and examine the content. It is a straightforward *view* file which uses the JSTL c : out to print some value.

2.6.2.1   Code Generation and Calling Web Service to Complete the Client App

Now we need to do some coding to fill in the gaps. Since the codegen plug-in will try to access the WSDL of your service (TopDownSimpleService), you need to have Tomcat running to code this part. Make sure that Tomcat is running and the service is accessible.

1. Run 'Maven generate-sources' from the project menu. You should see the generated classes in the folder /src/main/java-generated. You should also notice that the classes generated closely match the ones implemented on the service side (i.e., SEI, the request/response beans).
2. Now that you have access to these objects, you can use them in the controller code to make a call to the Web service. You can refer to the file named MarketServiceController.java provided for the exercise to complete the controller MarketServiceController.
3. Run 'Maven install' from the project menu. Deploy it onto Tomcat. The console should not show any error.
4. If everything is fine, test the client application by connecting to the following URLs:

   • http://localhost:8080/TopDownServiceClient/importMarket
   • http://localhost:8080/TopDownServiceClient/downloadFile

Something you can do as an extra exercise: The current implementation does not gracefully handle cases where the Web service operations throw SOAP faults. Modify the implementation of the client code so that it recognises SOAP faults and displays their content properly.

Chapter 3
Web Services – REST or Restful Services

Following on from the previous chapter, we now present RESTful services: the alternative yet equally (or recently even more) popular implementation method for Web services.

REST is an acronym standing for *Re*presentational *S*tate *T*ransfer, first introduced by Roy T. Fielding in his Ph.D. dissertation *Architectural Styles and the Design of Network-Based Software Architectures*. In proposing a new approach to building distributed applications unlike WS-*, where the focus was on standardising the messages and protocols, Fielding focused on the rationale behind the design of the modern Web architecture itself and highlighted how it differs from other distributed software system architectural styles. In doing so, he proposed a set of design principles for building distributed applications that is naturally suited to the Web architecture.

3.1 REST Design Principles

Most importantly, REST is an *architectural style* of networked systems (not a protocol, not a specification) whose objective is to expose *resources* on a networked system, especially on the Web. As mentioned, REST itself does not contain official standards or even a recommendation. It offers the following key concepts as component elements of its *"design guideline"* for building a service over the Web. However, these core component elements are in fact based on the core Web standards:

- *Resource identification* – all resources are uniquely identified using a URI (Uniform Resource Identifier). That is, all resources in a REST-based system are identified by a Web standard naming scheme.
- *Unified resource interface* – all resources are accessible to their potential client applications via a set of HTTP operations. That is, all resources in a REST-based system are manipulated via a uniform interface. The HTTP operations will allow the resources to be retrieved, created, deleted and updated.

© Springer International Publishing AG 2017
H.-y. Paik et al., *Web Service Implementation and Composition Techniques*,
DOI 10.1007/978-3-319-55542-3_3

- *Links and hypermedia* – the resources in a REST-based system can be linked via various relation link types. These links are used by potential client applications to navigate between different states of the same resource or different resources.

In the rest of the chapter, we will examine the individual principles in the design guideline set out in REST.

3.2   Resources

Before we go into the design principles that are applied to REST-based resources, let us take a step back and see what a resource in REST is.

It is generally agreed that a resource in REST is a "thing" (noun) that is *unique* (i.e., can be identified uniquely) and has at least one *representation*. A few examples of a resource in REST, depending on its application domain, could be Web pages, résumés, a song, movies, purchase orders, transaction records, employees, a blog posting, etc. Resources are a very generic concept and indeed some people would say 'anything' can be represented as REST resources.

However, in this book, we will assume that all resources must have a representation (i.e., a form in which the current state of a resource is transmitted to the client application). A resource must contain one or more *attributes* beyond the unique ID that can describe the resource. These attributes may also have a formal *schema* to define them. For example, for a student to be a resource, we would create a few attributes to describe him or her, such as name, address, phone number, program enrolled in, graduation year. The attributes of a resource and their values then can provide its context at any given moment.

A resource in REST has multiple representations. For example, a student named Jane Doe can be represented through an image (e.g., a picture of Jane Doe), or an XML document containing the name, address and phone number details of Jane Doe). The same details may also be transmitted via JSON format.

Based on this overview, let us go through the individual design principles that should be applied to REST-based resources.

3.3   Resource Identification

One of the core principles in REST is resource identification. Resources are identified by a URI (Uniform Resource Identifier). For example, the following is is an identification pointing to a piece of software.

```
http://www.example.com/software/release/1.0.3.tar.gz
```

It is a zipped tar file representation of the software, release version 1.0.3. The syntax of the identification used above is URL (Uniform Resource Locator).

The resource identification principle in REST says a resource has to have at least one URI. The most common forms of URI are URL and URN (Uniform Resource Name). The URN scheme is meant to allocate a unique name to a resource and there are a few well-known URN schemes such as ISBN for books or ISAN audio/visual recordings. The URL scheme is meant to allocate a means to obtain the resource referenced. For example, as shown below, `urn:isbn:0451450523` is a URN using the ISBN scheme and it corresponds to the 1968 book *The Last Unicorn*. The URL `file:///home/username/mybooks/TheLastUnicorn.pdf`, however, allows the client application to obtain a PDF representation of the book by following the URL. Although URN and URI support different usage in REST, in practice URLs are commonly used as means to identify as well as locate/obtain a resource.

- URN (Uniform Resource Name)

    `urn:isbn:0451450523`

- URL (Uniform Resource Locator)

    `file:///home/username/mybooks/TheLastUnicorn.pdf`

Every URI designates exactly one resource. It is possible that a resource is referenced by multiple URIs at a given time. For example, in the following two URLs, the version 1.0.3 release of software by the company example.com is referenced by its URL (which is not likely to change over time) and another URL which is resolved to the latest release of the resource (i.e., software v. 1.0.3).

```
http://www.example.com/software/releases/1.0.3.tar.gz
http://www.example.com/software/releases/latest
```

3.4 Addressability

Another important principle of REST is addressability. An application is deemed 'addressable' if its data set can be exploded as resources. For example, the file system on your computer is an addressable system. That is, every file in your computer is uniquely addressable. The cells in a spreadsheet are addressable via individual cell referencing.

From the REST point of view, this would mean that an addressable application should expose its data set as a set of URIs. The individual resources in the application should be directly accessible via their URIs (given that such access is allowable). We can see Google, the search engine application, as addressable. Take a resource identified by URL 'http://www.google.com.au/search?q=unsw'; this resource corresponds to the search result of the keyword 'unsw'. Although the content of the resource may change, this URL always points to the search results of the keyword 'unsw'. This uniquely addressable resource ID can be bookmarked, emailed or used as a link in some other program.

Flickr is another good example of an addressable application in that the easily identifiable resources of the system, namely the users, photos and albums, are organised in a way such that they can be individually accessed via their URLs.

REST advocates addressability as a main feature of its principles. The idea that all resources are individually accessible may seem natural, as people are used to accessing Web pages via URLs. However, not all Web applications are built this way. For example, it is quite common to come across situations where one has to navigate to a resource A (e.g., a user) before some resources relating to A are accessible (e.g., individual comments made by the user).

3.5   Statelessness

The next principle to discuss is 'Statelessness'. Being stateless means every HTTP request happens in complete isolation. The interaction 'context' (i.e., conversation sessions) between the REST service and its client application is maintained by the client application, and the client application is considered responsible for including all necessary information for the server to fulfill the request at any given stage of the interactions.

To explain what a stateless REST application means, let us think of a typical client-server interaction in many modern websites. Most conventional Web applications expect the client to make requests in a certain order, creating a trail of interaction data. For example, a user navigates to page A, then page B, then page C. It often gets confused when page C is directly accessed somehow because the server is expected to remember some data when the client visits page B, which will be used when the same client visits page C. This is because the state (interaction context between the client and server) is maintained on the server side as the *client application's state* and it expects a certain sequence of actions from the client depending on the stored state.

However, REST principles advise against storing the conversation state on the server side, because any information that the server has to maintain about a client makes the server less scalable.

Of course, HTTP interactions are by nature stateless. But introducing a session id concept, for example, we break the stateless nature of the HTTP interactions. Below, the string (PHPSESSIONID) is a key into a data structure on the server and the data structure would contain the state of the corresponding client.

```
http://www.example.com/forum?PHPSESSIONID=27314962133
```

This means any server-side scale-up (e.g., data duplication, migration) exercises will have to take the management of this session data into account.

The statelessness REST principle states that all HTTP requests (in the form of URI) need to contain the relevant client application state within it. This means a request should contain all information that the server needs to process the request, rather than relying on something like a session key. A RESTful service requires that the client application state stay on the client application side. A client should transmit its state to the server for every request that needs it. The server can nudge the client application toward new states by sending 'next links' for the client in its response, but it does not keep any state on behalf of a client.

However, a RESTful service is responsible for managing the state of its resources. That is, the resource states live on the server. A photo management service would create, update and delete photos and persist its states on the server. However, a client application state (i.e., particular conversational context during an interaction session) is kept off the server and managed by the client application itself. This is not too dissimilar to the Google search application scenario. Let us say that the resources in the Google search application are indexed Web pages. The states of the Web pages are globally the same to all clients. The states of individual client applications, e.g., query histories and pages visited, are different for every client because each client takes a different 'path' to its current state.

3.6 Resource Representations

A resource needs a representation for its state to be sent to the client. A representation of a resource contains some data about its 'current state'. Take a list of open bugs in software as a resource. Such a list could have multiple representational formats in that it can be represented in an XML document, an HTML page, as comma-separated values, etc. A representation of a resource may also contain metadata about the resource (e.g., creator, last update date). Normally, it is up to the client to decide which representation is required of a resource.

The server can offer two access paths. One is to assign a distinct URI for each representation of a resource, as shown below. This also meets the addressability and statelessness principles in that the client's request fully expresses the information necessary for the server to fulfill the request.

- the list in XML format – http://www.example.com/bugs/xml
- the list in HTML format – http://www.example.com/bugs/html
- the list in CSV format – http://www.example.com/bugs/csv

The other way is to use HTTP content negotiation in HTTP HEAD. In this case, the server will allocate one URI to the resource: http://www.example.com/bugs. The client requests will then contain in its HEAD section which format is the accepted/preferred content type. During content negotiation, other types of preferences can be set to indicate all kinds of *client preferences*, e.g., file format, payment information, authentication credentials, IP address of the client, caching directives, and so on.

In the following, the request expresses that the client prefers HTML content, and if not possible, any format in text.

```
HTTP GET  http://www.example.com/bugs
Accept: text/html; q=1.0, text/*; q=0.8
```

3.7 Uniform Interfaces in REST

Another important principle to discuss is the idea of using the standard HTTP operations a uniform interface for REST-based services. The most commonly employed HTTP operations for this purpose are the following four:

- **PUT**: Create a new resource (new URI) or update a resource (existing URI).
- **GET**: Retrieve a representation of a resource.
- **POST**: Modify the state of a resource. POST is a read-write operation and may change the state of the resource and have side effects on the server. Web browsers warn you when refreshing a page generated with POST.
- **DELETE**: Clear a resource after the URI is no longer valid

The operations are similar to the CRUD (Create, Read, Update, Delete) database operations. These are referred to as "Uniform Interface" because they are the standard HTTP operations performed on resources and they follow the same operation syntax and semantics. For example, to delete a customer who is represented as a resource, the operation will be DELETE(URI) (where URI is the URI of the customer to be deleted), instead of a custom operation like DeleteCustomer(customer_obj).

The REST Uniform Interface principle, if properly followed, gives us two properties:

- being Safe: Read-only operations. The operations on a resource do not change any server state. The client can call the operations 10 times; this has no effect on the server state.
- being Idempotent: Operations that have the same "effect" whether you apply them once or more than once. An effect here may well be a change of the server state. An operation on a resource is idempotent if making one request is the same as making a series of identical requests.

The two properties let a client make reliable HTTP requests over an unreliable network. This means if a response to a GET operation is lost in the network, the client can make another request without worrying about affecting the server state. By the same token, if a PUT request gets no response, the client can make the same request again. Even if the earlier one got through, the second PUT will have no side effect.

The point about REST Uniform Interface is in 'uniformity', whereby every service uses HTTP's interface the *same* way. It means, for example, GET means 'read-only' across the Web no matter which resource it is being used on. It means we do not use methods in place of GET, such as doSearch or getPage or nextNumber. This is not just using GET in your service, it is about using it the way it was meant to be used.

3.8   Web API Design for RESTful Services

Considering the principles we have discussed so far in this section, we will look into some of the best practices on designing a REST service. A well-designed API should make it easy for the clients to understand your service without having to "study" the API documents in depth. It should be self-describing and self-documenting as much as possible. The RESTful service principles (e.g., resources, addressability, uniform HTTP actions) actually give us a straightforward guideline for designing the Web API.

3.8.1   Designing URIs

URI Patterns

Let us start with the URIs (i.e., the addresses/identifications for the resources). One should move away from choosing URI patterns that represent the RPC-style interface design where lots of 'operation names' are used (e.g., /getCoffeeOrders, /createOrder, /getOrder?id=123). Instead, separate the *resources* (e.g., orders) from the actions (e.g., create or update) and use appropriate nouns (preferably plurals form) to represent the resources (e.g., /orders, /renewal_notices). Using URL paths in some cases can effectively show the relationships between resources (e.g., /orders/{order}/payment, /customers/{*customer_id*}/orders).

URIs should have *clear* identifiers that lead to individual resources. Mostly you'd use a primary key type like an *order Id* or an *invoice Id*. However, the identifiers do not have to be the same as the resource's internal key (e.g., database id). For example, the following URL (in one line) is perfectly unique and also descriptive of the resource it represents, a news article.

```
http://www.smh.com.au/it-pro/security-it/hacker-admits
-hijacking-plane-midair-fbi-20150517-gh3fne.html
```

URI patterns could also utilise URL query strings. For example, the URL /orders?date=2015-04-15 would correspond to all order resources that match the search criteria specified in the query string. Not every exposed URI needs to be in a "clean path"; query strings can be used when appropriate.

Adding Actions to the URIs

Once the resources' URIs are determined, we should decide which 'actions' should be performed on the URIs and determines what the consequences are of the applied actions. The following Table 3.1 illustrates a scenario using "coffee orders" resources.

Table 3.1 URIs and actions

Resource (URI)	GET	POST	PUT	DELETE
/coffeeOrders	get orders	new order	batch update	ERROR (?)
	return a list, status code 200	return new order + new URI, status code 201	status code (200, 204)	status code (e.g., 400 – client error)
/coffeeOrders/123	get 123	ERROR (?)	update 123	delete 123
	return an item, status code 200	return error status code (400 – client error)	updated item, status code (200, 204)	status code (204, 200)

Note PUT could also return 201 if the request resulted in a new resource

Let us take the *collection of coffee orders* to start. An appropriate URI to represent the collection is /coffeeOrders. Given that the URI represents a collection, performing a GET operation on it should return a list of all coffee orders. Also, performing a POST operation would mean adding a new order to the collection. In this case, the URI of the newly created coffee order resource will be returned. A PUT operation on the collection could mean a batch update of multiple orders. However, a DELETE operation, which would mean deleting the entire collection, should be mapped to an ERROR response because deleting an entire collection of coffee orders will not be a good course of action.

When the same HTTP operations are applied to a single coffee order resource, the expected behaviour of the operations is a little different. Say, there is a coffee order which is numbered 123 and its URI is /coffeeOrders/123). Performing a GET operation on the coffee order 123 would mean retrieving the details of the order. A POST operation would not make sense here and should be mapped to an ERROR response because it would mean creating a new coffee order 123, something that already exists. Performing a PUT operation means updating the order 123. A DELETE operation should delete the resource coffee order 123.

3.8.2   Design of the Responses

Using Status Code

Another aspect to consider for each operation is the design of the appropriate response. In such a consideration, the content of the response is not the only issue. The response may have to deal with error cases. Using proper status codes, and using them consistently in your responses, will help the client understand the interactions better.

The HTTP specification has a guideline for the status codes, but at minimum an operation should return the codes 200, 400 and 500. See Table 3.2.

Table 3.2 Basic status codes

Code	Description	When
200	OK	normal response, no errors
400	Bad Request	the client request contained something that was not expected or wrong
500	Internal Error	the server encountered internal errors during processing of the request

The following codes in Table 3.3 can also be utilised in appropriate situations. In fact, it is considered good practice to return an appropriate code that reflects the situations on the server as closely as possible. For example, a POST operation, when successful, should return 201 (instead of 200) because it is likely that the effect of the operation is a new resource.

Table 3.3 More meaningful status codes

Code	Description	When
201	Created	the client request created new resource(s)
304	Not Modified	the requested resource is cached
404, 401, 403	Not Found, Unauthorised, Forbidden	for managing authentication and authorisation on the requested resources

Response Formats

Ideally, a REST service will support a wide range of client applications by providing multiple content formats in its response. Commonly, JSON and XML are supported and the client application may engage in the content negotiation mechanism to choose the suitable response format.

It is recommended that the response format represent simple objects. A single result should return a single object. As shown in the Fig. 3.1 below, if a response contains multiple objects, it should return a collection as the container of the simple objects. This idea is demonstrated in the 'results' entry in the JSON object shown. resultSize means the returned response contains 25 coffee order objects.

3.8.3 HATEOAS – Taking Your API to the Next Level

It is said that for a REST-based service to be truly "RESTful", it has to follow the HATEOAS principle. The acronym HATEOAS stands for **H**ypermedia **A**s **T**he

```
/coffeeOrders/123                      /coffeeOrders

{                                      {
    "Id": "123",                           "resultSize": 25,
    "type": "latte",                       "results": [ {
    "extra shot": "no",                        "id": "100",
    "payment": {                               "type": "latte",
        "date": "2015-04-15",                  "extra shot": "no",
        "credit card": "123457"                "payment": {
    },                                             "date": "2015-04-15",
    "served_by": "mike"                            "credit card": "22223"
}                                              },
                                               "served_by": "sally"
                                           },
                                           { ... },
                                       ]

                                       }
```

Fig. 3.1 Returning simple object vs. multiple objects

Engine **O**f **A**pplication **S**tate. The following quote from Wikipedia explains the concept rather well.[1]

> The principle is that a client interacts with a network application entirely through hypermedia provided dynamically by application servers. A REST client needs no prior knowledge about how to interact with any particular application or server beyond a generic understanding of hypermedia.

To explain this further, let us think about how people interact with the Web generally. When someone visits a website for the first time, there is no need to look up a manual to know how to use a website. The way hypertext/hypermedia works is that the Web pages themselves can serve as a self-explanatory guide for the users. The HATEOAS principle aims to realise this in API design.

In a SOAP-based service, normally a single endpoint is exposed. The same endpoint receives requests for operations. The body of each request details which operation to run with what parameters. In SOAP, HTTP is merely a carrier of the SOAP messages. HTTP itself does not play a big role in the protocol of the service interaction.

In REST, HTTP is at the centre of the API in that the operations are defined by way of HTTP standard actions. Given that **HTTP** (Hypertext) is about allowing the users to navigate the site using links, an HTTP-based API also should allow the clients to navigate the service using links.

Let us consider an API that is designed without following the HATEOAS principle. Not implementing the links in REST API would look as in Fig. 3.2.

That is, in the scenario illustrated in Fig. 3.2, it is assumed that the client knows – maybe through studying the API documents – how to construct the *next request path*. That is, the client will combine /coffeeOrders and id:100. However, if the same API was designed using HATEOAS, it would look as in Fig. 3.3. Note in the illustration in Fig. 3.3 the links entries in the CoffeeOrders object. Each

---

[1] https://en.wikipedia.org/wiki/HATEOAS.

/coffeeOrders

```
{
    "resultSize": 25,
    "results": [ {
        "id": 100,
        "type": "latte",
    },
    {   "id": "101",
        "type": "cap",
        { ... },
    ]
}
```

GET /coffeeOrders/100

```
{
    "Id": "100",
    "type": "latte",
    "extra shot": "no",
    "payment": {
        "date": "2015-04-15",
        "credit card": "22223"
    },
    "served_by": "sally"
}
```

Fig. 3.2 Without *links* between resources

of the links is a complete reference to a resource. To access `Coffee Order 100`, the client just needs to follow the given address `coffeeOrders/100`. The idea of links applies to a single resources as well. In the same figure, `Coffee Order 123` has two links: one that links to *self*, and another that leads to a `Payment 123`. This link, for example, can be used to create a payment for the order, or to check the details of the payment made.

/coffeeOrders

```
{
    "resultSize": 25,
    "links": [{
        "href": "/coffeeOrders",
        "rel": "self"
    },
    {   "href": "/coffeeOrders?page=1",
        "rel": "alternative"
    }
    {   "href": "/coffeeOrders?page=2",
        "rel": "nextPage"
    }
    ],
    "results": [ {
        "id": "100",
        "type": "latte",
        "links": [ {
            "href": "/coffeeOrders/100",
            "rel": "details"
        }]
    },
    { ... },
    ]
}
```

/coffeeOrders/123

```
{
    "Id": "123",
    "type": "latte",
    "extra shot": "no",
    "payment": {
        "date": "2015-04-15",
        "credit card": "123457"
    },
    "served_by": "mike"
    "links": [ {
        "href": "/coffeeOrders/123",
        "rel": "self"
    },
    {
        "href": "/payments/123",
        "rel": "next"
    }
    ]
}
```

Fig. 3.3 With *links* between resources

Applying the HATEOAS principle encourages you to think about developing an API in a way that could help the clients understand it easily (as self-descriptive as possible). For example, include page navigation so that it is easy to retrieve the next set of objects (or traverse back to the previous set of objects). Also, having links that help create new or related resources would always be useful. If the client application state is such that update and delete on resources are allowed, there should be links that lead to those operations.

Although the REST principles are well understood, how they are considered and applied in practice is different from one implementation to another. For example, one may ignore the HATEOAS principle altogether and not provide various links in the responses as part of the API return formats.

The Richardson Maturity Model, proposed by Leonard Richardson, gives a way to measure to what level your service is "RESTful". According to the model (Level 0 being not RESTful, and Level 3 "fully complying with REST principles"):

- Level 0: One URI (single endpoint) exposed, requests contain operation details,
- Level 1: Expose resource URIs – individual URIs for each resource. Requests could still contain some operation details,
- Level 2: HTTP Methods – use the standard HTTP methods, status codes with the resource URIs,
- Level 3: HATEOAS – self-documenting responses, responses include links that the client can use

3.9   REST-Based Service Implementation

3.9.1   Building REST Web Services

Building a RESTful service does not require a specific client- or server-side framework for you to write your Web services. All you need is a client or server that supports the HTTP protocol.

- Choose a language of your choice.
- You do not need a big server infrastructure (HTTP/Web servers are enough).

3.9.1.1   A Very Simple REST – Without Any Framework

To demonstrate a very simple case of REST, let us consider the following scenario. We will use Java servlets, and we will show how you can override doGet(), doPost(), doPUT() and doDelete() to implement REST services.

In the following, every URL contains servlet path + path info (all you need to process a request in REST). You could use a third-party library for generating specific content type (CSV, JSON or XML, etc.) or use strings concatenations for simple responses.

The following servlet in the example supports a GET operation (with multiple representations: XML, CSV and JSON). Some quick overview about the servlet:

- The servlet is mapped to /places/sydney/* in the configuration file, web.xml, and it contains 'places to visit in Sydney' as resources.
- The GET operation returns some interesting places to visit in Sydney.
- Default representation is XML, but other formats can be added in the path info: JSON and CSV.
- Uses http://www.JSON.org/java/index.html for the JSON encoding.

Let us write a very simple REST Web service as a Java servlet. First, write a servlet class as follows (Listing 3.1).

```
1  public class SydneyServlet extends HttpServlet {
2      private static final String[] places = {
3          "Harbour Bridge",
4          "Circular Quay",
5          "Opera House",
6          "Hyde Park",
7          "Darling Harbour",
8          "Bondi Beach",
9          "Coogee Beach"
10     };
11
12     protected void doGet(HttpServletRequest req,
       HttpServletResponse res)
13         throws ServletException, IOException {
14         if ("/json".equals(req.getPathInfo())) {
15             jsonReply(res);
16         } else if ("/csv".equals(req.getPathInfo())){
17             csvReply(res);
18         } else {
19             xmlReply(res);
20         }
21     }
22 }
```

Listing 3.1 A simple servlet class

This servlet checks the request path to see if the client has requested the resources in JSON, CSV or XML. Now we want to build a method that will generate the right representation per request. Here is an implementation of xmlReply() (Listing 3.2).

```
1  private void xmlReply(HttpServletResponse res)
2      throws ServletException, IOException {
3
4      res.setContentType("text/xml");
5
6      Document doc = DocumentFactory.getInstance().createDocument();
7      Element root = doc.addElement("cityplaces");
8      root.addElement("city").setText("Sydney");
9      Element list = root.addElement("places");
10     for (int i = 0; i < places.length; ++i) {
11         list.addElement("places").setText(places[i]);
12     }
13
14     res.getWriter().write(doc.asXML());
15 }
```

Listing 3.2 Generating responses (XML)

When XML is requested, the servlet will produce something like this as the response (resulting screenshot shown in the bottom right corner of Fig. 3.4):

Here is an implementation of csvReply() (Listing 3.3).

```
1  private void csvReply(HttpServletResponse res)
2      throws ServletException, IOException {
3
4      res.setContentType("text/csv");
5
6      Writer writer = res.getWriter();
7      writer.write("City.Place\textbackslash{r}\textbackslash{n});
8      for (int i = 0; i < places.length; ++i) {
9          writer.write("Sydney,");
10         writer.write(places[i]);
11         writer.write("\textbackslash{r}\textbackslash{n}");
12     }
13 }
```

Listing 3.3 Generating responses (CSV)

When CSV is requested, the servlet will produce something like this as the response (resulting screenshot shown in the bottom right corner of Fig. 3.5):

Here is an implementation of jsonReply() (Listing 3.4).

```
1  private void jsonReply(HttpServletResponse res)
2      throws ServletException, IOException {
3
4      res.setContentType("text/json");
5
6      JSONObject root = new JSONObject();
7      root.put("city","Sydney");
8      JSONArray list = new JSONArray();
9
10     for (int i = 0; i < places.length; ++i) {
```

```java
private void xmlReply(HttpServletResponse resp) throws ServletException, IOException {
    resp.setContentType("text/xml");

    Document doc = DocumentFactory.getInstance().createDocument();
    Element root = doc.addElement("cityplaces");
    root.addElement("city").setText("Sydney");
    Element list = root.addElement("places");
    for (int i = 0; i < places.length; ++i) {
        list.addElement("place").setText(places[i]);
    }

    resp.getWriter().write(doc.asXML());
}
```

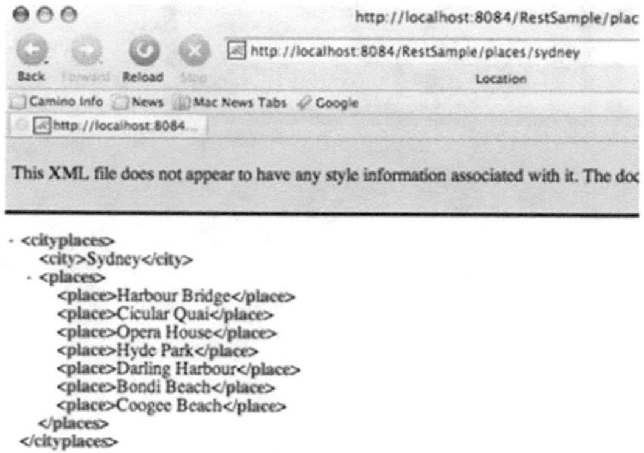

```
This XML file does not appear to have any style information associated with it. The doc

<cityplaces>
    <city>Sydney</city>
  - <places>
        <place>Harbour Bridge</place>
        <place>Cicular Quai</place>
        <place>Opera House</place>
        <place>Hyde Park</place>
        <place>Darling Harbour</place>
        <place>Bondi Beach</place>
        <place>Coogee Beach</place>
    </places>
</cityplaces>
```

Fig. 3.4   Simple REST – XML response

```
private void csvReply(HttpServletResponse resp) throws
ServletException, IOException {
    resp.setContentType("text/csv");

    Writer writer = resp.getWriter();
    writer.write("City,Place\r\n");
    for (int i = 0; i < places.length; ++i) {
        writer.write("Sydney,");
        writer.write(places[i]);
        writer.write("\r\n");
    }
}
```

Fig. 3.5 Simple REST – CSV response

```
private void jsonReply(HttpServletResponse resp) throws ServletException,
IOException {
    resp.setContentType("text/json");

    JSONObject root = new JSONObject();
    root.put("city", "Sydney");
    JSONArray list = new JSONArray();
    for (int i = 0; i < places.length; ++i) {
        list.add(places[i]);
    }
    root.put("places", list);

    resp.getWriter().write(root.toString());
}
```

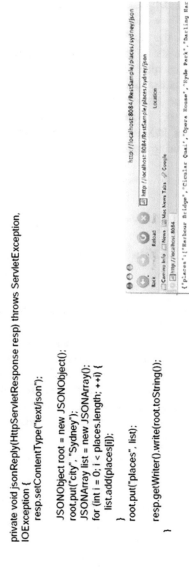

Fig. 3.6 Simple REST – JSON response

```
11        list.add(places[i]);
12      }
13    root.put("places",list);
14    res.getWriter().write(root.toString());
15  }
```

Listing 3.4 Generating responses (JSON)

When JSON is requested, the servlet will produce something like this as the response (resulting screenshot shown in the bottom right corner of Fig. 3.6):

In reality, it would still be nice to have some support (a framework). Having a framework can help reduce boilerplate-type coding. In Java, the libraries that help RESTful service development are specified in the JAX-RS (http://jcp.org/en/jsr/detail?id=311) standard specification. There are many implementations of JAX-RS. Through the lab exercise, we will see an example of JAX-RS support using Apache CXF.

Practical Exercise III

3.10   Lab Exercise 03: A Simple REST Service with Apache CXF (JAX-RS)

In this lab exercise, we are going to build a simple RESTful service. A RESTFul Web service is designed and implemented using the HTTP methods and the principles of the REST architectural style. A typical API document for a REST-based service will provide the base URI for the service, the MIME types it uses to communicate (e.g., XML or JSON) and the set of operations (POST, GET, PUT, DELETE) supported.

Java community defines standard REST support via JAX-RS (the Java API for RESTful Web Services) in JSR 311. There are a few implementations of this standard available now (e.g., Apache CXF, RESTEasy by JBoss, Jersey by Sun). We will use the Apache CXF implementation.

Exercise Files

The exercise files involved in the lab can be downloaded from the Github site:

- https://github.com/SOA-Book

  Follow the repository exercises to lab03.

3.10.1   Activity 1: Start with Hello World

We will start by getting a template from Apache CXF Maven Archetype. Of course, this is not the only way to get yourself started with REST and Apache CXF, but since we tried their template for SOAP (JAX-WS), let us go with their template for REST as well.

1. In a terminal window, navigate to your workspace.
2. Type in the following (mind the ':' at the end):

```
$ mvn archetype:generate -Dfilter=org.apache.cxf.archetype:
```

3. You will be prompted to 'Choose archetype:', enter number 1 (i.e., cxf-jaxrs-service (Simple CXF JAX-RS webapp service using Spring configuration))
4. At the next prompt, 'Choose a version:', enter number 51.
5. Then, at 'Define value for property groupId:', enter the groupId value as au.edu.unsw.soacourse.
6. Then, at 'Define value for property artifactId:', enter the artifactId value as HelloWorldCxfRest.
7. Then, at 'Define value for property version:', The default value is 1.0-SNAPSHOT (case sensitive). Leave the value as is, and hit Enter.
8. Next, at 'Define value for property package:', enter the package name as au.edu.unsw.soacourse.hello.
9. Now Maven will generate the template code. You should see a 'Build Success' message. You should also see a new directory called 'HelloWorldCxfRest' under your workspace.
10. The pom.xml file given from this template includes some plug-ins that we do not require. Replace it with the pom.xml provided for this exercise. We have removed unnecessary plug-ins and set maven-compiler-plugin to use JDK 1.7.

Let us import this into the Eclipse IDE as an *Existing Maven Project* and examine what has been generated.

1. Open Eclipse, and navigate to File → Import → Maven → Existing Maven Project. Navigate to HelloWorldCxfRest and complete the import process.
2. After importing, you should have a project structure similar to that in Fig. 3.7:
3. There are a few things to note. First, open web.xml. You will see a declaration of CXFServlet. The implementation of the servlet is provided by Apache CXF, as the name org.apache.cxf.transport.servlet.CXFServlet suggests. The servlet is mapped to a URL pattern /*. That is, all requests starting with http://localhost:8080/HelloWorldCxfRest are directed to this servlet.

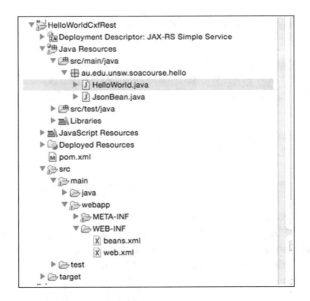

Fig. 3.7 JAX-RS HelloWorld project structure

4. The rest of the configuration details come from WEB-INF/beans.xml. Open beans.xml. Pay attention to the jaxrs:server declaration. This is where you will declare your REST implementation class. For example, in this current template, class au.edu.unsw.soacourse.hello.HelloWorld provides the implementation code. The jaxrs:providers part is for registering JSON support class org.codehaus.jackson.jaxrs.JacksonJsonProvider so you can consume/produce JSON in your service.

5. Now, open HelloWorld.java.

   • class HelloWorld is annotated with @Path("/hello"). @Path can be applied to resource classes or methods. When marked on a class, it means the class will handle the requests starting with /hello/{...}. With the current mapping in web.xml, the URL path will be:

     http://localhost:8080/HelloWorldCxfRest/hello

   • The ping() method is annotated with the following. Let us go through them one by one.
     – @Path(/echo/{input}) indicates that this method will handle the request path matching:
       http://localhost:8080/HelloWorldCxfRest/hello/echo/{input}
     – @GET indicates that the method will handle the GET request method on the said request path.

- – @Produces("text/plain") indicates that the response will contain plain text. @Produces({MediaType.TEXT_PLAIN}) has the same meaning.
- – @PathParam("input") annotation applies to the String input parameter of ping(). It will map the text value of the path parameter appearing after /echo to String input.
- – The method itself simply returns the input as a String.
- The modifyJson() method is annotated with:
  - – @Path(/jsonBean), indicates that this method will handle the request path matching:
    http://localhost:8080/HelloWorldCxfRest/hello/jsonBean
  - – @POST, indicates that the method will handle the POST request method on the said request path
  - – @Produces("application/json"), indicates that the response will contain JSON.
  - – @Consumes("application/json"), which applies to the input parameter JsonBean input. It will map the body content of the POST request (which will contain JSON) to JsonBean input.
  - – The method itself simply sets the value of Val2 to the value of Val1 and returns the object as response.

The template is actually functional as is. Let's compile and deploy to Tomcat and see how it behaves.

1. Run Maven Install – and add the project to the Tomcat server to run.
2. Open a browser. Type in:

http://localhost:8080/HelloWorldCxfRest/hello/echo/HelloWorld

You should see a plain text 'HelloWorld' returned.

3.10.2 Activity 2: Testing the HelloWorld Service

To test the REST service properly, we need a REST service client tool. There are many options, but one we settle with in this lab is Chrome POSTMAN. You can download it from the Chrome Web Store at the following address:

https://chrome.google.com/webstore/category/apps

NOTE: There are a plug-in version and an app version. We think the app version is easier to use. So download and install the app version of POSTMAN.
Once you have installed POSTMAN, open the app, then try the following:

1. type in the URL you want to test,
2. choose the request method you want to perform on the URL,

3. choose the data format you want to send and type in necessary text,
4. click Send.

For example, to test the POST implementation in HelloWorld.java, you would do something similar to what is shown in Fig. 3.8.

Fig. 3.8 Chrome POSTMAN

Play around with this tool to become familiar with what it does. It is a handy tool to learn for any REST service development task.

3.10.3   Activity 3: CRUD Operations on Resources

Now that we have tried the basic skeleton of Apache CXF on REST services, let us try and build a simple REST service from scratch.

Resources are at the centre of a RESTful Web service. The first thing in designing a RESTful Web service will be deciding what the resources you want to expose are – and coding some basic operations for them. As we have seen briefly in the HelloWorld template, In JAX-RS, resources are implemented by a POJO with an @Path annotation that associates an identifier (URI) to the resource.

A resource can also have sub-resources. In this case, such a resource is a resource collection while the sub-resources are member resources (e.g., class and students). For this exercise, let us use good old books as resources and develop a basic set of operations to create/read/update/delete them.

1. Use the HelloWorld project as a template and create a new Maven project out of that.
2. Edit pom.xml to reflect the following properties:

   - groupId: au.edu.unsw.soacourse
   - artifactId: RestfulBookService
   - package: au.edu.unsw.soacourse.books

3. Do Maven → Update Project to reflect the changes correctly.
4. Add a Data Model and a Data Access Model for the Resources. For this simple exercise, we are going to write a couple of Java classes for the data model and the data access model (not really useful in real applications, but will do for this lab exercise.)

   - **[A Book class (plain Java class)]** Using the Book.java file provided for the exercise, create the Book class with the given package detail. Note that this class also defines automatic mapping to XML (i.e., the class is automatically mapped to XML and back for serialisation). This is done via Java JAXB and the @XmlRootElement annotation.[2]
   - **[BookDao class]** Using the BooksDao.java file provided for the exercise, create the BookDao class with the given package details. Note that this class is just a HashMap-based in-memory data store, so to speak, which has no significance outside this lab guide. In a more realistic development, you will have a proper Data Access Object (DAO) which interacts with a real data store through queries. You may later turn the design into a proper DAO with full database access when needed.

5. Implement a REST-based service based on this model. We are going to write a class that exposes book resources in different ways (i.e., GET, PUT, DELETE, etc.).
   [BooksResource Class] Using the BooksResource.java file provided for the exercise, create the BooksResource class with the given package detail. Note that this class exposes the main REST interface for the book collection. It exposes GET (get the list of books, get the size of the list) and POST (for creating a book

---

[2]https://docs.oracle.com/javase/tutorial/jaxb/intro/.

under the collection). Also, it has a path param mapping for handling single book resources.

6. Configure the service and compile, then deploy. Open `WEB-INF/beans.xml`. You should configure the `jaxrs:server` declaration so that the implementation bean correctly points to `au.edu.unsw.soacourse.books.BooksResource`. Now run 'Maven install' and deploy the service to Tomcat.

7. Using POSTMAN, try out each method in the service and see its behaviour (especially the input/output).

3.10.3.1   Issues with `BooksResource.java`

Although functional, there are a few issues with the way we have implemented the REST operations in our previous activity. Let us go through the issues here so that you can address them. We would like to implement the operations so that their behaviour reflects the correct interpretation of RESTful HTTP operations.

In `BooksResource.java`, there are a few things to improve. Especially, we should consider what each operation's input and output should be.

Take the POST operation. Two things to note here:

• The input values are passed in as form params. In doing so, the 'id' of the resource is expected from the user as well. This is not correct behaviour of a POST operation, as POST should generate the id and let the user know what it is in response to.

• The POST operation returns nothing. We should generate a response that will contain links to the new resource (if created), and also to other resources that the client might be interested in.

Take the DELETE operation. Instead of returning a normal response with a status code (e.g., NOT_FOUND), it throws an error when the given id is not found in the data store. You always want to return something sensible to the user.

Take the PUT operation; the idea implemented in `putAndGetResponse()` seems to be that if the given key exists in the data store, it will update the value associated with the key. If it doesn't, it creates it. What are the status codes used here? For example, what does `Response.created().build()` return? Are they appropriate given that the implementation logic here deals with two possible scenarios?

Think about how you might improve these operations and make them truly RESTful operations. We leave this as an exercise for you.

3.10.4   Activity 4: Developing a Client for RESTful Services

There are many choices for building REST clients. For this lab, we will show what Apache CXF provides you with in terms of accessing REST services from a client. There are two sources of documents you can refer to:

- Apache CXF Client API documentation,[3]
- Apache CXF WebClient class documentation.[4]

[BookServiceClient Class] The `BookServiceClient.java` file provided for this exercise contains most of the features of the client API. Using the file provided, create the BookServiceClient class with the given package details in the current working project. Note that this class (which has its own main()) is a demonstrator of the WebClient class in Apache CXF. Look through the code. Compile and run the code. The results should be in the Console view.

---

[3]`http://cxf.apache.org/docs/jax-rs-client-api.html#JAX-RSClient`
`API-CXFWebClientAPI`.

[4]`https://cxf.apache.org/javadoc/latest/org/apache/cxf/jaxrs/`
`client/WebClient.html`.

Chapter 4
Web Services – Data Services

In this chapter, we introduce another form of service that we refer to as data service. The primary goal of data services is to give uniform access to the data layer of an application. This chapter explains the motivation behind the concept of data services and implementation techniques.

4.1 Data Services

4.1.1 WS-* and RESTful Services

To understand the what and why of data services, let us first briefly examine the two flavours of the Web services we have discussed so far in terms of their characteristics.

WS-* services: the services that are implemented based on SOAP and WSDL standards. This type of Web service naturally represents the logical/functional view of the underlying application functionality the service exposes. That is, a SOAP service is defined in terms of what it does, typically carrying out a business-level operation.

Because the SOAP standard is at the centre of the implementation, we can say WS-* services are message oriented. A service is formally defined in terms of the messages exchanged between provider agents and requester agents.

An important aspect of a SOAP service is that the contract is described by a machine-processable language. Such a contract in SOAP-based services tends to represent a small number of operations with relatively large and complex messages; i.e., the focus is on the message and its structure. The messages are sent in standard, platform-neutral format XML.

RESTful services: in comparison, the services implemented using the REST principles represent the resources and the management of the resources as the core elements they expose. Instead of a service representing a 'remote function' (i.e., a

© Springer International Publishing AG 2017
H.-y. Paik et al., *Web Service Implementation and Composition Techniques*,
DOI 10.1007/978-3-319-55542-3_4

business-level operation), it is expected to provide the uniform HTTP operations
on the resource it represents. Although there are some standards emerging (e.g.,
WADL[1]), most RESTful services are not documented with a machine-processable
contract. Rather, they tend to rely on API documentations to communicate what
the service does. Because the REST design principles set a few conventions,
such as the names of the operations, their parameters and expected behaviour,
the API documentations can be written and understood by the so-called "REST
conventions".

Figure 4.1 describes these two different views of service design conceptually.
In the SOAP services, what is exposed to the client is a contract (i.e., WSDL) and
the remote operations defined within it. In the RESTful services, what is exposed is
the resource itself through the uniform interfaces defined within the REST service
design guidelines.

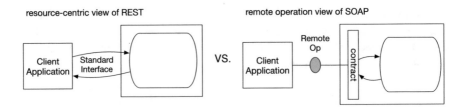

Fig. 4.1   RESTful service view vs. SOAP service view

4.1.2   Data Access as a Service

One important thing to note though is that both approaches are used in exposing
the functional or application logic layer of an information system (via either remote
operation viewpoint or the resource-oriented view point). The fundamental purpose
of these services is that they allow the client applications to access the business
functionality of the provider system (e.g., registering a customer).

Up until this point, it can be said that the data layer that the application layer
is relying on to service its functionality is still kept behind the wall of the application layer. That is, there is no direct/open access to the data layer from the client
application's viewpoint.

In recent years, the thinking around the data and the management of its access
has evolved. Due to easy access to the technologies that allow publishing content,
we have seen a proliferation of various data sources on the Web. For example, in
Australia, now every state-level as well as the federal government set up a website

---

[1]Web Application Description Language, http://www.w3.org/Submission/wadl/.

dedicated to disseminating various public records and government data. The advent of the services and the API concepts has also brought about wide spread provision of access end points that are primarily producers of data feeds. This trend has also become apparent within many of the big enterprises as the move towards the Web and API-based access has accelerated within enterprise management systems.

Many applications are now built to utilise these data sources to analyse, aggregate and repurpose the data from different areas. They tend to showcase some insights that were not possible to gain from looking at one data source only.

However, from the standpoint of the application integration topic, we can observe the classic heterogeneity problem again in this situation, where the available data sources use different data formats (e.g., CSV, XML or Word documents) to publish their data. In particular, as far as enterprise systems are concerned, the access mechanism to the data source may vary (e.g., from JDBC/SQL to FTP file transfers) as well.

The idea of **Data as Services** stems from the need to provide "uniform access" to available data for the data consuming application without the clients having to resolve the access and representation problems. One could characterise the data services as services with a data-oriented view, and it is providing 'data access' as a service. That is, the data services expose data directly to the data consuming application over simple/standard access interfaces (bypassing the application logic layer).

This enables a new way of thinking about data integration and interoperability across a broad range of data consumer applications.

4.2 Implementing Data Services

Just as conventional Web Services are built around "agreed standards/protocols", the design and implementation of data services should be supported by standards. However, there is no consensus around how to adequately design and build data services. However, it is apparent that the implementation techniques used for SOAP or RESTful services can also be used for data services, as the main focus of a data service is to *expose* data to its client. The mechanism to *expose* could be either in a remote-operation manner or a resource-oriented manner, as both techniques are capable of carrying and representing data in a standard format.

In fact, a more commonly adopted implementation technique for data services is the approach involving REST principles due to its simplicity. In the commercial solutions provided for enterprise systems (e.g., BEA AquaLogic Data Service Platform,[2] Microsoft WCF Data Services[3]), we can see a more comprehensive design methodology, models/templates, and development tools.

---

[2]Oracle/BEA, http://docs.oracle.com/cd/E13167_01/aldsp/docs21/index.html.

[3]Microsoft Astoria Project, https://msdn.microsoft.com/en-us/data/odata.aspx.

Regardless of the choice we make in terms of the implementation technique, when it comes to data services, there is a more important technology that forms the core of all data service implementation approaches, XML, in particular, XML Schema for Web-enabled feeds, XPath and XQuery for querying data to create the common access layer and XSLT for transforming data representations and resolving the heterogeneity problem at the presentation level.

For this reason, in this chapter we will introduce these XML technologies as the core enabler of data services. Later in the chapter, we will show how these are utilised to build a data service.

4.3   XML Transformation and Query Techniques

Whether speaking from the SOAP-based Web services camp or the resource-oriented Web services camp, the common data format in both approaches is XML. In consequence, the implementation of data transformation logic relies on various XML technologies; within this section we look in detail at three – probably the most common ones – of these technologies: XPath, XQuery (XML querying) and XSLT (XML transformation) (Fig. 4.2).

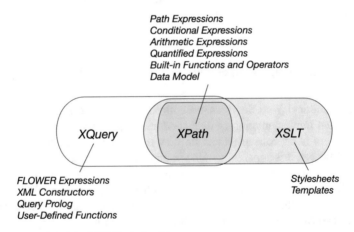

Fig. 4.2   XQuery, XPath and XSLT relationships

4.3.1   XPath

XPath is a query language for XML documents. The main objective of XPath is to provide a language to select parts of XML documents. Although it supports operations, that is not its main purpose. It appears as the value of attributes in other XML languages (e.g., XSLT, Schema, BPEL).

4.3.1.1 Representation

XPath represents an XML document as a Document Object Model (DOM) tree, a hierarchical tree whose elements are nodes. Seven different types of nodes are defined: document nodes (root), element nodes, text nodes, attribute nodes, comment nodes, processing rule nodes, and namespace nodes. Each node, depending on its type, has different properties; four are the properties that the XPath language describes: name, parent, children and value.

Figure 4.3 shows the XPath tree representation (right side) of an XML document (left side). The XML document contains data about a bunch of lonely office dwellers; the data in the XML document is presented in different types of nodes, depending on its characteristics, and the nodes are organized hierarchically in a tree.

4.3.1.2 Syntax

XPath has some rules for converting data types; however, the XPath language is famous for its *location path expressions*. In this section we focus on how to specify a location path. A location path expression evaluates a set of nodes and returns a new set of nodes as a result of the evaluation. Figure 4.4 depicts the syntax structure of a location path. To explain the syntax of XPath, we present the definitions of all the

possible elements composing an expression. Let us start from the simplest element, AxisSpecifier, and work our way up to a complete location path expression.

4.3.1.3 AxisSpecifier

An AxisSpecifier is an axis name followed by '::'. An **axis** is a particular direction through an XML document; the direction is determined from the context node. The **context node** represents the "current" location in the document. For illustration, let us say our context node is the first person node in the sample document shown in Fig. 4.3. There are 13 XPath axes as shown below.

- **self** represents the context node itself
- **child** represents the children of the context node. In our example, this will include the grade, age and phone nodes just below the first person node.
- **parent** represents the parent of the context node. In our example, this will point to the office node.
- **ancestor** represents all ancestors (parent, grandparent, etc.) of the context node. In our example, this will select the office node.

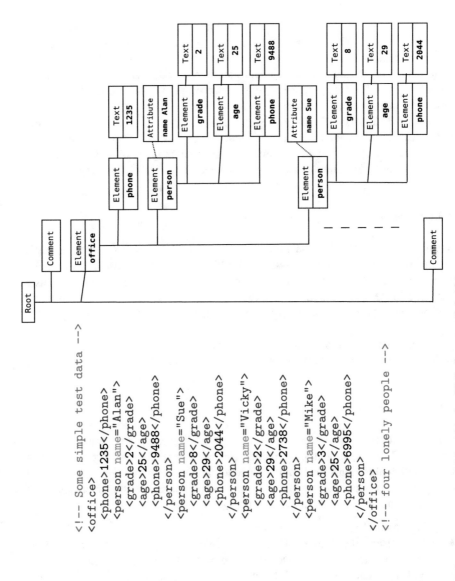

```
<!-- Some simple test data -->
<office>
   <phone>1235</phone>
   <person name="Alan">
      <grade>2</grade>
      <age>25</age>
      <phone>9488</phone>
   </person>
   <person name="Sue">
      <grade>8</grade>
      <age>29</age>
      <phone>2044</phone>
   </person>
   <person name="Vicky">
      <grade>2</grade>
      <age>29</age>
      <phone>2738</phone>
   </person>
   <person name="Mike">
      <grade>3</grade>
      <age>25</age>
      <phone>6995</phone>
   </person>
</office>
<!-- four lonely people -->
```

Fig. 4.3 XPath tree representation (*right side*) of an XML document (*left side*)

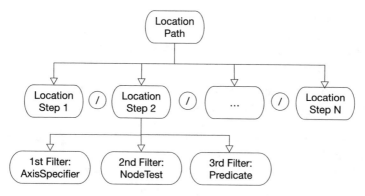

Fig. 4.4 Location path components

- **ancestor-or-self** represents all ancestors (parent, grandparent, etc.) of the context node as well as the context node itself. In our example, this will select the office and the first person nodes.
- **descendant** represents all descendants (children, grandchildren, etc.) of the context node. In our example, this will select the grade, age, phone, 2, 25 and 9488 nodes just below the first person node.
- **descendant-or-self** represents all descendants (children, grandchildren, etc.) of the context node as well as the context node itself. In our example, this will select the first person, grade, age, phone, 2, 25 and 9488 nodes just below the first person node.
- **following-sibling** represents all siblings after the current node. In our example, this selects the second, third and fourth person nodes.
- **preceding-sibling**: represents all siblings before the current node. In our example, this selects the phone node just below the office node.
- **following** represents all nodes that come after the context node, excluding any descendants and attribute and namespace nodes. In our example, this selects the second person and its grade, 8, age, 29, phone, 2044, the third person and its grade, 2, age, 29, phone, 2738, the fourth person and its grade, 3, age, 25, phone, 6995, and the comment node four lonely people.
- **preceding**: all nodes that come before the context node, excluding any ancestors and attribute and namespace nodes. In our example, this selects the phone, 1235 and the comment Some simple test data nodes.
- **attribute**: the attribute nodes of the context node. In our example, this will select the name = "Alan" attribute node.
- **namespace**: the namespace nodes of the context node. In our example, the context node has no namespace declaration attached to it.

An AxisSpecifier is the first filter of the location step. Some of the examples of the syntax for this component are: child::, descendant-or-self, and parent::.

4.3.1.4   NodeTest

XPath defines several node tests to select nodes from the XPath tree. The node tests can be divided into three types: name, asterisk and pseudo-function.

- **Name**: A node test returns true if the name of a node matches the name specified in the test. Examples of names from our sample XML document are office, person, grade, etc.
- **Asterisk**: this test returns true for all nodes, regardless of their type. It selects all element nodes and attribute nodes.
- **Pseudo-functions**: there are four pseudo-functions used for node tests.
  - node(): acts exactly like the asterisk.
  - text(): selects all the text-node children of the context.
  - comment(): selects all the comment-node children of the context.
  - processing-instruction(): selects all the nodes that are processing instructions. If the name of the processing instruction is entered in the parentheses, it will select just the entered processing instruction.

The NodeTest is the second filter of the location step, and it is added right next to an AxisSpecifier. Some of the examples of the two components put together are shown below.

- child::grade. This could be read as "from the context node, first apply the child axis specifier, then from the selected nodes, choose the nodes whose names match the grade".
- child::text(). This could be read as "from the context node, first apply the child axis specifier; from the selected nodes, choose all nodes whose node type is text".

4.3.1.5   Predicate

The predicate is a Boolean test. If the result is true for a node, the node gets included in the result; otherwise the node is ruled out. The predicate is the third filter of a location path. This filter is optional and does not need to be included. See below for some examples:

- child::room = "B501". This could be read as "from the context node, first apply the child axis specifier; from the selected nodes, choose all nodes whose name is room and text value is B501."
- attribute::born < 1976. This could be read as "from the context node, first apply the attribute axis specifier and then choose attributes whose name is born and value is 1976."

4.3.1.6 Location Step

The grammar for a complete location 'step' is defined as:

```
Step :: = AxisSpecifier NodeTest Predicate*
```

Each step is a series of "three filters", where the first filter is the *AxisSpecifier*, the second filter is the *NodeTest*, and the third filter is the *Predicate*, the last one being optional. Here are a few examples that could apply to the XML shown in Fig. 4.3:

- `parent::person[attribute::name = 'Sue']`
- `child::person[last()]`
- `child::person[1]`
- `child::name[child::phone = '56789']`

XPath also supports functions that permit manipulation of data, such as string (e.g., *string-join*, *contains*, *substring*), Boolean (e.g., *false*, *lang*), and number (e.g., *sum*, *ceiling*, *floor*) functions. The last() function in the second example will return the last person node from the child axis of the context node.

4.3.1.7 Location Path

A location path is composed by one or mode location steps separated by '/'. Location pats can be relative or absolute. Relative location paths start from the context node,

```
child::office/child::person/child::grade
```

while absolute location paths start at the document root (denoted by the first '/'),

```
/child::office/child::person/child::grade
```

4.3.1.8 XPath Abbreviated Syntax

For convenience, the commonly used XPath syntax can be abbreviated using the following shorthand:

- `//` is short for `/descendant-or-self::node()`
- `.` is short for `self::node()`
- `..` is short for `parent::node()`
- `@` is short for `attribute::`
- 'nothing' (i.e., empty) is short for `child::`

We show some of the examples here to illustrate the use of shorthand.

- full expression
  `child::office/child::person[attribute::name = 'Sue']`
  shorthands
  `office/person[@name = 'Sue']`

- full expression
  `/descendant-or-self::person[`*attribute*`::`*name* = '*Sue*']
  shorthand
  `//person[@name = 'Sue']`

4.3.1.9 XPath Exercises

Using the sample XML document shown in Fig. 4.3, let us try and solve the following queries using XPath expressions. We will be using both the full and shorthand expressions.

Query 1: Identify all person elements (how about first person element?)

   Long: `child::office/child::person`
   Abbreviated: `office/person`

We could try a little variation on this. The first person node could be chosen by using a function as below.

   Long: `child::office/child::person[1]`
   Abbreviated: `office/person[1]`

Query 2: Identify all person elements with grade 2.

   Long: `child::office/child::person[child::grade = 2]`
   Abbreviated: `office/person[grade = 2]`

Query 3: Identify Sue's age.

   Long:
   `child::office/child::person[attribute::name =' Sue']/child::age`
   Abbreviated: `office/person[@name =' Sue']/age`

Query 4: Identify all phone elements.

   Long:
   `/descendant-or-self::phone`
   Abbreviated: `//phone`

 Query 5: Identify persons names with age 29.

   Long:
   `child::office/child::person[child::age = 29][attribute::name]`
   Abbreviated: `office/person[age = 29][@name]`

4.3.2 XSLT

XSLT is a language for transforming the structure of an XML document. This language is versatile and has many use cases in XML applications. In particular, it is commonly used in the following scenarios:

- Converting an XML document to another XML document with different structure (xml → xml). One can add add/remove elements, rearrange elements, sort elements, perform calculations, etc.
- Providing different presentation/publication formats for the same piece of data. From a single XML document, the language can generate HTML, mobile device format, PDF, plain text, and more. This scenario is useful when you want to separate the data from its possible presentations.
- Transmitting data between applications. As a simple but effective application integration approach, the language could be used to transform a message from one format to another, mediating any structural or semantic mismatches in the communication messages.

XSLT has given the means to transform XML documents. Before XSLT, one could only do 'transformation' via writing custom applications with XML parsers, by working with the parser's API and a programming language to define a specific sequence of steps to be followed in order to produce the desired output.

For facilitating the transformation, XSLT employs a high-level declarative language approach. The required transformation is expressed as a set of 'rules'. Each rule describes the required transformation, rather than specifying a sequence of steps of how it should be done.

An XSLT process engine takes two types of input documents, XML and XSLT stylesheet. It applies the instructions in the stylesheet to the input document. An intermediary output is generated from which the serialisation process produces the resulting document. This process is depicted in Fig. 4.5. There are a few XSLT

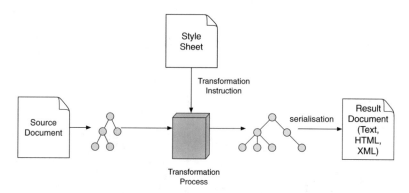

Fig. 4.5 XSLT performance. *Source* W3C

processors available, Xalan-Java by the Apache Software foundation, and Saxon by Michael Kay to name a couple, and many modern browsers have built-in support for XSLT.

The transformation process can be carried out on the server side or on the client side. On the server side the process can be either on demand or in advance and by means of XSLT processors (e.g., Xalan-Java, Saxon). On the client side the process occurs on demand by using XSLT-supported browsers, which include all major browsers (e.g., Mozilla Firefox, Google Chrome).

The documents are represented as trees; XSLT relies on the XML parser to obtain the trees. Figure 4.6 reveals how the Green-Eyed Monster document shown in Listing 4.1 is represented as an XSLT tree.

```
1  <!-- Green-Eyed Monster -->
2  <GEM>
3  <JealousyRecord>
4      <Person>Sue</Person>
5      <Job Earnings="peanuts">lecturer</Job>
6      <Holiday>
7          <Year>1996</Year>
8          <City>Nairobi</City><Country>Kenya</Country></Holiday>
9      <Holiday>
10         <Year>1994</Year>
11         <City>Paris</City><Country>France</Country></Holiday>
12     <Holiday>
13         <Year>1995</Year>
14         <City>Acapulco</City><Country>Mexico</Country></Holiday>
15 </JealousyRecord>
16 <JealousyRecord>
17     <Person>Bill</Person>
18     <Job Earnings="heaps">plumber</Job>
19     <Holiday>
20         <Year>1995</Year>
21         <City>Cairns</City><Country>Australia</Country></Holiday>
22     <Holiday>
```

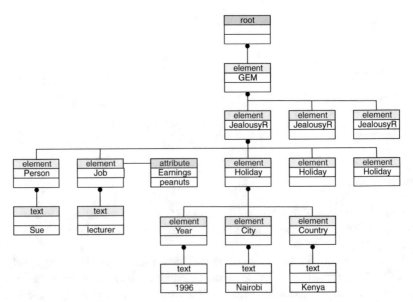

Fig. 4.6 An XSLT tree representation

```
23        <Year>1998</Year>
24        <City>Acapulco</City><Country>Mexico</Country></Holiday>
25     <Holiday>
26        <Year>1999</Year>
27        <City>Nairobi</City><Country>Kenya</Country></Holiday>
28 </JealousyRecord>
29 <JealousyRecord>
30     <Person>Doug</Person>
31     <Job Earnings="heaps">doctor</Job>
32     <Holiday>
33        <Year>1998</Year>
34        <City>Hong Kong</City><Country>China</Country></Holiday>
35     <Holiday>
36        <Year>1997</Year>
37        <City>Paris</City><Country>France</Country></Holiday>
38 </JealousyRecord>
39 </GEM>
```

Listing 4.1 Green-Eyed Monster document

Let us take the following example to get a quick overview of how XSLT works. In Listing 4.2, we see the details of a person's name, age and owned pets in XML. From this document, we would like to display the person's name, age and the number of pets owned in HTML.

```
1  <person>
2    <name>
3      <given>David</given>
4      <family>Edmond</family>
5    </name>
6    <age>57</age>
7    <pets>
8      <dog>Winnie</dog>
9      <cat>Misty</cat>
10   </pets>
11 </person>
```

Fig. 4.7 HTML Presentation

David Edmond

| How old? | 57 |
| Nr of pets | 2 |

Listing 4.2 A Person document

Here is the first glimpse of XSLT. Using the person document, the following XSL document generates the required transformation.

```
1 <?xml version="1.0"?>
2 <xsl:stylesheet
3   xmlns:xsl="http://www.w3.org/1999/XSL/Transform" version="2.0">
4 <xsl:template match="/">
5 <html>
6  <head>
7   <title><xsl:value-of select="person/name/given"/></title>
8  </head>
9  <body>
```

```
10    <h3>
11      <xsl:value-of select="person/name/given"/>
12      <xsl:text>    </xsl:text>
13      <xsl:value-of select="person/name/family"/>
14    </h3>
15    <table border="1">
16      <tr><td>How old?</td>
17          <td><xsl:value-of select="person/age"/></td></tr>
18      <tr><td>Nr of pets</td>
19          <td><xsl:value-of
20            select="count(person/pets/child::node())"/></td></tr>
21    </table>
22  </body>
23 </html>
24 </xsl:template>
25 </xsl:stylesheet>
```

Listing 4.3 XSLT for the Person Document

For now, we do not have to understand completely what is going on in this XSLT program. There are few things to note in the program though. An obvious observation is that the XSLT language itself is in XML. The XSLT related tags are pre-fixed with the conventional namespace label 'xsl'. Another thing to note is that the program seems to specify the output of the HTML code shown in Fig. 4.7, but in between the HTML tags there are some embedded lines that seem to contain XPath expressions (e.g., person/name/given, person/pets/child::node()).

4.3.2.1 The Transformation Process of XSLT

The transformation is a rule-based push process. The dominant feature of a typical XSLT consists of a sequence of so-called "template rules". Notice Line 4 in Listing 4.3, for example. Rules are not arranged in any particular order; as stated before, XSLT is declarative, not procedural. In each template rule, it is specified what output should be produced when particular patterns occur in the input. Notice Lines 5–22 in Listing 4.3 which contain the desired HTML output.

These are the steps of the XSLT transformation process:

1. XSLT first reads and parses the source document and the stylesheet.
2. Then, it finds a template rule that matches the root node.
3. Then, the processor instantiates the content of the template rule.

For example, when the XSLT code shown in Listing 4.4 is applied to the person document (Listing 4.2), the XSLT first reads both the person document and the stylesheet, looks for a template rule that matches the root note (Line 4), then instantiates the content of the template. In this case, the content is some HTML tags. In fact, this XSLT example will produce the same output with any XML input.

```
1 <?xml version="1.0"?>
```

```
2  <xsl:stylesheet
3    xmlns:xsl-"http://www.w3.org/1999/XSL/Transform" version="2.0">
4  <xsl:template match="/">
5    <html>
6      <head>
7        <title>Green Eyed Monster</title>
8      </head>
9      <body>
10        I found the Green Eyed Monster!
11      </body>
12    </html>
13  </xsl:template>
14  </xsl:stylesheet>
```

Listing 4.4 XSLT with a template rule

A template rule can contain another template rule in the form of 'apply-templates', in which case XSLT finds the matching template rule and instantiates the content. This basic process is repeated until there is no more template to apply. Listing 4.5 shows a simple case of this to illustrate the idea.

```
1  <?xml version="1.0"?>
2  <xsl:stylesheet
3    xmlns:xsl="http://www.w3.org/1999/XSL/Transform" version="2.0">
4  <xsl:template match="/">
5    <html>
6      <head>
7      <title>Green Monster</title>
8      </head>
9      <body>
10        <xsl:apply-templates select="GEM/JealousyRecord"/>
11      </body>
12    </html>
13  </xsl:template>
14  <xsl:template match="JealousyRecord">
15    <xsl:text>I found a Jealousy Record!</xsl:text><br/>
16  </xsl:template>
17  </xsl:stylesheet>
```

Listing 4.5 XSLT with apply-template

When this code is applied to the Green-Eyed Monster document (Listing 4.1), the XSLT processor first finds the template rule matching the root node (Line 4) and instantiates its content. Within the content, it comes across the apply-template statement that calls another template rule that matches the nodes Jealousy Record. This is specified by an XPath expression GEM/JealousyRecord. At this point, the processor finds the template (Line 14) and instantiates its text content "I found a Jealousy Record!". This content is then placed in between the <body>

tags. Note that there are three JealousyRecord nodes in the input document. So, this apply-template will be repeated three times (one for each match).

Here is the output of the XSLT, using the Green-Eyed Monster document as input (Listing 4.6).

```
1  <html>
2     <head>
3       <meta http-equiv="Content-Type" content="text/html;
          charset=UTF-8">
4       <title>Green Monster</title>
5     </head>
6     <body>
7     I found a Jealousy Record!<br>
8     I found a Jealousy Record!<br>
9     I found a Jealousy Record!<br>
10    </body>
11 </html>
```

Listing 4.6   Expected output

4.3.2.2   Quick Overview of XSLT Syntax Elements

In this section, we will briefly introduce the basic constructs of XSLT. There are six different types of basic constructs:

- Stylesheet Structuring
  - <xsl:stylesheet>
  - <xsl:include>
  - <xsl:import>
- Template Structuring
  - <xsl:template>
  - <xsl:apply-template>
  - <xsl:call-template>
- Conditional Processing
  - <xsl:if>
  - <xsl:choose>
  - <xsl:when>
  - <xsl:otherwise>
  - <xsl:for-each>

- Generating Output
  - <xsl:value-of>
  - <xsl:element>
  - <xsl:attribute>
  - <xsl:comment>
  - <xsl:processing-instruction>
  - <xsl:text>
- Variables and Parameters
  - <xsl:variable>
  - <xsl:param>
  - <xsl:with-param>
- Sorting and Numbering
  - <xsl:sort>
  - <xsl:number>

Let us go through the usage of the most common constructs.

Using *xsl:template*

A **template** contains a fragment of output to be generated when a suitable match is found in the input source document. The attribute *match* is used to indicate the nodes in the source document to which the template applies. The *match* is followed by an XPath expression.

- `<xsl:template match="/">` will match the root node of the source
- `<xsl:template match="Report/Intro">` will match any Intro element

Note that we are not allowed to nest <xsl:template> tags. You should use <xsl:apply-templates> or other syntax constructs like <xsl:for-each> tags to reference other templates.

Using *xsl:value-of*

The element **value-of** selects the text value of the specified node. For example, from the person document shown previously:

- `<xsl:value-of select="person/age"/>` retrieves the text value '57' from the age node.
- `<xsl:value-of select="."/>` retrieves the value of the current node (e.g., 'David' if the context node was 'person/name/given'.
- `<xsl:value-of select="count(person/pets/*)"/>` returns a count of all the child nodes under the pets node ('2' in this case).

It is also used to retrieve the value of XSLT parameters and variables. For example, to declare a variable `myVar`, we use the element **variable**.

```
<xsl:variable name="myVar" value="20"/>
```

To retrieve the value assigned to `myVar`, **value-of** is used as follows.

```
<xsl:value-of select="$myVar"/>
```

Using *xsl:if*

The **if** element inserts a conditional test. The syntax for specifying the **if** element is *<xsl:if test="XPath expressions"> element body </xsl:if>*.

To demonstrate how this element is used, consider the following documents: XML input and XSLT stylesheet for processing the input.

```
1 <poem>
2    <line>And suddenly the wind comes soft,</line>
3    <line>And Spring is here again;</line>
4    <line>And the hawthorn quickens with buds of green</line>
```

```
5    <line>And my heart with buds of pain.</line>
6  </poem>
```

Listing 4.7 A Poem

```
1  <xsl:stylesheet
2   xmlns:xsl="http://www.w3.org/1999/XSL/Transform" version="2.0">
3    <xsl:template match="/poem">
4      <html>
5        <head>
6         <title>A Poem</title>
7        </head>
8        <body>
9         <p>
10          <xsl:apply-templates select="line"/>
11         </p>
12        </body>
13      </html>
14 </xsl:template>
15 <xsl:template match="line">
16    <xsl:if test="position() mod 2 = 0">  </xsl:if>
17    <xsl:value-of select="."/><br/>
18 </xsl:template>j
19 </xsl:stylesheet>
```

Listing 4.8 XSLT Processing – adding "if" condition

In the XSLT code in Listing 4.8, the "if" element checks the position of the current line node. If it is an even number, it inserts two extra empty spaces (Line 16) before selecting the text value of line to create an indentation every second line. The serialised output in HTML is shown in Listing 4.9. Note   in the output.

```
1  <html>
2     <head>
3        <meta http-equiv="Content-Type" content="text/html;
       charset=UTF-8">
4        <title>A Poem</title>
5     </head>
6     <body>
7        <p>And suddenly the wind comes soft,<br>
8          And Spring is here again;<br>
9        And the hawthorn quickens with buds of green<br>
10         And my heart with buds of pain.<br></p>
11    </body>
12 </html>
```

Listing 4.9 Poem output

Using *xsl:choose*

The conventional Else-If construction is not available in XSLT; instead, the element
xsl:choose allows you to test multiple conditions. For example, we are given the
XML elements shown below (Listing 4.10):

```
1 <stocks>
2 <stock sec="IAG" open="31.00" high="32.61" low="30.15"
      close="30.51" />
3 <stock sec="CLS" open="29.32" high="30.01" low="29.15"
      close="29.35" />
4 <stock sec="BHP" open="33.35" high="34.60" low="32.80"
      close="33.50" />
5 </stocks>
```

Listing 4.10   Stock list XML

The following XSLT code compares the values of the attributes open and close
and, depending on the evaluation results, inserts different image files (Lines 18–28
in Listing 4.11).

```
1 <xsl:stylesheet
2  xmlns:xsl="http://www.w3.org/1999/XSL/Transform" version="2.0">
3   <xsl:template match="/stocks">
4     <html>
5       <head>
6        <title>Stocks</title>
7       </head>
8       <body>
9         <ol>
10          <xsl:apply-templates select="stock"/>
11         </ol>
12       </body>
13     </html>
14   </xsl:template>
15   <xsl:template match="stock">
16    <li>
17    <xsl:value-of select="@sec"/>
18    <xsl:choose>
19      <xsl:when test="@close &lt; @open">
20         <img src="down.gif" />
21      </xsl:when>
22      <xsl:when test="@close &gt; @open">
23         <img src="up.gif" />
24      </xsl:when>
25      <xsl:otherwise>
26         <img src="same.gif" />
27      </xsl:otherwise>
28    </xsl:choose>
29    </li>
```

```
30    </xsl:template>
31  </xsl:stylesheet>
```

Listing 4.11 XSLT processing – adding xsl:choose

The expected output of the code when applied against the above XML input is shown in Listing 4.12.

```
1  <html>
2     <head>
3        <meta http-equiv="Content-Type" content="text/html;
       charset=UTF-8">
4        <title>Stocks</title>
5     </head>
6     <body>
7        <ol>
8           <li>IAG<img src="down.gif"></li>
9           <li>CLS<img src="up.gif"></li>
10          <li>BHP<img src="up.gif"></li>
11       </ol>
12    </body>
13 </html>
```

Listing 4.12 Expected output

Using *xsl:element*

The element **xsl:element** is used to create XML element nodes in the output. To illustrate the usage, take the Office People Document in Listing 4.13 as input and consider the XSLT code shown in Listing 4.14.

```
1  <office>
2     <person name="Alan">
3        <phone>9488</phone>
4     </person>
5     <person name="Sue">
6        <phone>2044</phone>
7     </person>
8     <person name="Vicky">
9        <phone>2738</phone>
10    </person>
11    <person name="Mike">
12       <phone>6995</phone>
13    </person>
14 </office>
```

Listing 4.13 Office People XML

The XSLT code first creates an XML element named office_people as the document element. Then, it looks for person nodes. In each person node, an element named name is created and the element is filled with the value of the person's name attribute. The **xsl:output** element (Line 3) instructs the XSLT processor to format the output as XML.

```
1  <xsl:stylesheet
2    xmlns:xsl="http://www.w3.org/1999/XSL/Transform" version="2.0">
3  <xsl:output method="xml" indent="yes"/>
4    <xsl:template match="/office">
5      <xsl:element name="office_people">
6          <xsl:apply-templates select="person"/>
7      </xsl:element>
8  </xsl:template>
9  <xsl:template match="person">
10     <xsl:element name="name">
11         <xsl:value-of select="@name"/>
12     </xsl:element>
13 </xsl:template>
14 </xsl:stylesheet>
```

Listing 4.14 XSLT processing – Creating XML elements

Listing 4.15 shows the expected output when the code is run against the input. Note that the content is a well-formed XML document.

```
1  <?xml version="1.0" encoding="UTF-8"?>
2  <office_people>
3      <name>Alan</name>
4      <name>Sue</name>
5      <name>Vicky</name>
6      <name>Mike</name>
7  </office_people>
```

Listing 4.15 XSLT output – The content is XML

It is also possible to directly type in the elements you want to create. That is, the following code will achieve the same results.

```
1  <xsl:stylesheet
2    xmlns:xsl="http://www.w3.org/1999/XSL/Transform" version="2.0">
3  <xsl:output method="xml" indent="yes"/>
4    <xsl:template match="/office">
5      <office_people>
6          <xsl:apply-templates select="person"/>
7      </office_people>
8  </xsl:template>
9  <xsl:template match="person">
10     <name>
11         <xsl:value-of select="@name"/>
12     </name>
13 </xsl:template>
14 </xsl:stylesheet>
```

Listing 4.16 XSLT output – Directly creating elements

Using xsl:attribute

Although XML elements can be created by literally typing the names, sometimes using the explicit **xsl:element** method is necessary, especially when attributes are added to an element. The **xsl:attribute** adds an attribute declaration to an XML element. Consider the following XML fragment:

```
1 <person id="hpaik">
2    <homepage>http://www.cse.unsw.edu.au/~hpaik</homepage>
3 </person>
```

Let us say we would like to create an XML element that contains the following information.

```
1 <anchor addr="http://www.cse.unsw.edu.au/~hpaik">hpaik</anchor>
```

The following XSLT code may look reasonable, but it is not correct as the XSLT **value-of** element cannot be used as the value of `addr`.

```
<xsl:template match="person">
   <anchor addr=" <xsl:value-of select="homepage"/>   ">
      <xsl:value-of select="@id"/>
   </anchor>
</xsl:template>
```

Instead, **xsl:attribute** is used as follows.

```
1 <xsl:stylesheet
2   xmlns:xsl="http://www.w3.org/1999/XSL/Transform" version="2.0">
3 <xsl:output method="xml" indent="yes"/>
4 <xsl:template match="/person">
5    <anchor>
6       <xsl:attribute name="addr">
7        <xsl:value-of select="homepage"/>
8       </xsl:attribute>
9      <xsl:value-of select="@id"/>
10    </anchor>
11 </xsl:template>
12 </xsl:stylesheet>
```
Listing 4.17 Adding attributes to an element

Since this is a commonly used element creation pattern, there is a shorthand provided as shown below.

```
1 <xsl:stylesheet
2   xmlns:xsl="http://www.w3.org/1999/XSL/Transform" version="2.0">
3 <xsl:output method="xml" indent="yes"/>
4 <xsl:template match="/person">
5    <anchor addr="{homepage}">
6       <xsl:value-of select="@id"/>
```

```
7      </anchor>
8  </xsl:template>
9  </xsl:stylesheet>
```

Listing 4.18   Adding attributes to an element (shorthand)

Using *xsl : variable*

XSLT supports variables. XSLT variables are slightly different from those of other languages in that these variables are set once and are not allowed to be updated. Once set, they become 'read-only'. Variables in XSLT can be declared using the **xsl:variable** element:

```
<xsl:variable name="{variable name}" select="{variable value}" />
```

e.g., `<xsl:variable name="bodyTextSize" select="10pt"/>`

There are two types of variables: global and local. Global variables are available throughout the whole stylesheet, while local variables are only available within a particular template body.

```
1  <xsl:stylesheet
2    xmlns:xsl="http://www.w3.org/1999/XSL/Transform" version="2.0">
3  <xsl:variable name="width" select="50"/>
4  <xsl:template match="/office">
5      The value of width is <xsl:value-of select="$width" />
6      <xsl:apply-templates select="person" />
7  </xsl:template>
8  <xsl:template match="person">
9      The value of width is <xsl:value-of select="$width" />
10        <xsl:apply-templates select="/office/person/name" />
11 </xsl:template>
12 <xsl:template match="name">
13     The value of width is <xsl:value-of select="$width" />
14 </xsl:template>
15 </xsl:stylesheet>
```

Listing 4.19   Global variable

The output of this XSLT should be 50 from Line 5, 50 from Line 9 and 50 from Line 13, as the variable width is visible throughout the stylesheet.

```
1  <xsl:stylesheet
2    xmlns:xsl="http://www.w3.org/1999/XSL/Transform" version="2.0">
3  <xsl:variable name="width" select="50"/>
4  <xsl:template match="/office">
5      The value of width is <xsl:value-of select="$width" />
6      <xsl:apply-templates select="person" />
7  </xsl:template>
8  <xsl:template match="person">
```

```
9    <xsl:variable name="lwidth" select="$width*2"/>
10   The value of width is <xsl:value-of select="$width" />
11   The value of lwidth is <xsl:value-of select="$lwidth" />
12   <xsl:apply-templates select="/office/person/name" />
13  </xsl:template>
14  <xsl:template match="name">
15   The value of width is <xsl:value-of select="$width" />
16   <!--The value of lwidth is <xsl:value-of select="$lwidth" />-->
17  </xsl:template>
18  </xsl:stylesheet>
```

Listing 4.20   Local variable

The output of this XSLT should be 50 from Line 5, 50 from Line 10, 100 from Line 11, and 50 from Line 15. Note that if Line 16 were included, it would give an error stating "Variable lwidth has not been declared", as lwidth is only visible in Lines 8–13.

An interesting feature of an XSLT variable is that it is possible to create a temporary tree structure of XML elements and assign a variable to it. Figure 4.8 depicts the tree structure constructed by the variable declaration code in Listing 4.21.

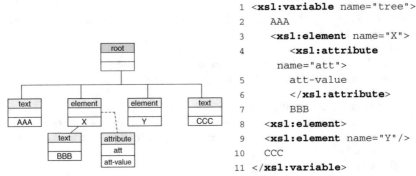

Fig. 4.8   XSLT temporary tree

```
1  <xsl:variable name="tree">
2    AAA
3    <xsl:element name="X">
4      <xsl:attribute
         name="att">
5      att-value
6      </xsl:attribute>
7      BBB
8    <xsl:element>
9    <xsl:element name="Y"/>
10   CCC
11  </xsl:variable>
```

Listing 4.21   A variable declaration

Once the tree is constructed, one can apply several functions on it. For example,

- To get the value of the attribute ("att-value"):
  ```
  <xsl:template match="/">
      <xsl:value-of select="$tree/X/@att" />
  </xsl:template>
  ```
- To get the total number of elements (2):
  ```
  <xsl:template match="/">
      <xsl:value-of select="count($tree//*)" />
  </xsl:template>
  ```

Using *xsl : param*

An XSLT program can take parameters. Parameters in XSLT can be declared using
xsl:param.

```
<xsl:param name="param_name">
```

Like variables, parameters have two different types: global and local. The values for
the global parameters are set outside the stylesheet and passed into the stylesheet
scope at runtime (e.g., command line). The local parameters are defined for a template, and their values are set using the **xsl:with-param** element when the template
is called.

For example, the following command line:

```
% java -jar saxon.jar aus.xml aus.xsl short=QLD
```

runs the XSLT stylesheet aus.xsl with aus.xml as input. It also passes a parameter called short with a value 'QLD'. This means that inside aus.xsl we should
find a global parameter declaration named short.

```
1 <xsl:stylesheet
2   xmlns:xsl="http://www.w3.org/1999/XSL/Transform" version="2.0">
3 <xsl:param name="short" />
4 <xsl:template match="Australia">
5     <xsl:apply-templates select="states/name[@abbr=$short]" />
6 </xsl:template>
7 <!-- details snipped -->
8 </xsl:stylesheet>
```

The following code snippet illustrates a local parameter declaration and its use.
As mentioned before, a local parameter value is set via the **xsl:with-param** element.

```
1 <xsl:stylesheet
2   xmlns:xsl="http://www.w3.org/1999/XSL/Transform" version="2.0">
3 <xsl:template match="Products">
4     <xsl:apply-templates select="Customers/Customer"
5         <xsl:with-param name="Filter" select="C10001" />
6     </xsl:apply-templates>
7 </xsl:template>
8 <xsl:template match="Customer">
9     <xsl:param name="Filter"/>
10 <!-- details snipped -->
11 </xsl:template>
12 </xsl:stylesheet>
```

Using *xsl : sort*

By default, the nodes are processed in document order: the order in which they
appear in the source document. The order can be changed in the output document via

xsl:sort. The following example demonstrates how to organize a list of cars based on the price (descending order).

```
1  <cars>
2      <car>
3          <make>Toyota</make>
4          <model>Corolla</model>
5          <price>30000</price>
6      </car>
7      <car>
8          <make>BMW</make>
9          <model>3.18</model>
10         <price>50000</price>
11     </car>
12     <car>
13         <make>Ford</make>
14         <model>Mustang Coupe</model>
15         <price>120000</price>
16     </car>
17 </cars>
```

Listing 4.22   Cars document

```
1  <xsl:stylesheet
2    xmlns:xsl="http://www.w3.org/1999/XSL/Transform" version="2.0">
3  <xsl:template match="/cars">
4      <xsl:apply-templates select="car">
5          <xsl:sort
6            data-type="number"
7            order="descending"
8            select="price"/>
9      </xsl:apply-templates>
10 </xsl:template>
11 <xsl:template match="car">
12     <xsl:value-of select="model" />
13 </xsl:template>
14 </xsl:stylesheet>
```

Listing 4.23   XSLT processing – Sorting nodes

When this code is executed against the input file, the printed order should be 'Mustang Coupe', '3.18' and then 'Corolla'. Note the attributes declared in the sort element. `data-type="number"` (Line 6 in Listing 4.23) converts the content of the price element into a number so that the sorting can be done semantically correctly.

Using *Text Nodes and White Spaces*

When there are two adjacent nodes in the output document, such as two `value-of`s inside a template rule, they are merged into one node, separated by a single space.

```
1 <xsl:template match="Entry">
2    <xsl:value-of select="LastName"/> <xsl:value-of
     select="FirstName"/>
3 </xsl:template>
```

Just like Web browsers, the XSLT processor ignores white spaces. XSLT does not support ' '; therefore the options to use instead are the following:

- space ( )
- tab (	)
- new line (
)
- carriage return ()

These characters can be directly typed into the code.

```
1 <xsl:template match="Entry">
2    <xsl:value-of select="LastName"/>
3    &#x20;&#x20;
4    <xsl:value-of select="FirstName"/>
5 </xsl:template>
```

The spaces within **xsl:text** are preserved.

```
1 <xsl:template match="Entry">
2    <xsl:value-of select="LastName"/>
3       <xsl:text>      </xsl:text>
4    <xsl:value-of select="FirstName"/>
5 </xsl:template>
```

There are three methods to control white spaces:

- *Insignificant whitespaces inside nodes*: to normalize insignificant whitespaces within elements, XSLT provides the function **normalize-space()**. For example, on the following node <description>

```
1 <a>
2 <description>   This ... is
3
4 a test.
5 </description>
6 </a>
```

the output of the following template (i.e., applying the function on the description node) is "This ... is a test.".

```
1 <xsl:stylesheet
2   xmlns:xsl="http://www.w3.org/1999/XSL/Transform"
      version="2.0">
3 <xsl:template match="/a">
4    <xsl:value-of select="normalize-space(description)"/>
5 </xsl:template>
6 </xsl:stylesheet>
```

- *Whitespace-only text nodes:*
  - If the whitespace-only text nodes (e.g., new lines, tabs in the source document) are to be treated as insignificant, the **xsl:strip-space** function tells the processor to ignore them. As shown below, *<xsl:strip-space elements="*">* used at top-level element will strip off all whitespace-only text nodes from the source document.

```
1 <xsl:stylesheet
2   xmlns:xsl="http://www.w3.org/1999/XSL/Transform"
     version="1.0">
3 <xsl:strip-space elements="*"/>
4 <xsl:template match="/">
5 <!-- snip -->
6 </xsl:stylesheet>
```

  - If the whitespace-only text nodes are significant and they have to be preserved, the tag *<xsl:preserve-space>* is to be used.

- Keep whitespaces: if the whitespaces are to be kept, use *xml:space="preserve"* in the XML document to instruct XML parsers to keep them.

4.3.2.3   Push vs. Pull Processing

This section explains two different approaches to authoring XSL code. To illustrate with an example, let us consider an XML document belonging to a rental company, containing a list of cars with their details (make and model) and three rental prices, two prices depending on the season and one special price for employees; the company wants to generate an HTML table showing only some of the information from the XML document, specifically, the car model and make and the prices for the high and the low season. Listing 4.24 shows the Cars XML document.

```
1 <cars>
2    <car class="intermediate">
3       <make>BMW</make>
4       <model>3.18</model>
5       <prices>
6          <price_per_day_hi>120</price_per_day_hi>
7          <price_per_day_lo>107</price_per_day_lo>
8          <price_employee>84</price_employee>
9       </prices>
10   </car>
11   <car class="specialty">
12      <make>Mustang Coupe</make>
13      <model>Ford</model>
14      <prices>
15         <price_per_day_hi>300</price_per_day_hi>
16         <price_per_day_lo>278</price_per_day_lo>
```

```
17              <price_employee>199</price_employee>
18          </prices>
19      </car>
20 </cars>
```

Listing 4.24   Cars XML document

The target output our XSLT code needs to generate is shown in Listing 4.25.

```
1  <html>
2  <body>
3  <h2>BMW 3.18</h2>
4  <table width="180px">
5    <tr>
6      <th>Price Low<br>Season</th>
7      <th>Price
       High<br>Season</th>
8    </tr>
9    <tr>
10     <td align="center">107</td>
11     <td align="center">120</td>
12   </tr>
13 </table>
14 <h2>Ford Mustang Coupe</h2>
15 <table width="180px">
16   <tr>
17     <th>Price Low<br>Season</th>
18     <th>Price
       High<br>Season</th>
19   </tr>
20   <tr>
21     <td align="center">278</td>
22     <td align="center">300</td>
23   </tr>
24 </table>
25 </body>
26 </html>
```

Fig. 4.9   HTML Presentation

Listing 4.25   Target output (in HTML)

In achieving the target output, we will introduce two different approaches, namely, push and pull (Fig. 4.9).

Push

The push style consists of writing a template rule for each kind of node that will be encountered in the source document. In push style processing, the processor pushes out every node in the source document; the template rules should be defined for these nodes so that they are caught for processing. An XSLT stylesheet using the push style to obtain the target output is presented in Listing 4.26.

```
1  <xsl:stylesheet
2      xmlns:xsl="http://www.w3.org/1999/XSL/Transform" version="2.0">
3  <xsl:output method="html" indent="yes"/>
4  <xsl:template match="/cars">
5  <html>
6      <body>
7       <xsl:apply-templates select="car"/>
8      </body>
9  </html>
10 </xsl:template>
11 <xsl:template match="car">
12     <h2>
13          <xsl:apply-templates select="make"/>
14          <xsl:text> </xsl:text>
15          <xsl:apply-templates select="model"/>
16     </h2>
17     <table width="180px">
18       <tr>
19         <th>Price Low  <br/>Season</th>
20         <th>Price High  <br/>Season</th>
21       </tr>
22       <xsl:apply-templates select="prices"/>
23     </table>
24 </xsl:template>
25 <xsl:template match="make">
26     <xsl:value-of select="."/>
27 </xsl:template>
28 <xsl:template match="model">
29     <xsl:value-of select="."/>
30 </xsl:template>
31 <xsl:template match="prices">
32     <tr> <xsl:apply-templates /> </tr>
33 </xsl:template>
34 <xsl:template match="price_per_day_hi">
35       <td align="center"> <xsl:value-of select="."/> </td>
36 </xsl:template>
37 <xsl:template match="price_per_day_lo">
38       <td align="center"> <xsl:value-of select="."/> </td>
39 </xsl:template>
40 <xsl:template match="text()"/>
41 </xsl:stylesheet>
```

Listing 4.26 Push style processing

It can be observed that the templates are defined to catch the nodes naturally following the tree structure. When the context node reaches prices (Line 31–33), <apply-templates /> is called (Line 32) without specifying the nodes to match. This causes the XSLT to visit every child node of the context node (i.e., `prices_per_day_hi`, `prices_per_day_lo` and `prices_employee`).

The 'do-nothing' template in Line 40 will catch the text value of `prices_employee`, eventually ignoring it in the output.

Pull

Pull style is based on extracting the desired content from the XML document with a template and copying it directly to the output. If the rental company were to apply the push style, the style sheet produced would be similar to the following:

```
1  <xsl:stylesheet
2     xmlns:xsl="http://www.w3.org/1999/XSL/Transform" version="2.0">
3  <xsl:output method="html" indent="yes"/>
4  <xsl:template match="/cars/car">
5  <html>
6     <body>
7       <h2>
8         <xsl:value-of select="make"/>
9         <xsl:text> </xsl:text>
10        <xsl:value-of select="model"/>
11      </h2>
12      <table width="180px">
13       <tr>
14         <th>Price Low  <br/>Season</th>
15         <th>Price High  <br/>Season</th>
16       </tr>
17       <tr>
18         <td align="center">
19           <xsl:value-of select="prices/prices_per_day_lo"/>
20         </td>
21         <td align="center">
22           <xsl:value-of select="prices/prices_per_day_hi"/>
23         </td>
24       </tr>
25      </table>
26     </body>
27  </html>
28  </xsl:template>
29  </xsl:stylesheet>
```

Listing 4.27 Pull style processing

In the presented example the push style is easier to use, and in general, for most of the XML documents, the push style is easier to read and apply. However, the decision should be made based on the type of document and the transformation one wants to perform. Push can result in a better style when the order of the information in the XML document is not very obvious and when the transformations are complex.

4.3.2.4   Example: Rule-Based Processing

Let us take an example to illustrate the practical use of applying rules though XSLT. Suppose you have phone book data with some entries in an XML document (phonebook.xml in Listing 4.28) and you want to obtain HTML output formatted as tables with the different details of each entry organized in columns and a single row per entry. To obtain the table, some transformation rules have to be applied. The rules are described in "pb.xsl" (Listing 4.29).

```xml
1  <?xml version="1.0"?>
2  <Phonebook>
3     <Entry>
4        <LastName Title="Miss">Edgar</LastName>
5        <FirstName>Pam</FirstName>
6        <School>Optometry</School>
7        <Campus>GP</Campus>
8        <Room>B501</Room>
9        <Extension>5695</Extension>
10    </Entry>
11    <Entry>
12       <LastName Title="Dr">Edmond</LastName>
13       <FirstName>David</FirstName>
14       <School>Information Systems</School>
15       <Campus>GP</Campus>
16       <Room>S842</Room>
17       <Extension>2240</Extension>
18    </Entry>
19    <Entry>
20       <LastName Title="Dr">Edmonds</LastName>
21       <FirstName>Ian</FirstName>
22       <School>Physical Sciences</School>
23       <Campus>GP</Campus>
24       <Room>M206</Room>
25       <Extension>2584</Extension>
26    </Entry>
27 </Phonebook>
```

Listing 4.28   phonebook.xml (source document)

```xml
1  <?xml version="1.0"?>
2  <xsl:stylesheet xmlns:xsl="http://www.w3.org/1999/XSL/Transform"
3       version="2.0">
4
5  <xsl:template match="/Phonebook">
6     <HTML><BODY><TABLE>
7     <xsl:apply-templates select="Entry"/>
8     </TABLE></BODY></HTML>
9  </xsl:template>
10
```

```
11 <xsl:template match="Entry">
12    <TR><TD><xsl:value-of select="LastName"/></TD>
13    <TD><xsl:apply-templates select="LastName"/></TD>
14    <TD><xsl:value-of select="FirstName"/></TD>
15    <TD><xsl:value-of select="School"/></TD>
16    <TD><xsl:value-of select="Campus"/></TD>
17    <TD><xsl:value-of select="Room"/></TD>
18    <TD><xsl:value-of select="Extension"/></TD></TR>
19 </xsl:template>
20
21 <xsl:template match="LastName">
22    <xsl:value-of select="@Title"/>
23 </xsl:template>
24 </xsl:stylesheet>
```

Listing 4.29 pb.xsl (XSL document)

The output of the transformation is shown in Listing 4.30 (Fig. 4.10).

```
1  <HTML>
2  <BODY>
3     <TABLE>
4        <TR><TD>Edgar</TD>
5        <TD>Miss</TD>
6        <TD>Pam</TD>
7        <TD>Optometry</TD>
8        <TD>GP</TD>
9        <TD>B501</TD>
10       <TD>5695</TD></TR>
11       <TR><TD>Edmond</TD>
12       <TD>Dr</TD>
13       <TD>David</TD>
14       <TD>Information
       Systems</TD>
15       <TD>GP</TD>
16       <TD>S842</TD>
17       <TD>2240</TD></TR>
18       <TR><TD>Edmonds</TD>
19       <TD>Dr</TD>
20       <TD>Ian</TD>
21       <TD>Physical
       Sciences</TD>
22       <TD>GP</TD>
23       <TD>M206</TD>
24       <TD>2584</TD></TR>
25    </TABLE>
26 </BODY>
27 </HTML>
```

Fig. 4.10 HTML presentation

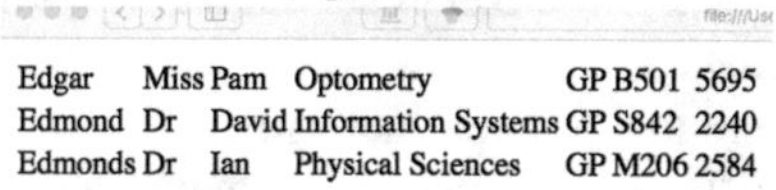

Edgar	Miss	Pam	Optometry	GP	B501	5695
Edmond	Dr	David	Information Systems	GP	S842	2240
Edmonds	Dr	Ian	Physical Sciences	GP	M206	2584

Listing 4.30 Output (in HTML)

4.3.2.5   Exercise: Generating XML Documents

Assume that you have the XML input specified in Listing 4.31 and you want to obtain the output specified in Listing 4.32. As an exercise, generate an XSLT program that performs the necessary transformation respecting the rules listed below. We present a solution here, but attempt to write a solution before looking it up.

```
1  <Phonebook>
2  <Entry>
3  <LastName Title="Miss">Edgar</LastName>
4  <FirstName>Pam</FirstName>
5  <School>Computer Science</School>
6  <Room>B501</Room>
7  <Extension>5097</Extension>
8  </Entry>
9  </Phonebook>
```

Listing 4.31 Input XML

```
1  <Phonebook>
2  <Entry Extension="5097">
3  <Name Title="Miss"
4       LastName="Pam"
5       FirstName="Edgar"/>
6  <Room Building=
7  "B">501</Room>
8  </Entry>
9  </Phonebook>
```

Listing 4.32 Target output XML

Rules:

- The Entry element will have a new attribute 'Extension'
- Create a new element called 'Name' with 'Title', 'LastName' and 'FirstName' as attributes
- Ignore the 'School' element
- The 'Room' element must have a new 'Building' attribute containing the first character of the Room

```
1  <?xml version="1.0"?>
2  <xsl:stylesheet xmlns:xsl="http://www.w3.org/1999/XSL/Transform"
3          version="2.0">
4  <xsl:output method="xml" indent="yes"/>
5
6      <xsl:template match="Phonebook">
7          <Phonebook>
8              <xsl:apply-templates />
9          </Phonebook>
10     </xsl:template>
11
12     <xsl:template match="Entry">
13         <Entry>
14             <xsl:attribute name="Extension">
15             <xsl:value-of select="Extension" /></xsl:attribute>
16         <Name>
17             <xsl:attribute name="Title">
18             <xsl:value-of select="LastName/@Title" /></xsl:attribute>
19             <xsl:attribute name="Lastname">
20             <xsl:value-of select="LastName" /></xsl:attribute>
21             <xsl:attribute name="FirstName">
```

```
22              <xsl:value-of select="FirstName" /></xsl:attribute>
23         </Name>
24         <Room>
25              <xsl:attribute name="Building">
26              <xsl:value-of select="substring(Room,1,1)"
         /></xsl:attribute>
27              <xsl:value-of select="substring(Room,2)" />
28         </Room>
29         </Entry>
30    </xsl:template>
31
32 </xsl:stylesheet>
```

Listing 4.33   XSLT program – Exercise solution

4.3.3   XQuery

XQuery is a declarative language, designed to query XML data, in which a query is represented as an expression. The aim is to provide a language to access collections of XML files just like you would in a conventional relational database.

XQuery is considered half programming language and half query language, due to its features that cover the aspects of both languages. For example, as programming language features, it has explicit iteration and variable bindings; recursive, user-defined functions; regular expressions; strong static typing; and ordered sequence data types much like lists or arrays. For its query language features, it provides filtering, grouping, and inner/outer joins.

XQuery presents some notable advantages, starting from its queries, which, in general, require less code than queries written in XSLT do. That, together with the strong influences on XQuery from XPath and SQL, makes XQuery an easy language to learn for users with previous knowledge of XPath and SQL. Another advantage is that XQuery can be used as a strongly typed language when the XML data is typed, which can improve the performance of the query by avoiding implicit type casts and provide type assurances that can be used when performing query optimization. On top of that, XQuery is supported by major database vendors.

XQuery capabilities go beyond simple data access in that it can also be used to implement information integration and transformation. The following lists some of the usage scenarios for XQuery:

- Selecting information based on specific criteria.
- Filtering out unwanted information.
- Searching for information within a document or set of documents.
- Joining data from multiple documents or collections of documents.
- Sorting, grouping, and aggregating data.
- Transforming and restructuring XML data into another XML vocabulary or structure.

- Performing arithmetic calculations on numbers and dates.
- Manipulating strings to reformat text.

Unlike the XSLT language, with its tree-based representation of XML elements, the XQuery language is designed to operate over ordered, finite sequences of items as its principal data type. These items can be atomic values (integers, strings, etc.) or unranked XML tree nodes. The evaluation of any XQuery expression yields an ordered sequence of $n >= 0$ items.

As a quick overview of the language structure, let us look over the different types of expressions defined in XQuery. Many of these expressions will become more familiar as we present more examples later on. A complete XQuery expression may consist of several of these expressions.

- **Primary expressions**: primitives of the language, including literals, variable references, context item expressions, constructors, and function calls.
- **Path expressions**: navigation expressions to extract nodes from XML documents.
- **Sequence expressions**: operators to manage sequences of items.
- **Arithmetic expressions**: arithmetic operators for addition, subtraction, multiplication, division, and modulus.
- **Comparison expressions**: XQuery provides operators to perform comparisons; three different kinds are defined: value comparisons, general comparisons, and node comparisons.
- **Logical expressions**: expressions with logical operators "and" and "or".
- **Constructors**: constructor operators can create XML structures within a query.
- **FLWOR expressions**: for the iteration and binding of variables to intermediate results. These are the most important expressions of XQuery and are explained in detail in the section "FLWOR Expression".
- **Ordered and unordered expressions**: describe operators to set the ordering mode for XQuery operations.
- **Conditional expressions**: expressions that contain an if-then-else statement.
- **Quantified expressions**: they support the existential and universal quantifiers.
- **Expressions on sequence types**: used to refer to a type in an XQuery expression.
- **Validate expressions**: used to validate a document node or an element node with respect to the schema definition.
- **Extension expressions**: expressions whose semantics indicates an aspect that may differ between implementations, but must be specified by the implementor for each particular implementation.

When creating an XQuery expression by means of combining the above-mentioned expressions, there are some syntax rules that should be taken into account. Here is a list of the syntax rules we can go over quickly.

- XQuery is a case-sensitive language.
- Keywords are in lowercase.
- No special end-of-line character.
- Every expression has a value and no side effects.

- Expressions are fully composable.
- Expressions can be nested with full generality.
- Expressions can raise errors.
- Comments look like this: (: *This is an XQuery Comment* :)

Figure 4.11 shows a complete XQuery expression. It is a FLWOR expression within which other expressions like Path expression, Comparison expression, Constructor, etc. are nested.

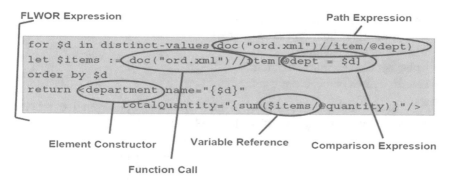

Fig. 4.11 XQuery nested expressions

In the following, we will introduce some of these expressions in detail with examples.

Constructors

Constructors create new XML elements. They are used to format the desired output from running an XQuery. For example, let us assume that a result of the query should be like what is shown in Listing 4.34. An XQuery constructor expression to construct the target XML is shown in Listing 4.35.

```
1 <emp empid="12345">
2    <name>John Smith</name>
3    <job>Anthopologist</job>
4 </emp>
```

Listing 4.34 Target output

```
1 <emp empid = {$id}>
2    {$name}
3    {$job}
4 </emp>
```

Listing 4.35 Constructor expression

This expression generates an <emp> element that has an "empid" attribute. The value of the attribute and the content of the element are specified by variables $name and $job, whose values are bound in other parts of the same query.

FLWOR Expression

XQuery defines FLWOR expressions which are used to iterate through the sequence of XML items. FLWOR is the acronym for **for, let, where, order by, and return**, and has a form analogous to SQL's **SELECT, FROM, WHERE, GROUP BY, and ORDER BY**. FLWOR is the most important expression in XQuery.

A FLWOR expression binds nodes (or node sets) to variables, operates over each legal combination of the bindings and produces a set of nodes. It does this through the following FLWOR statements:

- **for**: defines iterators that bind variables.
- **let**: defines collections (not to be iterated).
- **where**: defines conditions.
- **order by**: defines order conditions.
- **return**: defines output constructor.

The above four steps constitute a FLWOR expression execution process. Figure 4.12 depicts the process, which is as follows:

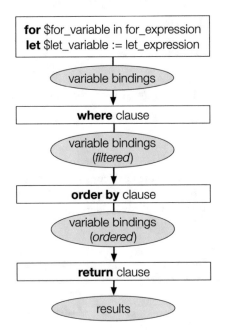

Fig. 4.12 XQuery steps

1. The *for* construct **successively binds** each item of an expression (*expr*) to a variable (*var*), generating a so-called *tuple stream*.
2. This tuple stream is then **filtered** by the *where* clause, retaining some tuples and discarding others.

3. The *return* clause is **evaluated** once for every tuple still in the stream.
4. The result of the expression is an **ordered** sequence containing the **concatenated** results of these evaluations.

To help the reader to understand the FLWOR expressions, we illustrate them with a few examples below. If the reader desires a more detailed theoretical description of XQuery, it can be found on its official website.[4]

For the examples, we use cars.xml, shown in Listing 4.36.

```
 1  <cars>
 2    <car class="compact">
 3        <id>1</id>
 4        <make>Toyota</make>
 5        <model>Corolla</model>
 6        <color>red</color>
 7        <color>blue</color>
 8        <prices>
 9            <price_per_day_hi>97</price_per_day_hi>
10            <price_per_day_lo>85</price_per_day_lo>
11            <price_employee>74</price_employee>
12        </prices>
13    </car>
14    <car class="compact">
15        <id>2</id>
16        <make>Toyota</make>
17        <model>Yaris</model>
18        <color>yellow</color>
19        <prices>
20            <price_per_day_hi>70</price_per_day_hi>
21            <price_per_day_lo>60</price_per_day_lo>
22            <price_employee>37</price_employee>
23        </prices>
24    </car>
25    <car class="intermediate">
26        <id>3</id>
27        <make>BMW</make>
28        <model>3.18</model>
29        <color>red</color>
30        <prices>
31            <price_per_day_hi>120</price_per_day_hi>
32            <price_per_day_lo>107</price_per_day_lo>
33            <price_employee>84</price_employee>
34        </prices>
35    </car>
36    <car class="specialty">
37        <id>4</id>
38        <make>Mustang Coupe</make>
39        <model>Ford</model>
```

---

[4] http://www.w3.org/TR/2001/WD-xquery-20010215/.

```
40          <color>black</color>
41          <prices>
42              <price_per_day_hi>300</price_per_day_hi>
43              <price_per_day_lo>278</price_per_day_lo>
44              <price_employee>199</price_employee>
45          </prices>
46      </car>
47 </cars>
```

Listing 4.36 Input XML document – cars.xml

FLWOR SQL Similarity

This example is to show how an XQuery syntax containing *for*, *where* and *return* is similar to the SQL syntax containing *select*, *from* and *where* statements.

```
1 xquery version "1.0";
2 for $car in doc("cars.xml")//car
3   where $car/@class = "compact"
4   return
5       <car>
6       {
7           $car/make,
8           $car/model,
9           <br/>
10      }
11      </car>
```

Listing 4.37 XQuery and SQL similarity – simple.xq

This XQuery generates a list of all the cars belonging to the class "compact". The list in this case will have two results: "Toyota Corolla" and "Toyota Yaris". The output of the query is:

```
1 <car>
2     <make>Toyota</make>
3     <model>Corolla</model>
4     <br/>
5 </car>
6 <car>
7     <make>Toyota</make>
8     <model>Yaris</model>
9     <br/>
10 </car>
```

Listing 4.38 Output of simple.xq

Note the output elements created as defined in the constructor expressions.

FLWOR: *for* and *let*

Let us look at the individual elements of a FLWOR expression. A FLWOR expression requires a for or let clause. The *for* clause iterates based on a sequence and it creates as many bindings as members the sequence has, which means that it binds a variable to each node, while the *let* clause binds a variable to the whole sequence.

Both of them are used in the example shown in offering.xq. The objective in this example is to obtain a list with the different models of a make and the number of their colours available.

The *for* clause here creates a sequence of *car* nodes and binds each node to the variable $car. The nodes in the variable $car can be interated. The *let* clause on the other hand binds the result of the Path expression '$car/color' into the variable $aux. The nodes bound to $aux are not meant for iteration; rather, the nodes are bound to the variable as a whole (i.e., collection).

```
1 <text>We currently offer: <br/></text>,
2 for $car in doc('cars.xml')//car
3   let $aux := $car/color
4   where contains($car/make, "Toyota")
5   return
6       <car>
7       {
8           <text>{count($aux)} different color/s of </text>,
9           $car/model,
10          <br/>
11      }
12      </car>
```

Listing 4.39 XQuery using *let* and *for* clauses – offering.xq

The output of the query is shown below. Note the results of count($aux) in the output.

```
1 <text>We currenly offer: <br/>
2 </text>
3 <car>
4   <text>2 different color/s of </text>
5   <model>Corolla</model>
6   <br/>
7 </car>
8 <car>
9   <text>1 different color/s of </text>
10  <model>Yaris</model>
11  <br/>
12 </car>
```

Listing 4.40 Output of offering.xq

FLWOR: Conditions

Conditions are expressed in XQuery by the syntax: IF expr THEN expr ELSE. In this example, given the XML document "cars.xml", we want to obtain the list of cars for which the low season price is less than 100. To get that list, a conditional clause has to be applied as follows. The output of the XQuery is shown right after.

```
1  for $car in doc("cars.xml")//car
2     return
3       <car>
4         {
5           if (($car//price_per_day_lo) < 100) then (
6               $car/make,  $car/model, $car//price_per_day_lo
7           ) else (
8               $car/make, $car/model
9           )
10        }
11      </car>
```

Listing 4.41 XQuery: if-else.xq

```
1  <car>
2     <make>Toyota</make>
3     <model>Corolla</model>
4     <price_per_day_lo>85</price_per_day_lo>
5  </car>
6  <car>
7     <make>Toyota</make>
8     <model>Yaris</model>
9     <price_per_day_lo>60</price_per_day_lo>
10 </car>
11 <car>
12    <make>BMW</make>
13    <model>3.18</model>
14 </car>
15 <car>
16    <make>Mustang Coupe</make>
17    <model>Ford</model>
18 </car>
```

Listing 4.42 Output: if-else.xq

FLWOR: Sorting

The purpose of this example is to sort the cars in alphabetical order. This is the XQuery. Note the *order by* clause position after *for*, but before *return*.

```
1 for $car in doc("cars.xml")//car
2    order by ($car/make)
3    return
4      <car>
5        {
6          $car/make,
7          $car/model,
8          <br/>
9        }
10     </car>
```

Listing 4.43 XQuery: sort.xq

```
1 <car>
2    <make>BMW</make>
3    <model>3.18</model>
4    <br/>
5 </car>
6 <car>
7    <make>Mustang Coupe</make>
8    <model>Ford</model>
9    <br/>
10 </car>
11 <car>
12    <make>Toyota</make>
13    <model>Corolla</model>
14    <br/>
15 </car>
16 <car>
17    <make>Toyota</make>
18    <model>Yaris</model>
19    <br/>
20 </car>
```

Listing 4.44 Output: sort.xq

FLWOR: Joins

Two kinds of joins can be used in FLWOR expressions: inner and outer. To perform a join, we would need at least one other XML file. "specialFeatures.xml" is an XML document that contains details about the special characteristics of the cars.

```
1 <?xml version="1.0"?>
2 <special_features>
3    <feature name="Recaro leather seat">
4      <car_id>4</car_id>
5      <color>red</color>
6    </feature>
7    <feature name="12 Speakers">
8      <car_id>4</car_id>
9      <brand>Pioneer</brand>
```

```
10      <power>600W</power>
11    </feature>
12    <feature name="Heated Seats">
13      <car_id>3</car_id>
14    </feature>
15 </special_features>
```

Listing 4.45 Second input for join: specialFeatures.xml

What is required in this example is to obtain a list of the cars (make, model) with the features they have, using first an inner join, and then an outer join.

First, the XQuery using an **inner join** expression looks as in Listing 4.46. In the output, we can expect that the cars that do not appear in the "specialFeatures.xml" file will not be included in the final output.

```
1 for $car in doc("cars.xml")//car,
2     $feature in doc("specialFeatures.xml")//feature
3 where $car//id = $feature//car_id
4 return
5   <car>
6      {$car/make}
7      {$car/model} <score> - </score>
8      <feature>{string($feature/@name)}></feature>
9      <br/>
10   </car>
```

Listing 4.46 XQuery: inner-join.xq

```
1 <car>
2    <make>BMW</make>
3    <model>3.18</model>
4    <score> - </score>
5    <feature>Heated Seats</feature>
6    <br/>
7 </car>
8 <car>
9    <make>Mustang Coupe</make>
10   <model>Ford</model>
11   <score> - </score>
12   <feature>Recaro leather seat</feature>
13   <br/>
14 </car>
15 <car>
16   <make>Mustang Coupe</make>
17   <model>Ford</model>
18   <score> - </score>
19   <feature>12 Speakers</feature>
20   <br/>
21 </car>
```

Listing 4.47 Output: inner-join.xq

Second, the outer join will look as follows. In the output, we can expect that the cars that do not appear in the "specialFeatures.xml" file will still be included in the final output.

```
1  for $car in doc("cars.xml")//car
2  return
3     <car>
4         {$car/make}
5         {$car/model} <score> - </score>
6         {
7         for $feature in doc("specialFeatures.xml")//feature
8         where $car//id = $feature//car_id
9         return
10        <feature>{string($feature/@name)}></feature>
11        }
12     </car>
```

Listing 4.48   XQuery: outer-join.xq

```
1  <car>
2     <make>Toyota</make>
3     <model>Corolla</model>
4     <score> - </score>
5  </car>
6  <car>
7     <make>Toyota</make>
8     <model>Yaris</model>
9     <score> - </score>
10 </car>
11 <car>
12    <make>BMW</make>
13    <model>3.18</model>
14    <score> - </score>
15    <feature>Heated Seats&gt;</feature>
16 </car>
17 <car>
18    <make>Mustang Coupe</make>
19    <model>Ford</model>
20    <score> - </score>
21    <feature>Recaro leather seat&gt;</feature>
22    <feature>12 Speakers&gt;</feature>
23 </car>
```

Listing 4.49   Output: outer-join.xq

As the reader can observe, none of the outputs is a perfect example; however, the objective is to show how to use the joins. The outputs can be polished, but that will generate more lines of code and make the example more difficult to read.

FLWOR: Text Match

There are two different styles to check for whether a text matches or not:

- Equality: *//car[make="Toyota"]*
- Full-text: *//car[contains(make,"Toy")]*

For example, here is a query (and its output) that selects cars whose maker's name contains "Toy".

```
1 for $car in doc('cars.xml')//car
2   where $car[contains($car/make, "Toy")]
3   return
4       <car>
5       {
6           $car/model,
7           $car/make
8       }
9       </car>
```

Listing 4.50   XQuery: match.xq

```
1 <car>
2     <model>Corolla</model>
3     <make>Toyota</make>
4 </car>
5 <car>
6     <model>Yaris</model>
7     <make>Toyota</make>
8 </car>
```

Listing 4.51   Output: match.xq

XQuery Update Facility

XQuery provides five different update statements. Not all implementations of XQuery support update facilities. The exact syntax of updates may differ slightly from one implementation to another. Let us consider the following XML document in order to apply the update facilities on it:

```
1 <animals>
2     <animal>lion</animal>
3     <animal>elephant</animal>
4     <animal>tiger</animal>
5 </animals>
```

Listing 4.52   Input document – animals.xml

The **insert** statement will create a new element and insert it into a given position. For example, to insert a new animal, a rhino, after the elephant, we do:

```
1 insert node <animal> rhino</animal> after
2 doc("animals.xml")/animals/animal[2]
```
Listing 4.53 Insert

```
1 <animals>
2    <animal>lion</animal>
3    <animal>elephant</animal>
4    <animal>rhino</animal>
5    <animal>tiger</animal>
6 </animals>
```
Listing 4.54 After insert

delete will remove an element. For example, to delete the elephant element from the document, we do:

```
1 delete node doc("animals.xml")/animals/animal[2]
```
Listing 4.55 Delete

```
1 <animals>
2    <animal>lion</animal>
3    <animal>rhino</animal>
4    <animal>tiger</animal>
5 </animals>
```
Listing 4.56 After delete

replace replaces the target element with a given node. For example, to replace the tiger with a zebra, we do:

```
1 replace node doc("animals.xml")/animals/animal[3]
2 with <animal>zebra</animal>
```
Listing 4.57 Replace

```
1 <animals>
2    <animal>lion</animal>
3    <animal>rhino</animal>
4    <animal>zebra</animal>
5 </animals>
```
Listing 4.58 After replace

You can also **rename** an element. For example, to change the name of the node "animal" which contains "lion" to "king", we do:

```
1 rename node doc("animals.xml")/animals/animal[1]
2 as 'king'
```
Listing 4.59 Rename

```
1 <animals>
2    <king>lion</king>
3    <animal>rhino</animal>
4    <animal>zebra</animal>
5 </animals>
```
Listing 4.60   After rename

The transform expression can be used to return modified copies of existing nodes. In the following example, the transform expression is used to return the list of animals excluding the "<king>" element.

```
1 copy $anim := doc("animals.xml")/animals
2    modify (delete nodes $anim/king)
3    return $anim
```
Listing 4.61   Transform

```
1 <animals>
2    <animal>rhino</animal>
3    <animal>zebra</animal>
4 </animals>
```
Listing 4.62   Transformation output

One thing to note here is that the input document remains exactly the same as before, as the transformation is performed on the copied nodes ($anim).

4.4   Exposing Data as Services

In the direct data access scenario depicted in Fig. 4.13, developing data-consuming applications over multiple data sources is rather painful. The difficulties arise from the fact that:

- There is no one single view of "X" for any "X"
  - What data do I have available about "X"?
  - How do I put together the information I need?
  - What else is "X" related to?
- There is no uniformity over the data model or representation language
  - Data about "X" is stored in many *different* formats.
  - Accessing or updating "X" involves many *different* APIs.
  - *Manual coding* of "distributed query plans" is required.

Data Consuming Applications

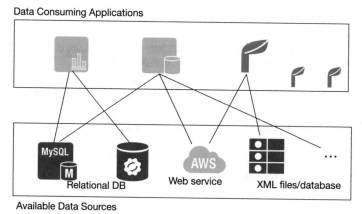

Available Data Sources

Fig. 4.13 Consuming data via direct data access to the sources

Now with the data services concept, we can create a scenario shown in Fig. 4.14 where data services are creating a uniform data access layer to the underlying data sources.

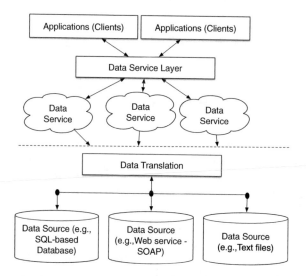

Fig. 4.14 Consuming data via direct data access to the sources

Conceptually, realizing a data service involves choosing an existing standard for the data representation model (e.g., XML, JSON) as the payload of a data service request/response, then choosing the interface scheme (e.g., SOAP or REST). XML is a good choice as there are readily available transformation and query techniques, as we have seen in the previous sections.

Let's say a company exposes various services around employees. You may have a Web-based portal which is a fully functioning Web application. You may also expose a SOAP-based service. For example, such a service may allow a client application to register a new employee, which sets up a few privileges automatically in the system. You may also expose a data service that allows lookup of employees. Figure 4.15 illustrates how a data service may coexist with other services. In the example, a data service which is registered with an endpoint `http://soacourse.unsw.edu.au/dataservice/empLookup/` receives an HTTP request (i.e., look up by employee ID A2219876).

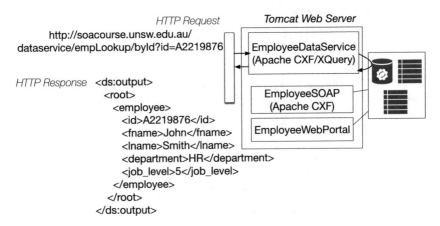

Fig. 4.15 A plain implementation of a data service using XQuery

In REST, this request can be mapped to a GET operation with a parameter "id". In the implementation of the GET operation, a pre-coded XQuery fragment can be called upon to run the query against the underlying data source. The returned record from the XQuery execution can be then formatted and returned in the HTTP response payload.

```
declare variable $id as xs:string external;
<root>{
    for $employee in collection("employee")/employee
    where $employee/emp_id = $id
    return $employee
}</root>
```

To summarise, the data as a service concept advocates the view that the actual platform on which the data resides does not matter. The data can cleaned and enriched as needed, and be "exposed/offered" to different consumer applications, irrespective of the format of their physical existence in the organizations or the Web. The main focus of a data service is to give data users access to any information in the enterprise/Web through a *single, query-based* access layer. Typically, a data service models a unit of information, such as a customer, sales order, or product.

XML technologies introduced in this chapter provide (i) a common data model and (ii) a common language for data extraction, transformation, and aggregation, which form the core techniques in generic design and implementation solutions for data services.

4.5 Lab04: Data Service Enablers – XSLT and XQuery

In this lab, you will work through some exercises in XSLT and XQuery to learn the basics of the languages.

Exercise Files

The exercise files involved in the lab can be downloaded from the Github site:

- https://github.com/SOA-Book

    Follow the repository exercises, then lab04.

4.5.1 Working Through XSLT Examples

First, we will work through some exercises in XSLT.

Installing Saxon:

Begin by installing Saxon, the XSLT processor.

1. Create a directory called saxon.
2. Saxon is freely available on the Web. There is a copy of the version 6.5.4. included in the exercise files.
3. Unzip the file into the 'saxon' directory you have created.
4. It has complete documentation and samples. In this lab, you are interested in using the saxon.jar file.

Downloading exercise files:

Download the source code of the examples available in the Github site given above. Unzipping the file will create a directory called `xslexample`. All XSLT files and related XML documents required for the example will be there.

To make the exercise simpler let us copy the necessary library to the directory where the example files are. So, first copy `saxon.jar` to the `xslexample` directory.[5]

Trying out the Examples

Before proceeding, make sure that your local environment variable JAVA_HOME is set correctly.

Now, test the examples and examine the output files. You should also examine the XSLT files and see if you can understand the transforming process in each example.

1. `java -jar saxon.jar edmond.xml edmond.xsl > out.html`
2. `java -jar saxon.jar books.xml BIBstyle.xsl > out.html`
   (Note: BIBstyle uses for-each element)
3. `java -jar saxon.jar books.xml BIBstyle2.xsl > out.html`
   (Note: BIBstyle2 uses apply-templates element)
4. `java -jar saxon.jar gem.xml MyFriends.xsl > out.html`
5. `java -jar saxon.jar gem.xml GEMholiday.xsl > out.html`
6. `java -jar saxon.jar scorers.xml gtimes.xsl > out.html`
7. `java -jar saxon.jar scorers.xml gcount.xsl > out.html`
8. `java -jar saxon.jar Phonebook.xml p2p.xsl > out.xml`
9. `java -jar saxon.jar sdb.xml q1.xsl > out.xml`
10. `java -jar saxon.jar sdb.xml q1a.xsl > out.xml`
    (Note: the one with weight more than 25)
11. `java -jar saxon.jar sdb.xml q2.xsl > out.xml`
12. `java -jar saxon.jar sdb.xml q3.xsl > out.xml`
13. `java -jar saxon.jar sdb.xml q4.xsl > out.xml`
14. `java -jar saxon.jar sdb.xml q5.xsl > out.xml`
15. `java -jar saxon.jar sdb.xml q6.xsl > out.xml`

Developing Your Own XSLT Program

Now write an XSLT program that produces a listing of all my friends and the number of holidays each has taken:

1. The output should be something like:

Sue   3
Bill 3
Doug 2

---

[5]Our sincere thanks to Dr. David Edmond, the original creator of the files, for generously allowing us to use his files in this exercise.

Sorting XSLT Output

In this section, we will examine the ability to sort the output produced as part of an XSL transformation.

1. Open the XML data file `aus.xml`. You should see a list of all eight Australian states and territories. They are classified as "divisions", and each division's name, abbreviation, capital city, area and population are provided.
2. Try `aussort1.xsl` via:

```
java -jar saxon.jar aus.xml aussort1.xsl > out.html
```

3. Examine the output file. You should see a list of all divisions in descending order of area (in square kilometres).
4. Open the XSLT program `aussort1.xsl`. Note the use of the `xsl:sort` element to sort the table in descending order of area. Also, note the location of the sort element (i.e., inside 'apply-templates')
5. In a new browser window, open this xslt reference link.[6] You should then scroll down to `xsl:sort`. The XSLT reference documentation shows a few different sorting options.
6. Now change the program so that it sorts the output in ascending order of population.

Providing Parameters to XSLT Programs

We will often wish to parameterise an XSLT program. A simple example is when we only want to select some of the possible output that might result from scanning the document. In the next program, we will display information about just one of the states or territories, depending upon a value supplied by the user. The value will be the abbreviation, for example, VIC for Victoria.

1. Try the following:

```
java -jar saxon.jar aus.xml ausparam1.xsl short=QLD > \
out.html
```

2. Examine the output file. You should see information specific to Queensland.
3. Open the file `ausparam1.xsl` file. You should make sure you understand the following features of the program:

   a. The declaration of the parameter "short".
   b. The use of the parameter in the form `$short` in the `<H2>` element.
   c. The use of the expression `division/name[@abbr=$short]` to ensure that the only divisions selected are those with a name that has an "abbr" attribute equal to the parameter provided. This expression has the effect of choosing *name* elements for template matching.
   d. The consequent appearance of `match="name"` to catch these elements.

---

[6]http://www.w3.org/TR/xslt20/.

   e. The use of `select="."` to display the name element.

   f. The use of `select="../cap"`, for example, to display sibling elements of name.

Indexing Elements in XSLT

We can tell an XSLT program that we want to build an index structure. This could be useful if the transformation requires repeated access to elements. Suppose that our program needs to frequently access divisions by means of abbreviations such as QLD. We can define a key that may then be used to access divisions by means of their abbreviations.

1. Try the following:

```
java -jar saxon.jar aus.xml auskey1.xsl short=QLD > \
out.html
```

2. Examine the output file. You should see information specific to Queensland, just as you did with the previous program.

3. Open the file `auskey1.xsl` file. You should make sure you understand the following features of the program:

   a. The use of the `xsl:key` element to state our need for an index and its three attributes: (1) the `name="by-abbr"`, which allows us to name the key structure; (2) the `match="name"`, which indicates that we want to access `name` elements by means of this structure; and (3) the `use="@abbr"`, which indicates that we want to access these elements by means of their abbreviations.

   b. The use of `select="key('by-abbr',$short)"` to indicate that we only want to access `name` elements that match the abbreviation indicated in the `short` parameter.

Developing Your Own Key Structure

Now, based on the previous example, develop a new program that defines an index to access divisions by means of their status.

1. The command line should be like this:

```
java -jar saxon.jar aus.xml auskey2.xsl \
status=Territory > out.html
```

2. Open the file `out.html` file. You should see information specific to territories only.

4.5.2 Working Through XQuery Examples

In this exercise, we provide examples of writing XQuery files to create a view (in the database sense) over some XML files. The source XML files are given in the exercise files. You can run the individual queries and observe the output to see how various syntax elements of XQuery work in practice.

1. First, create a directory called `saxon-xq`.
2. Download the exercise file provided. It contains the Saxon XQuery processor (version 9) and some XQuery files and XML source documents.
3. Unzip the file into the `saxon-xq` directory you have created.
4. Test the examples and examine the output files using the following command in a terminal window:

```
java -cp saxon9he.jar net.sf.saxon.Query -q:$1 -o:$2
```

Here, variable 1 ($1) represents the query file name (i.e., sample files with extension ".xq") and variable 2 ($2) represents the output file name. For example, to run the q1.xq file given in the exercise, Do:

```
java -cp saxon9he.jar net.sf.saxon.Query -q:q1.xq \
-o:q1out.xml
```

You should see the file `q1out.xml` created and be able to observe the content.

Chapter 5
Web Service Composition: Overview

This chapter aims to outline basic concepts about Web service composition before presenting a concrete technology. We will present views on processes, atomic services and composite services, the motivations behind the use of service composition technology, and the differences between service orchestration and choreography. Let us start with the definition of Web service composition in a few words:

> The activity of aggregating Web services to build a new Web service is known as *Web Service Composition*

A faithful graphical representation of a Web service is a workflow model, which contains a number of non-overlapping tasks ordered by directed flows. These altogether, represent a process. A workflow can be considered a virtual representation of a piece of real work. Each task in a workflow can represent a Web service, and the flows in the workflow represent how the Web services are coordinated (i.e., composed). Workflows can describe conversation rules and protocols between services as well. Figure 5.1 represents a composite Web service by means of a workflow.

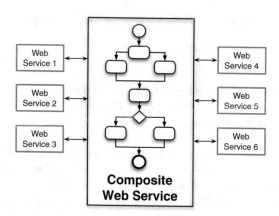

Fig. 5.1 Workflow representation of a composite service

© Springer International Publishing AG 2017
H.-y. Paik et al., *Web Service Implementation and Composition Techniques*,
DOI 10.1007/978-3-319-55542-3_5

5.1   From Atomic to Composite Services

Let us discuss, through a scenario, how Web service composition is used and why it is a useful technique. In real life, processes are rarely fully realised by simple, elementary Web services; for example, Fig. 5.2 illustrates an online book store that implements the process of selling a book. The implementation glues together three existing Web services: *Stock Availability* to check the availability of the requested book in the storehouse, *Online Payment* to contact the bank and verify all payment details, and *Shipping Request* to place an order with the shipping company. The approach of manually managing systems similar to that of the online book store

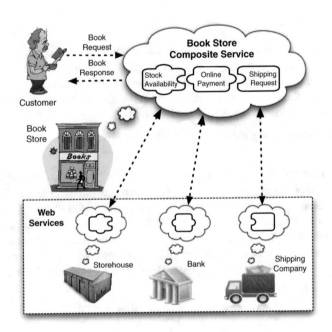

Fig. 5.2   An example of Web service composition

through atomic services, where the sequence of the process and the data interaction among the services have to be defined every time a purchase is made, is obviously complex, tedious and error prone.

By defining the process as a Web service composition, the "glue" logic is expressed in a self-describing manner, which creates a template from which multiple instances of the process are created and managed. This approach can generate integrated systems that offer a more efficient and flexible solution. It increases the opportunity for the companies and individuals involved to reuse Web services (e.g., the *Online Payment* service can participate in different Web service compositions in different contexts), or replace existing Web service with a new one.

The core concept in fact is easy to grasp. However, there are some basic characteristics that should be pointed out:

- Web services are not like application libraries which have to be compiled and
  linked as part of an application.
- The basic components (individual services) remain separated (i.e., exist independently) from the composite service.
- A composition of Web services mainly involves specifying which services need
  to be invoked, in what order, and how to handle exceptional situations, etc. This
  can be seen as a Web service-based workflow.
- Web Service composition can be nested: Web services can be considered as building blocks that can be assembled. This allows building of complex applications by
  progressively aggregating components. When a composite service is exposed as a
  Web service, it can be considered as a building block as well and, in consequence,
  used for another composition (see Example 5.1.1).

Example 5.1.1 *Nested Composition*

Consider the procurement *component in Fig. 5.3. The business logic of*
procurement *is realised by composing other "Web Services". The component
calls two suppliers, compares the quotes, follows up for approval if necessary and
makes a payment with a chosen supplier. Then,* Procurement *itself is exposed as
a Web service, servicing the* Supply Chain *application. Using the same idea, the
bigger application (*Supply Chain*) itself could service other applications as an
independent Web service.*

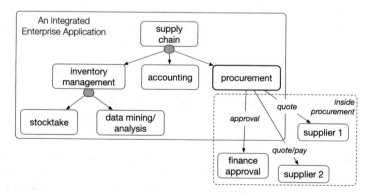

Fig. 5.3 An example of nested composition [2]

5.2 Service Orchestration vs. Service Choreography

These two terms describe two aspects of connecting Web services to create business processes. They are very closely related and that sometimes causes confusion and misinterpretations of their meaning. This section contains definitions for both terms and examples that should help clarify the place that these aspects occupy in Web service composition.

Orchestration comes from orchestras; in an orchestra there is a conductor leading it, and there are musicians who play their instruments following the instructions of the conductor. The musicians know their role; they know how to play their instruments, but not necessarily directly interact with each other. That is, in an orchestra, there is a central system (the conductor) that coordinates and synchronises the interactions of the components to perform a coherent piece of music.

Choreography is related to dance; on a dancing stage there are just dancers, but they know what they have to do and how to interact with the other dancers; each dancer is in charge of being synchronised with the rest.

These concepts have been adapted by SOA to service composition. The term **service orchestration** describes how Web services can interact with each other at the message level, including the business logic and execution order of the interactions, from the perspective and under control of a single endpoint (single party). In Fig. 5.4a, the central workflow (`Store BPEL Workflow`) coordinates `Warehouse`, `Carrier` and `Customer`.

Choreography is associated with the public (globally visible) message exchanges, rules of interaction and agreements between multiple business process endpoints. Choreography tracks the sequence of messages that may involve multiple parties and multiple sources, described from the perspectives of all parties (common view). Figure 5.4b shows a choreographed interaction between two parties, illustrating the fact that the two directly communicate without a central coordinator. Any one of the parties may also be participating in another interaction (e.g., between `Store` and `Shipment`) in the context of a bigger, global interaction.

5.3 Service Composition View from Orchestration and Choreography

In this section, we will illustrate, through an example, the different views of a service composition depending on the perspective used to look at it. The example composition is done with three services; in Fig. 5.5a they are represented in three different pools and their private content is shown (not just the interface but the logic of the service). In Fig. 5.5b the interfaces of the services are shown, in what is called the public or business protocol view, and they are visible from the other services. The view is called public because the other parties involved in the composition have access to it.

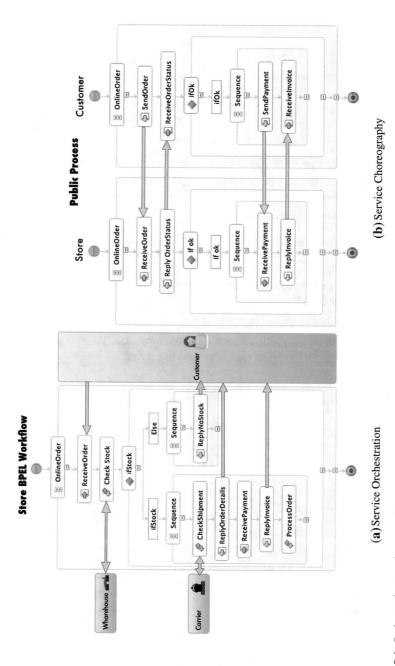

(a) Service Orchestration

(b) Service Choreography

Fig. 5.4 Orchestration *vs.* choreography

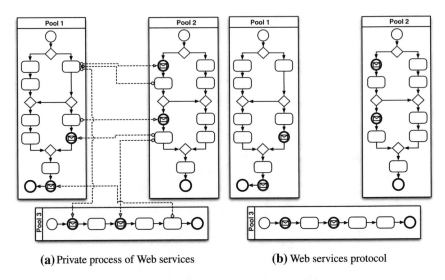

(a) Private process of Web services   **(b)** Web services protocol

Fig. 5.5 An example composition: Private view and its protocol view

Once these three services are composed, this composition can be observed from different points of view:

1. From the **choreography** point of view, the process is seen from a global perspective where all the parties have the same importance. There is a global view of the protocols and the data exchange (see Fig. 5.6a).

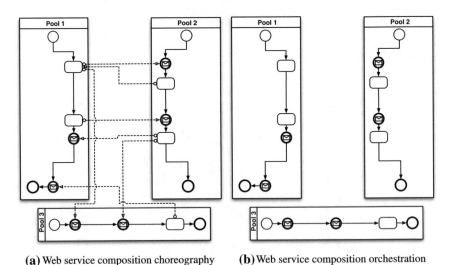

(a) Web service composition choreography   **(b)** Web service composition orchestration

Fig. 5.6 Web service composition: Different views

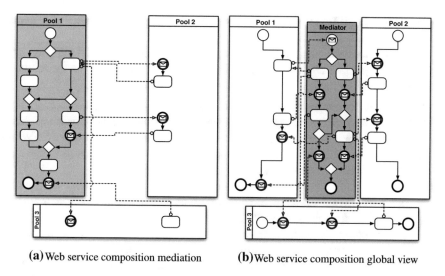

(a) Web service composition mediation   (b) Web service composition global view

Fig. 5.7 Web service composition: Different views, cont.

2. In the orchestration, the process is seen from the viewpoint of one partner (in this example from the partner corresponding to "Pool1"). It is similar to a private process but with connections to other processes. The connections among the other services are not considered (see Fig. 5.6b).

3. The orchestration can be applied with a "mediator" process; in this case it is called service mediation instead of service orchestration. The mediator is a Web service put in the middle of the other services, which interacts with the different protocols of the Web services. The mediator is regularly used to give more freedom to the developers of the other services by ensuring policy compliance within it (see Fig. 5.7a).

Finally, if we could use orchestration and choreography together, a global collaborative process would be obtained (see Fig. 5.7b). This is just theoretical, since usually internal parts of processes are not shared.

5.4 Benefits of Web Service Composition

Web service composition enables communication, cooperation, and coordination among disparate applications from different sources over the Internet. Nowadays the aggregation of services is used to create integrated tailored systems (i.e., EAI – Enterprise Application Integration, B2B – Business to Business, B2C – Business to Customer), to work with repetitive tasks (e.g., scientific processes, long-tail processes), to build mashups (e.g., feed aggregation, UI Widget aggregation) and for

many other things. This technology is now present in a growing number of systems
that are used daily (Fig. 5.8).

Thus, service composition technology plays an important role in a high number
of software systems. The reasons for adopting service composition as the method
for developing new applications lie mainly in the following benefits:

- Integration: the integration of services, whether it happens inside one company
  (EAI), between companies (B2B), or between companies and customers (B2C),
  is a general requirement to permit the services to interact and work together. With
  service composition technologies organizations can interoperate and be integrated
  to work together in the same system.
- Global view: before services could be composed, there was no global view; each
  service was "living" on its own. To compose them allows one to create a global
  view, which increases productivity and reduces costs.
- Extended role of IT: to provide environments where services can be composed
  facilitates the participation of non-pure IT people in the process.
- Merge and reduce code: the possibility of composing services creates the ability
  of reuse existing services (composite services, in turn, can be reused as well).
  Reusing reduces the need for coding and therefore the amount of code generated.
- Standardization: Web service composition is standards-based, which provides an
  environment where all the parts can interact seamlessly, which upholds some of
  the other mentioned benefits such as risk and cost reduction.

5.5   Web Service Composition Environment

Designing and implementing Web service composition involves activities that are just
like those in any other programming tasks. Therefore, a typical Web service composition development environment supports design, coding, deployment and testing
of Web service composition logic. Generally speaking, a development environment
for composite Web services includes the following features (see Fig. 5.9):

- **Composition Model and Language**: this enables the specification of the services to be combined, the order in which the different services are to be invoked,
  and the way in which service invocation parameters are determined. The written
  specification is referred to as a composition schema.
- **Integrated Development Environment**: this refers to the tool that gives users
  the ability to specify the composition, by textual or graphical means, using the
  elements provided by the composition model and language. A common type of
  a development environment is a graphical interface through which designers can
  specify a composition schema by dragging and dropping Web services onto a
  canvas; the graphs and other descriptive information are then translated into textual
  specifications (i.e., the composition schema).
- **Run-time Environment**: this refers to a composition engine that interprets the
  composition schema and executes its business logic.

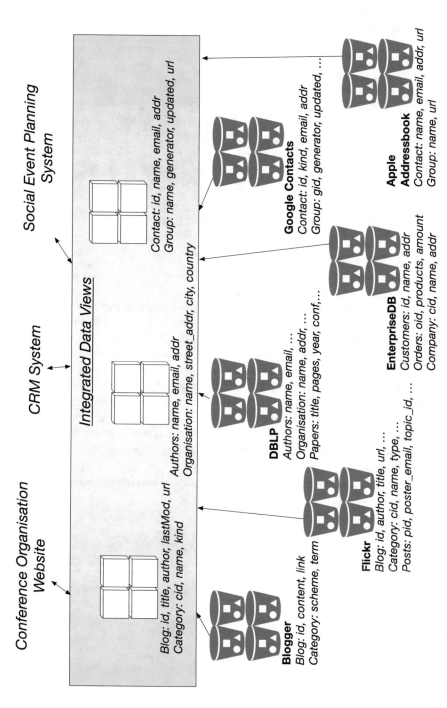

Fig. 5.8 Enterprise information integration

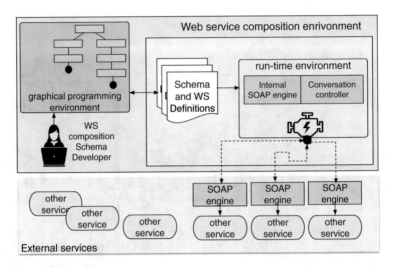

Fig. 5.9 Web service composition environment

There are two aspects to consider in defining the functional part of a composite service: *control flow* and data flow. The control flow of a composite Web service specifies the execution order of atomic Web services. The data flow of a composite Web service describes the message exchanges (i.e., message flows) between services. An important sub-task in specifying data flow is data mapping and transformation, which deals with the information regarding the treatment of the data.

There are other cross-cutting concerns involved in service composition, such as exception handling, transaction processing, and security. They are undoubtedly important concepts to deal with; however, they are not exclusive to service composition, as they are common to almost any programming language. We do not cover them in this book.

In the following chapters, we will discuss the design and implementation of the control and data flows.

Chapter 6
Web Service Composition: Control Flows

Defining the control flow of a composite service is equivalent to specifying in what order the atomic services are required to be executed.

This is necessary in every composition; this does not mean that it has to be explicit; control flow is always there, even if it is implicit in the composition. In next chapter, where data flow will be explained, we will show some examples where a service is composed by defining the data flow only. In these cases, the process flow is inferred from the data flow and it implicitly determines the control flow.

As mentioned previously, Web service composition needs a language to express its composition logic, such as control flow. In this chapter, we will introduce two of the most commonly used composition languages: BPEL (Business Process Execution Language) and BPMN (Business Process Model and Notation). There are some other composition languages that have the ability to define control flow by means of construct elements. But these two are the most popular Web Service composition standards and they are backed by important technological companies in the area. Another notable point is that in both languages, the control flows are always explicitly expressed.

6.1 BPEL (Business Process Execution Language)

BPEL is also known as BPEL4WS (BPEL for Web Services, before v2.0) and WSBPEL (from v2.0). It supersedes XLANG (by Microsoft) and WSFL (by IBM). To standardise the language, an OASIS committee consisting of BEA, Microsoft, IBM, SAP and Siebel Systems proposed the first version of BPEL4WS in 2003. Now it is widely supported by many Web service composition platforms.

BPEL defines a notation for specifying business process behaviour based on the operations available from the "partnering" Web services. It can be used to implement executable business processes (cf. orchestration) or to describe non-executable abstract processes (cf. protocol). The executable processes describe the composition

© Springer International Publishing AG 2017
H.-y. Paik et al., *Web Service Implementation and Composition Techniques*,
DOI 10.1007/978-3-319-55542-3_6

of different Web service interfaces expressed in the form of WSDL port types. The result of this composition using BPEL is recursively published as a Web service.

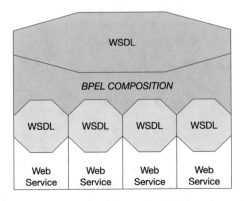

Fig. 6.1 An executable BPEL composition is exposed as a Web service

The language elements in BPEL are defined as XML elements. In a complete BPEL process document, written in XML, the following aspects of the process are described:

- The different roles that take part in the message exchanges with the BPEL process.
- The WSDL port types that must be supported by the roles and by the BPEL process itself.
- The coordination of control flows and the other aspects (e.g., transaction processing, exception handling)
- Any message correlation information that defines how messages can be routed to the correct instance of the BPEL process.

As explained in the previous chapter, when describing the orchestration of a business process, as BPEL does, the scope of it is not general, but is described from the point of view of one of the participants. Figure 6.2 shows the orchestration for a supplier defined by BPEL. In the figure, we see the Supplier as the main controller of the process with which three partner roles interact: Customer, Local Stock Service, Warehouse. Each role supports a WSDL port type through which messages are exchanged. The Supplier can define the coordination logic (the control flow), message variables, or the message correlation specification.

6.1.1 BPEL Model

The syntax of BPEL can be split into six categories: basic activities, structured activities, variables, partner links, handlers and correlation sets. It is not the intention

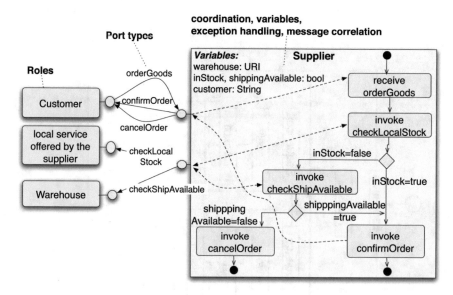

Fig. 6.2 Orchestration for supplier in BPEL [2]

of this book to describe the BPEL model in detail (if the reader is interested, the specification of WSBPEL by OASIS is freely available online); instead, the basic constructs, emphasizing the ones related with control flows, are described.

Activities

The control flow definition in a BPEL process is created by combining the basic process steps called BPEL basic activities with the process structure activities called BPEL structured activities.

The **Basic activities** are simple tasks and represent a unit of work/task. They do not have any control structure and they do not contain any other embedded activity. The **Structured activities** define the control flow. The activities represent the well-known business process or workflow constructs such as AND-split, OR-split, AND-join, etc. Using the structured activities the explicit control flow of a BPEL process (the order in which the basic activities are executed) can be expressed. BPEL allows recursively combining the structured activities to express arbitrarily complex processes (see Fig. 6.3).

Basic activities – simple tasks

- *Invoke* – invokes an operation of a WS.
- *Receive* – waits for a message from an operation.
- *Reply* – generates a message through an operation.
- *Assign* – copies data from one place to another.

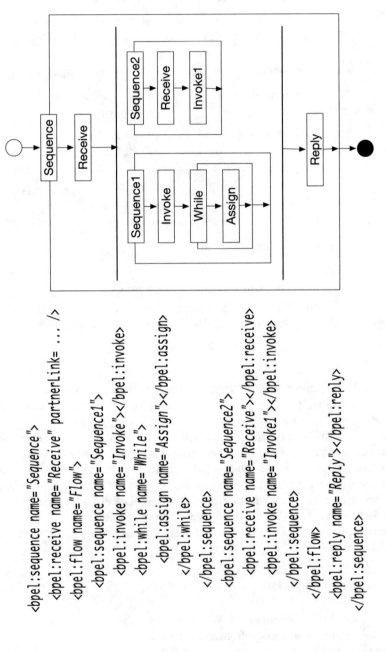

```
<bpel:sequence name="Sequence">
  <bpel:receive name="Receive" partnerLink= ... />
  <bpel:flow name="Flow">
    <bpel:sequence name="Sequence1">
      <bpel:invoke name="Invoke"></bpel:invoke>
      <bpel:while name="While">
        <bpel:assign name="Assign"></bpel:assign>
      </bpel:while>
    </bpel:sequence>
    <bpel:sequence name="Sequence2">
      <bpel:receive name="Receive"></bpel:receive>
      <bpel:invoke name="Invoke1"></bpel:invoke>
    </bpel:sequence>
  </bpel:flow>
  <bpel:reply name="Reply"></bpel:reply>
</bpel:sequence>
```

Fig. 6.3 Nesting activities and visual notations of BPEL

- *Throw* – signals an internal fault.
- *Wait* – waits for some time.
- *Empty* – does nothing.
- *Exit* – ends a process
- *Rethrow* – throws the original fault data again.

Structured activities – process structure

- *Sequence* – creates ordered steps of activities.
- *If* – provides conditional behaviour.
- *While* – repeats execution as long as the evaluated condition is true (Evaluation at the beginning of the iteration).
- *RepeatUntil* – repeats execution as long as the evaluated condition is true (Evaluation at the end of the iteration).
- *Pick* – waits for one of several events to occur.
- *Flow* – executes activities in parallel.

Partners and partner link types

Partners are the actors who play particular roles within a composition. Partner link types characterize the conversational relationship between two services by defining the "roles" played by each of the services; each of those roles in a partner link type is linked with a WSDL port type.

A partner link type can include one or two roles. It includes two roles when each of the services must implement its role by providing the port type specified (useful for asynchronous messaging); it includes one role when there is no restriction placed on the calling Web service regarding the provision of a port type (useful for synchronous messaging). Web services playing the role are required to support the operations defined in the port types associated with the role.

A partner type is a service type which is resolved to an actual Web service at deployment time or at run-time.

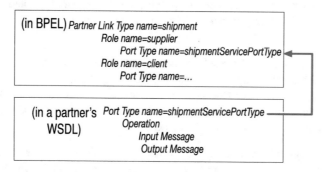

Fig. 6.4 Partner links, roles and WSDL portType

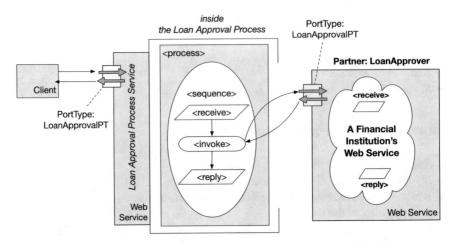

Fig. 6.5 Loan approval process as BPEL

6.1.2 BPEL Example

Let us walk through a basic BPEL example. There is a lab activity at the end of this chapter to help you practice some basic BPEL coding and deployment tasks. In this example, we will review the concepts introduced above to show how the different elements of the BPEL language fit together.

Figure 6.5 explains the overall scenario of the example, Loan Approval Process Service. The Loan Approval Process Service is a Web service that provides a port type: LoanApprovalPT, which has an operation named approve(). The client is expected to send an input message called creditInformationMessage and the service to return approvalMessage. The internal implementation of Loan Approval Process Service is defined as a BPEL process that partners with another Web service that happens to provide the same port type and operation: LoanApprovalPT.approve(). The control flow logic of the BPEL process is as follows:

1. receives a creditInformationMessage from the client;
2. invokes the partner's approve() operation (here, passing on the same message creditInformationMessage); note that the synchronous invoke activity will receive the output message approvalMessage from the partner service;
3. replies to the client passing on the approvalMessage.

To implement this, we define the messages (Fig. 6.6). The messages are the input/output of the approve() operation in LoanApprovalPT. In the partner's

```
1    <?xml version="1.0" encoding="UTF-8"?>
2    <xsd:schema xmlns:xsd="http://www.w3.org/2001/XMLSchema"
3       targetNamespace="http://soacourse.unsw.edu.au/loandefinitions"
4       xmlns:tns="http://soacourse.unsw.edu.au/loandefinitions"
5       elementFormDefault="qualified"/>
6
7    <xsd:complexType name="loanInputType">
8       <xsd:sequence>
9          <xsd:element name="firstName" type="xsd:string" />
10         <xsd:element name="name" type="xsd:string" />
11         <xsd:element name="amount" type="xsd:integer" />
12      </xsd:sequence>
13   </xsd:complexType>
14
15   <xsd:complexType name="approvalType">
16      <xsd:sequence>
17         <xsd:element name="accept" type="xsd:string" />
18      </xsd:sequence>
19   </xsd:complexType>
20
21   <xsd:element name="creditInformationMessage" type="tns:loanInputType" />
22   <xsd:element name="approvalMessage" type="tns:approvalType" />
23   </xsd:schema>
```

Fig. 6.6 Loan approval process messages

WSDL, we should then expect to see a definition of the operation and its messages as shown in Fig. 6.7.

Now, Loan Approval Process Service, which is a BPEL process, is going to define a WSDL file to expose itself as a Web service. This is shown in Fig. 6.8, where: (i) the import statement brings the definition of the `LoanApprovalPT` port type into this WSDL, (ii) a partner link type with a role `approver` is defined; a partner that plays this role will support the `LoanApprovalPT` port type; (iii) then, the binding and service definitions for the Loan Approval Process service are defined.

Using these definitions, the BPEL process can now be described. Let us examine the BPEL code in two parts. First, in Fig. 6.9, after importing the relevant WSDL definitions (i.e., the BPEL process' own WSDL file and the partner's WSDL file), there is a partner link definition. There is only partner link type and one role (approver) in this scenario. An important syntax to note in the partner link definition is in the way roles are defined. There are two partners to represent according to the scenario depicted in Fig. 6.5. One parter link is to represent the interactions between client and the Loan Approval Process (the BPEL process). The other link is to represent interactions between the Loan Approval Process (the BPEL process) and the partner service. These are declared as two partner links, `client` and `approver` respectively. In the client link, `myRole = "approver"` specifies that it is the Loan Approval Process that plays the approver role (providing the referenced port type), whereas in the approver link, it is the partner service that plays the role. Besides the partner link definition, there are two BPEL variables declared to hold the input/output messages.

The actual control flow part of the BPEL process in this example is fairly straightforward. As shown in Fig. 6.10, the orchestration logic starts with a `receive` activity (through the client link), then proceeds with an `invoke` activity (through the approver link) to call the partner service, and then with a `reply` activity (through the client link) to relay the response message. Thus a single pipeline of three activities is constructed with the BPEL-structured activity `sequence`.

6.2   BPMN (Business Process Model and Notation)

BPMN (Business Process Model and Notation), another composition language, uses a set of flow chart based notations for defining business processes. Before BPMN, there was no "formal" notation appealing to both technical and business users and having clear execution semantics. Earlier workflow modelling languages represented dynamic behaviour and execution semantics (e.g., Petri Nets), which could become quite complicated to comprehend for business users. The simple/conceptual processing modelling notations (e.g., conventional flow charts, UML activity diagrams) were not precise enough to fully express clear execution semantics.

```
1   <?xml version='1.0' encoding='UTF-8'?>
2   <wsdl:definitions
3   ...
4   name="loanApprovalPT" targetNamespace="http://soacourse.unsw.edu.au/loanapprover">
5
6       <wsdl:message name="approveResponse">
7           <wsdl:part element="ns2:approvalMessage" name="loanresp">
8           </wsdl:part>
9       </wsdl:message>
10
11      <wsdl:message name="approve">
12          <wsdl:part element="ns2:creditInformationMessage" name="loanreq">
13          </wsdl:part>
14      </wsdl:message>
15
16      <wsdl:portType name="loanApprovalPT">
17          <wsdl:operation name="approve">
18              <wsdl:input message="ns1:approve" name="approve">
19              </wsdl:input>
20              <wsdl:output message="ns1:approveResponse" name="approveResponse">
21              </wsdl:output>
22          </wsdl:operation>
23      </wsdl:portType>
24
25  </wsdl:definitions>
```

Fig. 6.7 Loan approval process: The partner's WSDL

```
 2   <definitions name="LoanApprovalService"
 3     ...
 4     targetNamespace="http://soacourse.unsw.edu.au/loanapproval"
 5     xmlns:tns="http://soacourse.unsw.edu.au/loanapproval"
 6     xmlns:approver="http://soacourse.unsw.edu.au/loanapprover">
 7
 8     <import namespace="http://soacourse.unsw.edu.au/loanapprover"
 9        location="loanapprover.wsdl" />
10
11     <plnk:partnerLinkType name="LoanApprovalLinkType">
12        <plnk:role name="approver" portType="approver:loanApprovalPT" />
13     </plnk:partnerLinkType>
14
15     <binding name="LoanApprovalServiceBinding" type="approver:loanApprovalPT">
16        <soap:binding style="document"
17          transport="http://schemas.xmlsoap.org/soap/http" />
18        <operation name="approve">
19          <soap:operation soapAction="http://soacourse.unsw.edu.au/loanapproval/approve" />
20          <input>
21            <soap:body use="literal" />
22          </input>
23          <output>
24            <soap:body use="literal" />
25          </output>
26        </operation>
27     </binding>
28
29     <service name="LoanApprovalServiceProcess">
30        <port name="LoanApprovalProcessPort" binding="tns:LoanApprovalServiceBinding">
31          <soap:address
32             location="http://localhost:6060/ode/processes/LoanApprovalServiceProcess" />
33        </port>
34     </service>
35   </definitions>
```

Fig. 6.8 Loan approval process: The BPEL process' WSDL

```
1   <!-- SimpleHomeLoan BPEL Process [Generated by the Eclipse BPEL Designer] -->
2   <bpel:process name="SimpleHomeLoan"
3       targetNamespace="http://soacourse.unsw.edu.au/loanapproval"
4       suppressJoinFailure="yes"
5       xmlns:tns="http://soacourse.unsw.edu.au/loanapproval"
6       xmlns:ns1="http://soacourse.unsw.edu.au/loanapprover"
7       xmlns:ns2="http://soacourse.unsw.edu.au/loandefinitions"
8       xmlns:bpel="http://docs.oasis-open.org/wsbpel/2.0/process/executable">
9
10  <bpel:import location="loanApprovalArtifacts.wsdl" namespace="http://soacourse.unsw.edu.au/loanapproval"
11      importType="http://schemas.xmlsoap.org/wsdl/" />
12  <bpel:import namespace="http://soacourse.unsw.edu.au/loanapprover"
13      location="loanapprover.wsdl" importType="http://schemas.xmlsoap.org/wsdl/" />
14
15  <bpel:partnerLinks>
16      <bpel:partnerLink name="client" partnerLinkType="tns:loanApprovalLinkType" myRole="approver" />
17      <bpel:partnerLink name="approver" partnerLinkType="tns:loanApprovalLinkType" partnerRole="approver" />
18  </bpel:partnerLinks>
19
20  <bpel:variables>
21      <bpel:variable name="request"
22          messageType="ns1:approve"/>
23
24      <bpel:variable name="approvalInfo"
25          messageType="ns1:approveResponse"/>
26
27  </bpel:variables>
```

Fig. 6.9 Loan approval process: The BPEL process (Part 1)

```
29  <!-- ============================================ -->
30  <!-- ORCHESTRATION LOGIC                          -->
31  <!-- Set of activities coordinating the flow of messages across the -->
32  <!-- services integrated within this business process -->
33  <!-- ============================================ -->
34  <bpel:sequence name="main">
35
36      <bpel:receive name="receiveInput" partnerLink="client"
37          portType="ns1:loanApprovalPT"
38          operation="approve" createInstance="yes" variable="request"/>
39
40      <bpel:invoke name="Invoke" partnerLink="approver"
41          portType="ns1:loanApprovalPT"
42          operation="approve" inputVariable="request"
43          outputVariable="approvalInfo" />
44
45      <bpel:reply name="replyOutput"
46          partnerLink="client"
47          portType="ns1:loanApprovalPT"
48          operation="approve"
49          variable="approvalInfo" />
50  </bpel:sequence>
51  </bpel:process>
```

Fig. 6.10 Loan approval process: The BPEL process (Part 2)

BPMN addresses this "niche". Many tools can generate an executable language (BPEL) from this business-level notation. Once a business process is developed (i.e. by a business analyst), it can be directly applied to a BPM engine, instead of going through human interpretations and translations.

In this chapter, we are presenting BPMN as an alternative language to BPEL in terms of expressing the control flow logic. Only the main elements of BPMN that could form an overview of the language are discussed here, with an example. More details about the language and available tools can be found at the BPMN specification site.[1]

6.2.1 BPMN Model

BPMN defines a set of graphical elements; when combined they generate a Business Process Diagram (BPD). A BPD can be easily interpreted by most of the business analysts. BPMN offers a wide variety of elements that can represent complex business processes while, at the same time, the graphic notation simplifies the creating of BPDs. There are four basic categories that embrace all the BPMN elements: Flow Objects, Connecting Objects, Swimlanes and Artifacts.

Flow Objects

They are the main elements in a BPD, representing the behaviour of business processes. The control flow is generated by means of flow objects connected together.

Events: Something that happens during the process is called *event*. Events are represented by circles; depending on when they act on the flow the circles will have a different appearance. There are three types: start, intermediate and end. The circles can be empty or contain different symbols, which indicate the subtype of message. An event needs a cause to be activated, meaning that an event could be catching something (the cause is called trigger), or to create an impact on the process, in which case the event is acting as a thrower.

Events can be placed in two different positions, within the process flow or attached to the boundary of an activity. In the first case, the event happens during the execution of the process and it does not modify the process flow. In the second case, if the event is triggered, it modifies the process flow by interrupting the activity the event is attached to and it follows the outgoing sequence flow of the event.

---

[1]http://www.bpmn.org, BPMN.

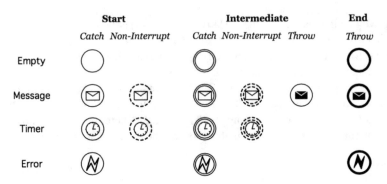

Fig. 6.11 Some of the event types in BPMN

Activities: An activity indicates the work that has to be done. Activities can be atomic, in which case they are called tasks, or non-atomic, in which case they are named sub-processes. Tasks, as atomic activities, cannot be broken down, while sub-processes can be broken down in sub-processes and/or activities. Sub-processes are useful to group activities in order to hide the complexity or to manage a group of activities all at the same time. Activities are represented by rounded-corner rectangles.

Gateways: Gateways provide the ability to define the control flow branching. They determine how the sequence flow is forking and merging. The branches to be executed will be defined by conditions or events, unless the parallel gateway is applied; this makes the process flow follow all the branches.

Connecting Objects

The flow objects explained in the previous section are linked in the BPD through connecting objects.

Sequence Flow: The order in which the activities are executed in a process is defined by the sequence flow.

Message Flow: A message flow indicates the exchange of messages between two participants of the system and their direction (who is the sender and who the receiver)

Association: By an association, artifacts or text can be connected to flow objects. An association can show the inputs and outputs of activities; it is commonly used to attach text annotations to objects.

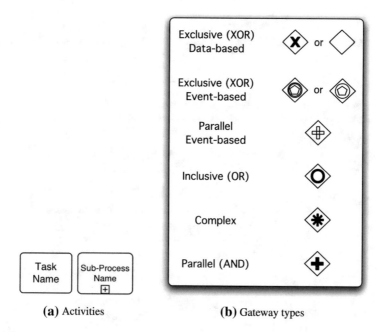

Exclusive (XOR) Data-based	
Exclusive (XOR) Event-based	
Parallel Event-based	
Inclusive (OR)	
Complex	
Parallel (AND)	

(a) Activities   (b) Gateway types

Fig. 6.12 Activities and gateway types

Fig. 6.13 Connecting objects: Sequence flow, message flow and association (from *left* to *right*)

Swimlanes

Swimlanes are introduced in BPMN with the intention of organizing the activities represented in the process.

Pools: A pool represents a participant in the process. A regular representation of a business process should have as many pools as participants in the business process, those a business role or a business entity use to be represented by pools. The interaction between pools is handled through message flow, which excludes the possibility of any sequence flow between pools.

Lanes: Lanes are sub-divisions of the pools. They split the pool with the objective of categorising or organising the activities within the pool. They are used to represent roles in the organization. Unlike pools, sequence flows can communicate with two different lanes.

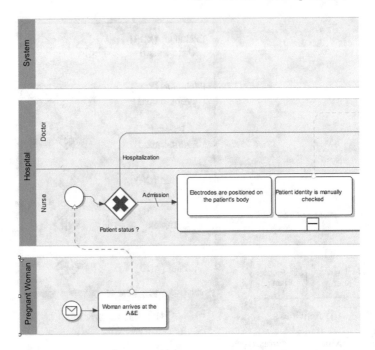

Fig. 6.14 Example of BPD with pools and lanes

Artifacts

Artifacts are used to add information to the diagram, information that is not modifying or affecting in any sense the sequence or message flow, but may be useful as complementary information for understanding the diagram.

Data Objects: They show how data and documents are used in a process. Regarding the data, they show the data required or generated by an activity. Regarding the documents, they show how a document is changed or updated during the process.

Groups: Groups are used to highlight a part of a diagram by a dashed square that groups some elements of the diagram. They do not affect the sequence flow and they do not generate or imply any constraint.

Annotations: Through annotations the modeller can provide additional text information.

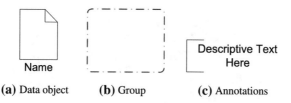

(a) Data object   (b) Group   (c) Annotations

Fig. 6.15 BPMN artifacts

6.2.2 BPMN Example

BPMN supports the representation of three different processes: private processes, abstract processes and collaborative processes. The following example, shown in Fig. 6.16, is a collaborative process where a sender who wants to ship dangerous goods is interacting with a shipping company. In order to send the goods the sender has to accomplish a set of tasks; he or she has to ask the government for the required permissions to send dangerous materials; at the same time he or she has to prepare the goods to be sent (i.e., buy the proper containers); once those tasks are done, the sender has to contact the freight company to arrange the shipment. The shipping company, in turn, will receive the petition and it will be taken over by an employee; if the value of the goods is higher than $5,000, the employee will drive the shipment to a manager who will contact an insurance company to insure the goods.

The process consists of the following elements:

- Three pools, which represent the three different roles in this process. The sender, the shipping company and the insurance company.
- Two start events, the one that is starting the activity from the sender, and the message from the sender that activates the shipping company process.
- Ten tasks with auto-explicative names.
- Four message exchanges, represented by the interactions among pools.
- Two end events, the one from the shipping company that ends the process by sending a message to the sender, and the one in the sender pool that finalizes the process.
- Four gateways; the gateways are always duplicated; one is used to start the part of the process related with the gateway and the duplicate is used to close the part of the process affected by it. Then, the four gateways delimit two blocks; the first one in the sender, containing a parallel gateway, indicates that the branches between the open and the close gateway are executed at the same time; the second block is delimited by two exclusive gateways; if the condition of the gateway is fulfilled, the flow will follow the branch tagged with the word "yes"; if not, it will follow the branch tagged with the word "no".

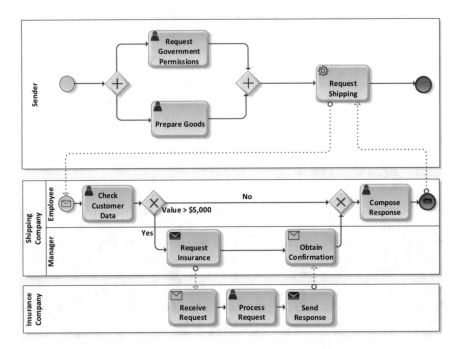

Fig. 6.16 BPMN example

Practical Exercise V

6.3   Lab Exercise 05: Web Service Composition with BPEL and Apache ODE

In this exercise, we will learn how to write a BPEL program to compose Web services and also see how the composed service (i.e., the BPEL program) itself runs as a Web service. We will use Apache ODE as a BPEL runtime engine. The version of the BPEL specification we are using in this lab is v2.0. For your information, the specification page is http://docs.oasis-open.org/wsbpel/2.0/OS/wsbpel-v2.0-OS.html.

Exercise Files

The exercise files involved in the lab can be downloaded from the Github site:

- https://github.com/SOA-Book

  Follow the repository exercises, then lab05.

6.3.1   Software Setup

In terms of new software to configure/install, we need the following items:

1. Apache ODE (v.1.3.6) – BPEL runtime engine and manager
2. Eclipse BPEL Designer (v1.0.4)
3. Tomcat 6 – as the hosting environment for Apache ODE

Although we can set up to run Apache ODE in the same Tomcat installation we have been using in the previous labs by running it on a different port, we will set up the environment in a way that we see a designated BPEL server and physically separate CXF servers for the external partner services. This may help us better understand the interactions between the service runtime engines involved. This also makes the development/deployment process of services more manageable.

Tomcat 6

Download Tomcat 6 (v6.0.43) from the Apache Tomcat website. The link is shown below.

```
https://tomcat.apache.org/download-60.cgi#6.0.43
```

We use version 6 because it is compatible with the version of Apache ODE we are using in this lab exercise. After unzipping and installing Tomcat 6, follow the next steps:

1. Let us first configure the port numbers so that they are different from the normal 8080 range. This is to distinguish the Tomcat with Apache ODE installation from the other instances of Tomcat in your environment. Open `conf/server.xml`. Find the following three port numbers and change them to the value specified.

   - Find: <Connector port="8080" protocol="HTTP/1.1"
   - Replace with: <Connector port="6060" protocol="HTTP/1.1"
   - Find: <Connector port="8009" protocol="AJP/1.3" ...
   - Replace with: <Connector port="6009" protocol="AJP/1.3" ...
   - Find: <Server port="8005" shutdown="SHUTDOWN">
   - Replace with: <Server port="6005" shutdown="SHUTDOWN">

   Note: This changing of port numbers is not a requirement to run Apache ODE. But changing the default ports here makes it easier to distinguish BPEL servers from other servers.
2. Now start this new Tomcat installation and test that it is running successfully. Entering `http://localhost:6060` into your browser should give you the Tomcat home page.
3. We will refer to this installation as `Tomcat6-ODE`

Apache ODE

We will use Apache ODE v1.3.6. You can download the WAR distribution file from the following location:

  `www.apache.org/dyn/closer.cgi/ode/apache-ode-war-1.3.6.zip`

1. Unzip the file. You will find `apache-ode-war-1.3.6/ode.war`.
2. Copy the `ode.war` file to `Tomcat6-ODE`/webapps.
3. Now start `Tomcat6-ODE`. This should deploy the `ode.war` file and create an application directory called `ode`.
4. Check that ODE is correctly deployed and is running on `Tomcat6-ODE`. Into your browser, type in: `http://localhost:6060/ode`. This should give you the home page of Apache ODE, and your ODE server is ready.

Eclipse BPEL Designer

For authoring and deploying BPEL code, we will use an Eclipse plug-in called 'Eclipse BPEL Designer'. For more information about the plug-in, refer to the Eclipse BPEL Designer home page.[2]

To install the plug-in, we will use the *Update/Install New Software* menu (under Help) in Eclipse. Since we have installed other plug-ins for lab exercises before, we will not detail the instructions here. The address of the site you should use to search for the plug-in is:

  `http://download.eclipse.org/bpel/site/1.0.4`

Choose and install all available components under '*Eclipse BPEL Designer*'. Figure 6.17 shows a screenshot from the installation process.

Follow through with the installation process to completion. When everything is done, you should see a new BPEL 2.0 option when you choose 'New → Other', as shown in Fig. 6.18.

Setting up Eclipse BPEL Designer with Apache ODE

Now we will configure the Eclipse BPEL Designer to work with the Apache ODE installation we set up before.

1. In the `Servers` window view tab, right-click and select "New → Server".
2. From the list, select "Apache → ODE v1.x Server". Select *Server runtime environment: Apache Ode 1.x Runtime*. Then click "Next".

---

[2]`https://eclipse.org/bpel/`.

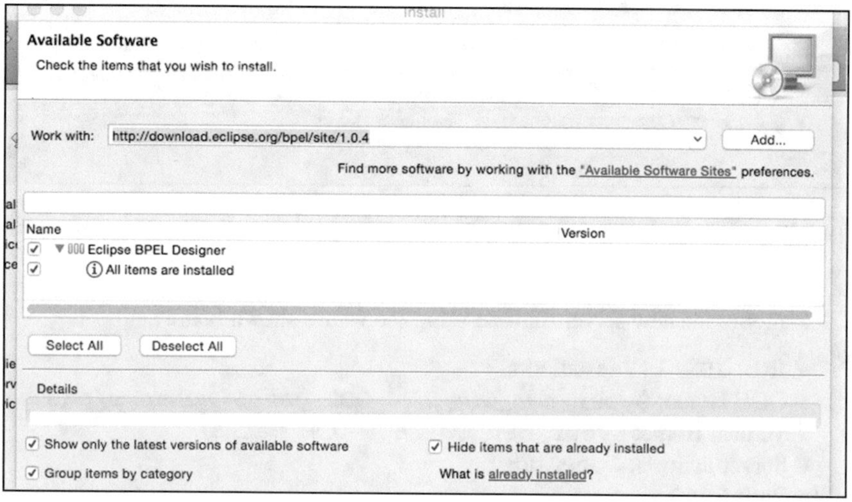

Fig. 6.17 Eclipse BPEL designer plug-ins

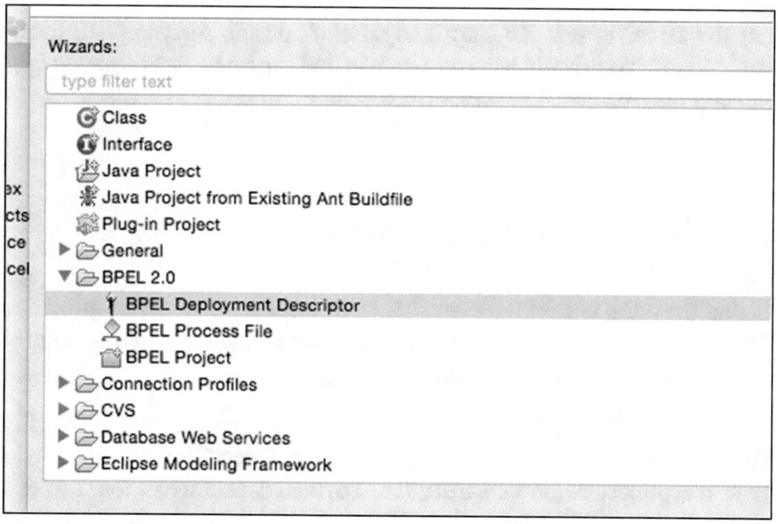

Fig. 6.18 Eclipse BPEL project options

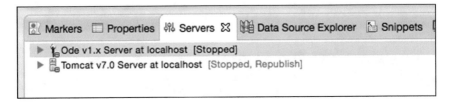

Fig. 6.19 Eclipse servers window view

3. Configure the new server runtime using the values shown below:

   - JRE: JDK 1.7 installation
   - ODE Home: $your_own_TOMCAT6-ODE_path$/webapps/ode
   - Tomcat Home: $your_own_TOMCAT6-ODE_path$
   - Server address: localhost
   - Port: 6060

4. Click "Finish". Your Servers window view now should have an extra server entry as in Fig. 6.19.
5. Start the server to test. To start it, right click on the Apache ODE entry and select "Start". You should have no errors in the Console view and you can now start/stop the Apache ODE server from Eclipse.

6.3.2   Activity 1: Hello World in BPEL

To test that the setup is working correctly, let us build a simple BPEL program. We will deploy a simple Hello World BPEL process which receives an input string from a client and echoes back the input as a response.

1. Create a new BPEL project named BPEL_HelloWorld by selecting File → New → Others → BPEL 2.0 → BPEL Project. Select "Next".
2. Type the project name as BPEL_HelloWorld and select the Target Runtime as Apache ODE 1.x Runtime. Choose the "Default Configuration" option. Click "Next". Leave the content folder as bpelContent. Click "Finish" (see Fig. 6.20).
3. Right click on the BPEL_HelloWorld project; select New → Others → BPEL 2.0 → New BPEL Process File. Click "Next".
4. Choose "Create a BPEL process from a template". Then, fill in the following details; then click "Next" (see Fig. 6.21).

   - BPEL Process Name: HelloWorld,
   - Namespace: http://helloworld.
   - Leave Abstract Process "unchecked".

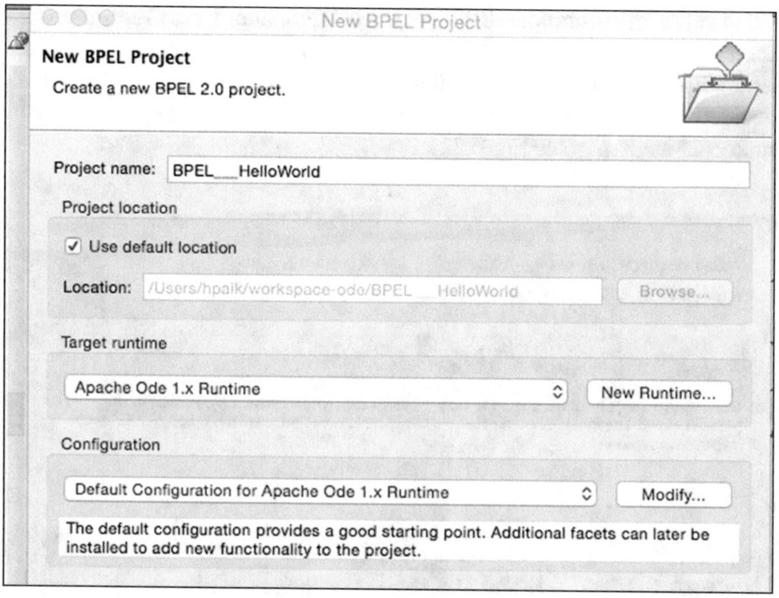

Fig. 6.20 Starting a new BPEL project in Eclipse

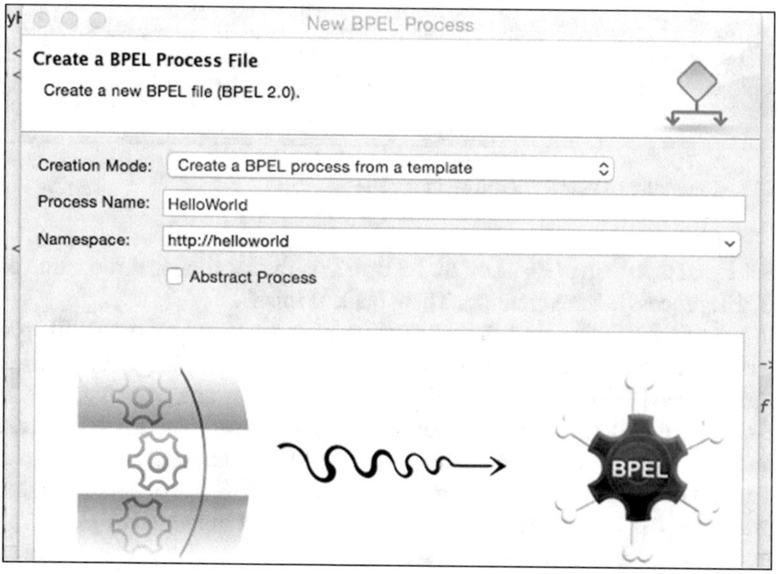

Fig. 6.21 Configuring a new BPEL process file

5. Choose the "Synchronous BPEL Process" template. Make sure to change the server address to `http://localhost:6060/ode/processes/HelloWorld`. That is, the default value `8080/HelloWorld` should be avoided as the port number is not correct. Then, choose the option for "Binding protocol" as `SOAP` (see Fig. 6.22).

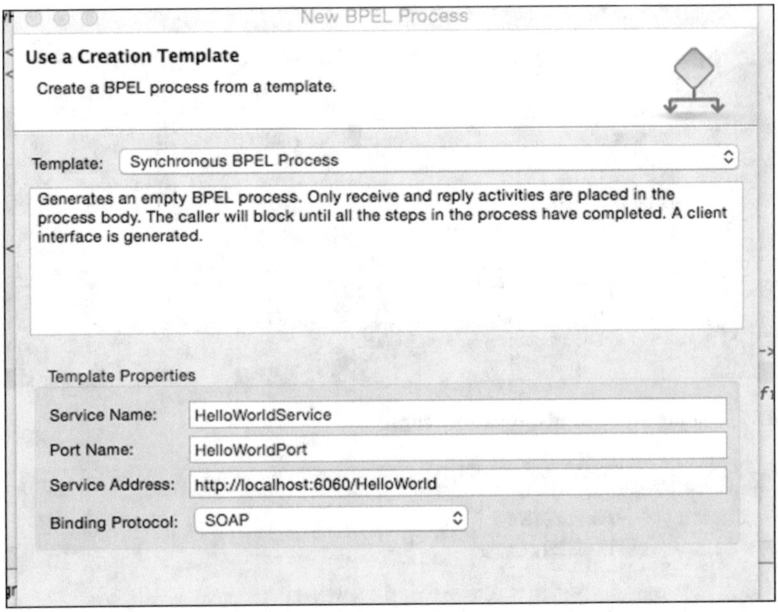

Fig. 6.22 Configuring a new BPEL project template

6. Set `bpelContent/HelloWorld.bpel` as the location and file name of the BPEL process we are creating. Then, click "Finish".
7. In the project folder, you should see two files generated by the BPEL project wizard process: `HelloWorld.bpel` and `HelloWorldArtifacts.wsdl`. First, let us quickly check the WSDL file. You will see one `portType` (named: `HelloWorld`) with an operation named `process`. The operation takes a message named `HelloWorldRequest` and outputs `ResponseMessage`. There is one `partnerLinkType` is defined. In it, we see one role defined and named as `HelloWorldProvider`, and this role is supported by `portType=HelloWorld` that we just have seen.
8. Now, examine the `HelloWorld.bpel` file using the `Source` view (rather than the `Design` view) first. A few things to notice here:

   - reference to the WSDL file.
   - `partnerLink` definition: It uses `partnerLinkType=HelloWorld`, and the role named `HelloWorldProvider` is fulfilled by the BPEL process

itself. That is, the BPEL process is the provider of the operation. This is expressed as `myRole=HelloWorldProvider`.

- variables: input and output; each corresponds to the `HelloWorldRequest` and `ResponseMessage` messages.

9. Now click on the `Design` view of `HelloWorld.bpel`. To add another action or control, you can use the `BPEL Palette`. To show this `Palette`, right click on the empty space in the editor and select "Show Palette in the Palette View".

10. We want to design this BPEL process to respond to the client with the same string that it received from the client (i.e., echo). Therefore, we have to add an activity which copies the received input to the output. To do this, delete the empty activity `FIX_ME xxx` (do right-click and delete). Click on the `Assign` activity on the `Actions` folder of the palette and drag it to the space between the `receiveInput` and `replyOutput` activities (or do right-click on the `replyOutput` activity and choose "Insert Before", then "Assign") (see Fig. 6.23).

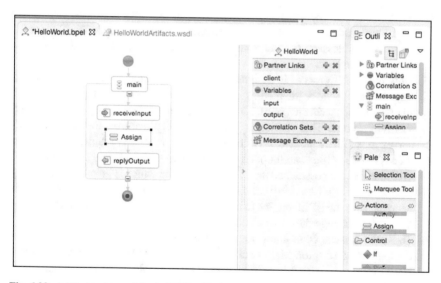

Fig. 6.23 Adding assign activity in BPEL

11. Switch back to `Source` view and see what has changed in the XML source.

12. Now to copy the input value to output; we will configure the `Assign` activity with the necessary details. Do right-click on the `Assign` activity. Select "Show in properties". In the `Properties tab`, select "Details".

13. Click on the "New" button to define an `assign` operator. You will see '? to ?' and possible options for `From` data sources and options for `Targets/To` data sources. Assign the following values to `From` and `To`. Set 'From' to input

→ payload → input. Then, set To to output → payload → result, by clicking and highlighting the message parts. After highlighting the from-to assignment, click somewhere outside the from-to mapping window; you will see an Initializer pop-up dialog. Click "Yes" to initialize the output variable and save the process. You will see something as in Fig. 6.24 when done.

Fig. 6.24 Adding details of the assign activity in BPEL

14. Switch back to the Source view; you will see that there are two copy instructions added to the Assign activity, one to initialise the HelloWorld Response message (output variable), the other to copy the input payload to the output payload.
15. Now the BPEL process is designed. We will check the WSDL file again, this time to double check the binding information for the service. Open the WSDL file HelloWorldArtifacts.wsdl and examine the binding details and service definitions. This service is going to be deployed on the Apache ODE server as a BPEL process service. So, make sure that the address of the service is http://localhost:6060/ode/processes/HelloWorld. This address is defined for the port named HelloWorldPort, which is linked to the binding details named HellowWorldBinding. This concrete binding information is necessary for the BPEL engine to know how to interact and act as a Web service. You should change the service address correctly and save it.
16. To let the Apache ODE know your declarations and designs, you have to add a deployment descriptor. Right click on the BPEL_HelloWorld project; select New → Others → BPEL 2.0 → Apache ODE Deployment Descriptor. Open deploy.xml with the ODE Deployment Editor. Here, you need to configure the binding information for the Inbound Interfaces. Choose PartnerLink 'client', then Associated Port 'HelloWorldPort' (the associated binding details will be automatically chosen). Save the configuration.
    Note: The PartnerLink "client" entry should already be listed in Inbound Interfaces. If you do not see it for any reason, click on the table and roll your mouse up and down. It should appear.

17. Now you have finished your design and it's time to run the process. Right click on the Ode v1.x Server at `localhost`; select "Add and Remove Projects". Select the `BPEL_HelloWorld` in the Available projects box and click "Add". Then, click "Finish". You may have to start/restart the ODE server. But you should get no errors and eventually get a message indicating that the deployment was successful in the `Console` View.

18. We will test the `Hello World` deployment with the Web Services Explorer provided by Eclipse. Right click on the `HelloWorldArtifacts.wsdl` file. Select Web Services → Test with Web Services Explorer. Select the operation process. Then, type "Hello from Me" in the input text box. If your deployment was a success, you will get the same string back in the SOAP response.

19. If everything works fine, your Apache ODE and BPEL designer setup is good to go to the next step. Resolve any issues here before you move on to the next activity.

6.3.3 Activity 2: Simple HomeLoan Process Service

In this exercise, we will implement one of the examples shown in this chapter – the Loan Approval Service.

The Loan Approval Service (which is a BPEL process service) interacts with a client and the Loan Approver Service through the `PartnerLinkType` named `loanApprovalLinkType`. In that link type, a role named `approver` and its associated PortType named `loanApprovalPT` are declared.

Partner Service Details

First, let us look at the external (partner) Web service Loan Approver.

1. Download the exercise code provided for Loan Approver. It is a zipped Maven project, `LoanApproverService.zip`. Import it into your Eclipse environment using "Existing Projects into Workspace".

2. Under the folders `src/main/resources/wsdl` and `src/main/resources/xsd`, you will find WSDL and XSD files respectively. First, open the XSD file `xsd/loanmessages.xsd`. Notice the XML types and elements declared in the file. Pay attention to the namespace under which these XML types and elements are declared:

```
http://soacourse.unsw.edu.au/loandefinitions
```

The risk message is definitely not necessary for Loan Approver Service. But having it declared here allows us to reuse this single XSD for the Risk Assessor Service later on. So for now you can ignore the risk message part.

3. Open `wsdl/loanapprover.wsdl`. First, notice the target namespace

   `http://soacourse.unsw.edu.au/loanapprover,`

   and also note the import statement to reference the XSD file with the namespace:

   `http://soacourse.unsw.edu.au/loandefinitions`

   Look further and examine the PortType (named `loanApprovalPT`) and the operation `approve`. Note that the message elements declared in the WSDL file (i.e., `LoanApprovalRequestMsg` and `LoanApprovalResponseMsg`) use the XML elements declared in the XSD file.
   Examine the binding and service definition parts. The actual `soap:address` in the service definition will be "corrected" by the Apache CXF server when this service is deployed. So you do not have to worry about the address for now.

4. The `src/main/java-generated` folder includes the generated classes based on this WSDL (and the imported XSD). The rest is pretty much straightforward:

   - `soacourse.unsw.edu.au.loanapprover.LoanApprovalPT` is the SEI.
   - `soacourse.unsw.edu.au.loanapprover.LoanApprovalPTImpl` is the actual provider class. The implementation logic is rather minimal here; you may change it. The main point is to return 'yes' or 'no'.

5. Open `src/main/webapp/WEB-INF/beans.xml`. Note the endpoint declaration. The address for the service is to be `/loanapprover`.

6. Now do "Maven Update", "Clean" and "Install". Add the service to the Tomcat server – the one we set up for Apache CXF services in the previous labs. Test that the service is running correctly. The address of the WSDL should be (if you haven't changed anything):

   `http://localhost:8080/LoanApproverServiceT2/loanapprover?wsdl`

BPEL Process (the WSDL Part)

We will now work on creating some BPEL code and related artifacts. In this exercise, have a look at the sample code given in the figures and change the template code in your own files accordingly. Pay attention to the changes you are asked to make and carefully consider why those changes are necessary.

1. Create a new BPEL project using the BPEL designer; New → Other → BPEL 2.0 → BPEL project. Follow through with the project widget. Some of the values to be set are here:

   - Project name: `BPEL_LoanApprovalService`
   - Target runtime: `Apache ODE 1.x`
   - Content folder: `bpelContent` (default)

2. In the project folder, we need to include the WSDL file of our partner service. It should be running at (make sure that the Tomcat server for the CXF services is running):

```
http://localhost:8080/LoanApproverServiceT2/loanapprover?wsdl
```

   - Go to the URL of the service.
   - Notice that the WSDL file served by the URL mainly contains the binding and service definition information (with `soap:address` correctly filled in). Save this file locally on your computer. Name it `loanapproverBinding.wsdl`.
   - In the WSDL, you will notice an import statement for another WSDL. This imported WSDL contains the abstract information (e.g., messages and port type) of the service. Type in the URL in the browser:

```
http://localhost:8080/LoanApproverServiceT2/
loanapproverwsdl=loanApprovalPT.wsdl
```

   Save this file locally on your computer. Name it `loanapprover.wsdl`

3. Once the project is created, right-click on the `bpelContent` folder. Do Import → General → File System. Choose the two WSDL files from the previous step and import them into the folder.
4. Open `loanapproverBinding.wsdl`. In `wsdl:import`, change the value of the location to `location="loanapprover.wsdl"` (i.e., remove the full URL reference). Apache ODE does not process imported content from a remote location.
5. Now, create a new BPEL process file. Do New → Other → BPEL 2.0 → BPEL Process File. Follow through with the widget. Some of the values to be set are here:

   - Process Name: `SimpleHomeLoan`
   - Namespace: `http://soacourse.unsw.edu.au/loanapproval`
   - Choose the "Synchronous BPEL Process" template
   - Service Name: `LoanApprovalServiceProcess`
   - Port Name: `LoanApprovalProcessPort`
   - Service Address:
     `http://localhost:6060/ode/processes/LoanApproval`
     `ServiceProcess`
   - Binding: SOAP

   Choose the location of the BPEL-related files to be `bpelContent/`, and the file name of the BPEL process to be `SimpleHomeLoan.bpel`. Then click "Finish".
6. Now in the `bpelContent` folder, you will find two files: `SimpleHomeLoan.bpel` (the BPEL process file) and a WSDL file, `SimpleHomeLoanArtifacts.wsdl`. The WSDL file is going to describe the service provided by the BPEL process `SimpleHomeLoan`. According to the Loan Approval Service scenario described in this chapter, this BPEL service is going to provide portType

loanApproverPT with operation approve – so we want this WSDL to reflect that.

7. Open SimpleHomeLoanArtifacts.wsdl. First note that this WSDL has its own target namespace (http://soacourse.unsw.edu.au/loanapproval) as we specified above.

8. We are going to reuse much of the information declared in loanapprover. wsdl. So, remove the existing type definition and message definition and the portType definition parts. Now you should have the partnerLinkType, binding and service definition parts left. Insert an import statement as below, just above the partnerLinkType definition:

```
<import namespace="http://soacourse.unsw.edu.au/loanapprover"
location="loanapprover.wsdl" />
```

Now, add a new namespace declaration for this import statement at the element wsdl:definitions. Name the prefix approver. Your WSDL up to now should look as in Listing 6.1.

```
1  <?xml version="1.0"?>
2  <definitions name="LoanApprovalService"
3     targetName space="http://soacourse.unsw.edu.au/loanapproval"
4    xmlns:tns="http://soacourse.unsw.edu.au/loanapproval"
5    xmlns:plnk="http://docs.oasis-open.org/wsbpel/2.0/plnktype"
6    xmlns="http://schemas.xmlsoap.org/wsdl/"
7    xmlns:soap="http://schemas.xmlsoap.org/wsdl/soap/"
8    xmlns:approver="http://soacourse.unsw.edu.au/loanapprover">
9
10   <import namespace="http://soacourse.unsw.edu.au/loanapprover"
11     location="loanapprover.wsdl" />
12
13   <plnk:partnerLinkType name="loanApprovalLinkType">
14     <plnk:role name="approver" portType="approver:loanApprovalPT" />
15   </plnk:partnerLinkType>
```

Listing 6.1 PartnerLinkType in SimpleHomeLoanArtifacts.wsdl

9. Change the partnerLinkType definition as shown in Listing 6.1 above as well. Note that we are declaring one partnerLinkType named loanApprovalLinkType with role=approver and its portType= approver:loanApprovalPT. You should mind the namespace prefix.

10. Now we need to correct the binding and service definition parts. Change the binding and service definitions to what is shown in Listing 6.2.

```
1  <binding name="LoanApprovalServiceBinding"
       type="approver:loanApprovalPT">
2    <soap:binding style-"document"
3    transport="http://schemas.xmlsoap.org/soap/http" />
4    <operation name="approve">
5    <soap:operation
       soapAction="http://soacourse.unsw.edu.au/loanapproval/approve"
       />
6    <input>
7      <soap:body use="literal" />
8    </input>
9    <output>
10     <soap:body use="literal" />
11   </output>
12   </operation>
13 </binding>
14
15 <service name="LoanApprovalServiceProcess">
16   <port name="LoanApprovalProcessPort"
       binding="tns:LoanApprovalServiceBinding">
17   <soap:address location=
18 "http://localhost:6060/ode/processes/LoanApprovalServiceProcess"
       />
19   </port>
20 </service>
21 </definitions>
```

Listing 6.2 binding and service in `SimpleHomeLoanArtifacts.wsdl`

BPEL Process (the BPEL Part)

In the previous step, we have effectively defined the service interface for the BPEL process. Now, all we need to do is code the BPEL process.

Open `SimpleHomeLoan.bpel`. In this, the main elements we need to have are: (i) `partnerLinks` (i.e., declaring which partnerLinkType this process is involved in, and what kind of role this process plays in that link), (ii) variables to store/manipulate the messages and (iii) the service coordination/orchestration logic.

1. First, some of the information this process needs is in other WSDLs. Let's import them. You will notice that there is an import statement to bring in the process' own WSDL (`SimpleHomeLoanArtifacts.wsdl`). Mind the namespace there. This process (`SimpleHomeLoan.bpel`) is going to share the same namespace as `SimpleHomeLoanArtifacts.wsdl`.
2. We need to import another WSDL (`loanapprover.wsdl`). Add an extra import statement for `loanapprover.wsdl`. After the import, also add the namespace of the imported WSDL to `bpel:process`. This part of your BPEL code should look something like what is shown in Listing 6.3.

```
1 <bpel:process name="SimpleHomeLoan"
2 targetNamespace="http://soacourse.unsw.edu.au/loanapproval"
3 suppressJoinFailure="yes"
4 xmlns:tns="http://soacourse.unsw.edu.au/loanapproval"
5 xmlns:ns1="http://soacourse.unsw.edu.au/loanapprover"
6 xmlns:ns2="http://soacourse.unsw.edu.au/loandefinitions"
7 xmlns:bpel=
8 "http://docs.oasis-open.org/wsbpel/2.0/process/executable">
9
10 <!-- Import the client WSDL -->
11 <bpel:import location=
12 "loanapprovalArtifacts.wsdl"
        namespace="http://soacourse.unsw.edu.au/loanapproval"
13 importType="http://schemas.xmlsoap.org/wsdl/" />
14 <bpel:import
        namespace="http://soacourse.unsw.edu.au/loanapprover"
15 location="loanapprover.wsdl"
16 importType="http://schemas.xmlsoap.org/wsdl/" />
```

Listing 6.3   import statement in `SimpleHomeLoan.bpel`

3. Now look at the `partnerLinks`. This process is interacting with two entities: the client (i.e., the requester) and its external Web service partner (the LoanApproval service). So, you should make two `partnerLinks` declarations. Change the `partnerLinks` section of the template BPEL with the code shown in Listing 6.4, minding the reference to `partnerLinkType` and `roles`.

```
1 <bpel:partnerLinks>
2     <!-- The 'client' role represents the requester of this
        service. -->
3     <bpel:partnerLink name="client"
4                 partnerLinkType="tns:loanApprovalLinkType"
5                 myRole="approver"
6                 />
7     <bpel:partnerLink name="approver"
8                 partnerLinkType="tns:loanApprovalLinkType"
9                 partnerRole="approver"
10                />
11 </bpel:partnerLinks>
```

Listing 6.4   partnerLinks in `SimpleHomeLoan.bpel`

4. For the variables, we are going to declare one for the input request message and another for the output/response. Mind the namespace of the message types (Listing 6.5).

```
 1 <bpel:variables>
 2      <!-- Reference to the message passed as input during
         initiation -->
 3      <bpel:variable name="request"
 4                  messageType="ns1:approve"/>
 5
 6      <!--
 7        Reference to the message that will be returned to the
         requester
 8        -->
 9      <bpel:variable name="approvalInfo"
10                  messageType="ns1:approveResponse"/>
11
12 </bpel:variables>
```

Listing 6.5   Variables in SimpleHomeLoan.bpel

5. Now the orchestration code goes like what is shown in Listing 6.6.

```
 1 <bpel:sequence name="main">
 2
 3      <!-- Receive input from requester.
 4          Note: This maps to operation defined in
         SimpleHomeLoan.wsdl
 5          -->
 6      <bpel:receive name="receiveInput" partnerLink="client"
 7              portType="ns1:loanApprovalPT"
 8              operation="approve" createInstance="yes"
         variable="request"/>
 9
10      <!-- Generate reply to synchronous request -->
11      <bpel:invoke name="Invoke" partnerLink="approver"
12              portType="ns1:loanApprovalPT"
13              operation="approve" inputVariable="request"
14              outputVariable="approvalInfo">
15      </bpel:invoke>
16      <bpel:reply name="replyOutput"
17              partnerLink="client"
18              portType="ns1:loanApprovalPT"
19              operation="approve"
20              variable="approvalInfo"
21              />
22 </bpel:sequence>
23 </bpel:process>
```

Listing 6.6   Orchestration logic in SimpleHomeLoan.bpel

6. Save the file. Fix errors if there are any. Now we need to create a deployment descriptor for this process service.

7. Right click on the `bpelContent` folder, do New → Other → BPEL 2.0 → BPEL Deployment Descriptor. In the Inbound Interfaces table, there should be Partner Link `client` listed. Associate "LoanApprovalProcessPort" (accessible from the definitions in `SimpleHomeLoanArtifacts.wsdl`) to the `client`. On the Outbound Interfaces table, there should be Partner Link `approver` listed. Associate "LoanApprovalPTImplPort" to the `approver` (accessible from `loanapproverBinding.wsdl`). Save the configuration.

8. Deploy the project to the Apache ODE server. Pay attention to the `Console` view and error messages that you may have. If everything goes OK, test the BPEL service. Right-click on `SimpleHomeLoanArtifacts.wsdl`. Select Web Services → Test with Web Services Explorer. Select the operation `approve`. Then, type in the inputs. If your deployment was a success, you will get `approvalInfo` (yes or no depending on your input) in the SOAP response.

These activities should give you enough basic knowledge to explore BPEL further.

Chapter 7
Web Service Composition: Data Flows

The data flow of a service composition specifies how data is exchanged between services. More specifically, it describes the actions performed on output message/data of a previously consumed service that is transferred to the input of a later executed service. The data-flow description encapsulates the data movement from one service to another and the transformations applied on this data. Practically every composition language, whether it graphically wires outputs to inputs (e.g., IFTTT[1]) or is programmatically defined (e.g., XPath expressions), supports the specification of data flow.

7.1 Data-Flow Paradigms

There exist two different paradigms based on the message passing style, namely, *blackboard* and *explicit data flow* [2]. In the next few paragraphs, we explain and exemplify them.

7.1.1 Blackboard

The blackboard paradigm is based on storing data centrally: every process instance has a set of variables, which are used as sources and targets of each Web service activity and are commonly shared by all the services;[2] hence the use of the term blackboard. The blackboard is the imaginary place where all the services read their inputs from and write their outputs to. The main implication of using the blackboard paradigm is value overwriting: if a service generates a value of a variable different from the value previously generated by another service, the value will be overwritten

---

[1] https://ifttt.com.

[2] Some authors prefer to name them activities rather than services. The term activity is more precise as it describes the invocation of a service operation. To maintain simple terminology and not create confusion with different terms, the authors use the word service.

© Springer International Publishing AG 2017
H.-y. Paik et al., *Web Service Implementation and Composition Techniques*,
DOI 10.1007/978-3-319-55542-3_7

and the last one will be the only one active and stored. The concept is similar to how conventional programming languages such as Java and C handle data. Several Web service composition languages also follow this paradigm, among them the Web Service Business Process Execution Language (BPEL).

BPEL Data Flow

As previously stated, BPEL handles data by a blackboard paradigm; more specifically, BPEL does not provide explicit constructs for the data-flow description. This is mentioned in the BPEL specification [16]: "The information is passed between the different activities in an **implicit** way through the sharing of globally visible data containers". In consequence, BPEL is considered a language that does not directly support data flows.

BPEL is built on several XML specifications: Web Service Description Language (WSDL), XML Schema Definition (XSD), Simple Object Access Protocol (SOAP), Extensive Markup Language Schema (XML Schema), and XML Path Language (XPath). SOAP is at the communication layer and is used for message exchanging. The message types and the operations provided by a Web service are defined by WSDL using XML Schema, which provides the data model. The data manipulation is described using XPath expressions, unless the manipulation requires complex transformations, at which point XQuery, XSLT, or even Java programs may be used.

Example 7.1.1 BPEL Data Flow: Loan Approval *This example is based on the example with the same name defined in the BPEL 2.0 specification.[3] This example has been reduced in order to cover principally the data flow, leaving aside other composition aspects such as the control flow. The example describes a simple loan approval service process to be specified using BPEL: the loan service receives loan requests from customers which include personal information and amount being requested. Based on that information the request is approved or denied. The information is analyzed in terms of amount requested and risk associated with the customer: for amounts under $10,000 the risk of the customer is evaluated by means of a risk assessment Web service; if the evaluation results in low risk associated with the customer, the request is approved; for amounts equal to or greater than $10,000 the request is further evaluated by the invocation of an external (to the process) service. Let us just consider the part of the process after the reply from the risk assessment service ('LoanAssesorWS') has been received (highlighted in Fig. 7.1). Once the risk assessment completes and the reply message is received and stored in the variable 'risk' (output variable), the risk result is evaluated using two transition conditions, which consists of two XPath conditional expressions:* $\$risk.level = 'low'$ *and* $\$risk.level = 'high'$ *(Listing 7.1, Lines 12–18).*

```
1 <process name="loanApprovalProcess"
2 ...
3   <variables>
4     <variable name="approval" messageType="lns:approvalMessage" />
```

[3]http://docs.oasis-open.org/wsbpel/2.0/OS/wsbpel-v2.0-OS.html.

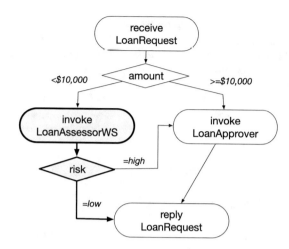

Fig. 7.1 BPEL data flow example – In diagram

```
5    </variables>
6    ...
7    <flow>
8    ...
9      <invoke partnerLink="assessor" portType="lns:riskAssessmentPT"
10     operation="check" inputVariable="request"
       outputVariable="risk">
11       <targets><target linkName="receive-to-assess" /><targets>
12       <sources>
13          <source linkName="assess-to-setMessage">
14             <transitionCondition>$risk.level='low'
15             </transitionCondition>
16          </source>
17          <source linkName="assess-to-approval">
18             <transitionCondition>$risk.level='high'
19             </transitionCondition>
20          </source>
21       </sources>
22     </invoke>
23     <assign>
24       <targets><target linkName="assess-to-setMessage" /><targets>
25       <sources><source linkName="setMessage-to-reply"/></sources>
26       <copy>
27          <from><literal>yes</literal></from>
28          <to variable="approval" part="accept" />
29       </copy>
30     </assign>
31   </flow>
32   ...
```

Listing 7.1 BPEL data flow example – in BPEL code

If the XPath expression that evaluates whether the risk level is low results in true, the response message has to be set to confirm the loan to the customer. For that, the literal 'yes' is copied to the 'accept' part of the 'approval' variable of the type 'approval message'. The BPEL code that specifies the copy is shown in Listing 7.1, Lines 25–28:

```
1  <copy>
2   <from>
3    <literal>yes</literal>
4   </from>
5   <to variable="approval" part="accept />
6  </copy>
```

Listing 7.2 BPEL copy statement

The copy defines the source (<from> element) and the target (<to> element). Any general XPath expression is allowed in the <from> element, as long as it returns a valid XPath value type (i.e., string, number or Boolean) and is compatible with the type of the <to> element.

This example shows the basics of how BPEL handles the data flow. It also alludes to some key concepts (e.g., expression, source, target) that will be further elaborated on throughout this chapter.

7.1.2 Explicit Data Flow

The explicit data-flow paradigm makes data flow a fully and clearly defined part of the composition. It does this by specifying the data flow between different services by means of data connectors. A data connector describes how data is manipulated and routed to or from Web services. Unlike in the blackboard paradigm, data is not overwritten: two services can generate the same variable as an output, and a third service can be designed to gather the value from one or the other by using a data connector. This paradigm is commonly used by data-centric systems which require simple control flow. Due to the data-centric approach of Web 2.0 (intensified in the Semantic Web), the Web composition languages designed for that environment (i.e., Mashup tools) principally follow the explicit data-flow paradigm.

Mashups Data Flow

A mashup is a Web application that is developed by composing data, application logic, and user interfaces originating from disparate Web sources. The result is a simple but powerful and useful application. It is simple because the process is composed in a few steps, namely gathering data, transforming it and presenting it. In general, mashup programs require neither the use of complex control-flow structures nor the coordination of multiple actors. This and the aim of keeping a user-friendly environment are the reasons why the vast majority of mashup development tools do not provide control-flow constructors [10]. The specification of data flow is enough to extract the implicit control flow.

The data flow in a mashup is defined as a sequence of operators that perform data manipulations on the input data received via input parameters whose result is stored in the output parameters. Operators are the building blocks of the data flow; they are programs that either invoke a Web service or call functions to act on the data. They operate in a manner similar to that of Extract, Transform and Load (ETL) processes in data warehousing environments.

An example of mashup is the HousingMaps application,[4] which is using data coming from two different sources to combine them in the same interface. HousingMaps extracts the list of apartment offers from Craigslist;[5] this data is sent to Google Maps[6] in the required format; Google Maps combines the data from Craigslist with its own data (maps) to create a map with the apartments Craigslist is offering marked on it (Fig. 7.2).

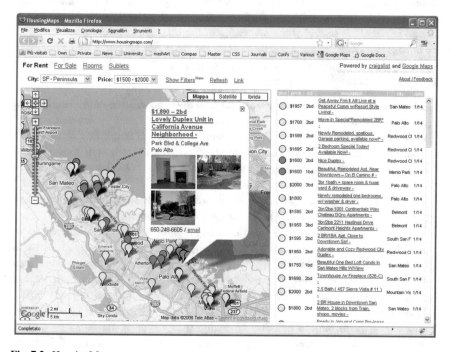

Fig. 7.2 HousingMaps

[4]http://www.housingmaps.com.
[5]http://www.craigslist.com.
[6]http://maps.google.com.

Yahoo! Pipes Mashup

Yahoo! Pipes, although it is now deprecated by Yahoo, provides a good example of a service composition paradigm through data flow. So, we show it here as an example of a mashup tool.

Yahoo! Pipes follows a data-flow-oriented approach, which implies that the composition is limited to data aggregation and manipulation through the application of data transformation operations. Therefore Yahoo! Pipes supports a number of data manipulation operators, such as filter, split, tail, union, rename, sort, and truncate, which, in turn, may be applied through the use of modules that encapsulate the functionality of the transformation operator. Next we exemplify how the data transformation occurs in Yahoo! Pipes.

Example 7.1.2 *Example: Yahoo! Pipes with Multiple Data Transformations. The goal of this example is to reduce and organize the results obtained from the combination of Yahoo! Local and Flickr. The results from Yahoo! Local are organized by their rating, reduced to 10 results, and the string "[Yahoo!]" is added at the beginning of the item title; the results from Flickr are also limited to 10 items and the string "[Flickr]" is added at the beginning of the title. These data transformations are introduced after the data has been gathered from Yahoo! Local and Flickr and before the data is combined through the union operator. The applied transformations are explained in the following list:*

1. *The first data transformation corresponds to the organization of the results from the Yahoo! Local Web service. To that end, the module "Sort" is applied; "Sort" organizes the received items into a specified order. It is applied to the items obtained from the "Yahoo! Local" module by wiring the output of Yahoo! Local to the input of the "Sort" module, which is one of the "Operators" that Yahoo! Pipes provides. The module includes dropping lists for the selection of sorting criteria. In this case the items are organized based on the value of the attribute "item.Rating.Average" and the type of order is "descending".*
2. *The number of result items is limited to 10 for both services (i.e., Yahoo! Local and Flickr) in this example. By reducing the number of results, the objective is to have a clearer and more tidy view of the map. The reduction is performed by means of the module "Truncate", which, like "Sort", is under the category "Operators". The module contains a text box where the number of feeds can be specified, 10 in this case.*
3. *The last transformation consists of changing the title of the items by adding an identifier to know whether the result comes from Yahoo! Local or Flickr. The*

   *appropriate module to perform this transformation is "Regex"; it searches for a regular expression in an item to replace it with a new expression. "Regex" allows the specification of a set of rules; for the current example a single rule is enough to carry out the transformation. The rule contains three fields: (i) "**In**" selects the element of the item where the rule will be applied. In this case for the items from both Yahoo! Local and Flickr, the item element is the title (i.e., "item.title");*

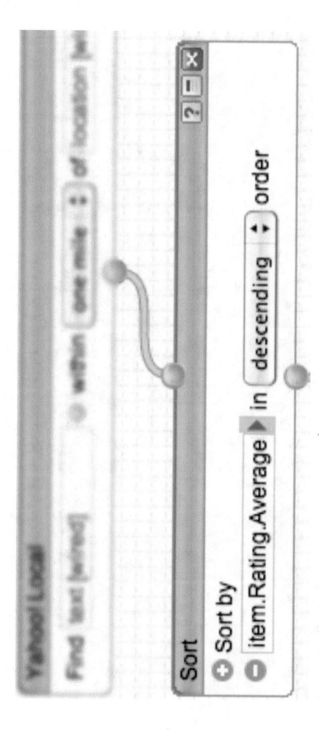

Fig. 7.3   Data transformation modules added (Sort)

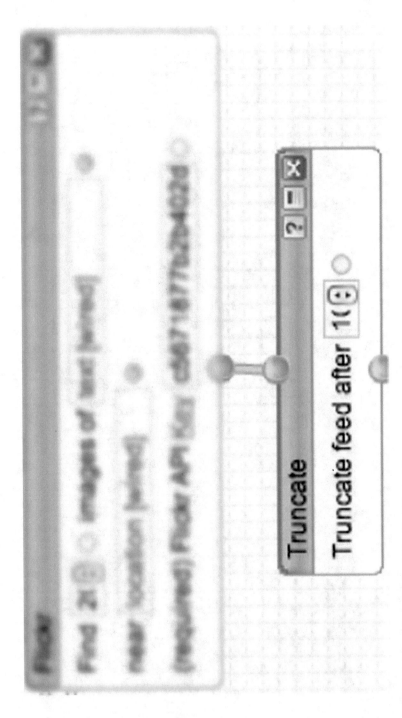

Fig. 7.4 Data transformation modules added (Truncate)

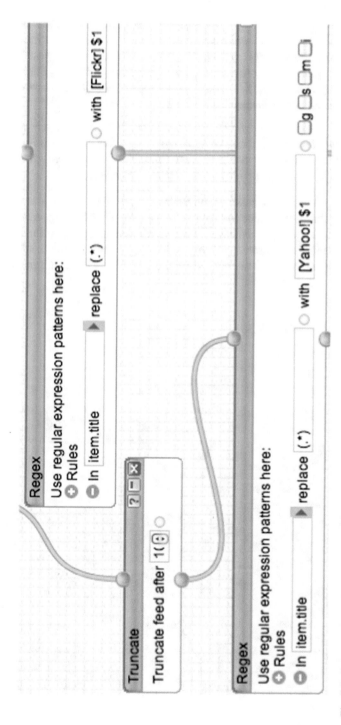

Fig. 7.5 Data transformation modules added (Regex)

*(ii) "**replace**" is the field where the regular expression is entered. The expression used in this example is "(.*)", which selects the whole text of the item element selected; and (iii) "**with**" indicates what the result of the regular expression is going to be replaced with. In both "Regex" modules, the field 'with' contains first the word that must precede the title (i.e., "[Yahoo!]" or "[Flickr]"), and subsequently the string "$1", which refers to the part of the "item.title" that matched the regular expression.*

Figures 7.3, 7.4 and 7.5 depict the modules that have been added to introduce the data transformations in the pipe. The result of the execution of the pipe is illustrated by a screenshot of the tool in Fig. 7.6. The transformations included are easily recognizable when comparing the two screenshots of results.

In general, any complete composition environment provides transformation logic to deal with data management and data heterogeneity. Data heterogeneity was not present in this last example; however, if the required transformation logic to solve data heterogeneity is not provided, composition may be impossible in some cases. Thus, the composition in the majority of mashups is, to some extent, limited in this aspect.

Fig. 7.6 Yahoo! Pipes result

Chapter 8
Service Component Architecture (SCA)

In the previous chapters we have described SOA as an architectural paradigm for building enterprise-class middleware applications. Conceptually, implementing an SOA-based solution is simple. We have a software component; it is packaged as a service and other components can thereby use this service. However, building a successful SOA solution is complex. Enterprise architects have found putting SOA into practice difficult due to the significant lack of standards and specifications that are otherwise needed to provide a definitive guideline on how service-oriented applications are developed. Business computing environments contain many different technologies and integrating these technologies is complex. Within a single application, you may be required to integrate Java objects, BPEL processes, REST Web services as well as Java Message Services (JMSs), and JSON-RPC protocols, to name but a few. What is needed is a consensus on how to describe an assembly of services regardless of the technology used to implement and access them. This chapter introduces a framework known as *Service Component Architecture* (SCA) that provides a technology-agnostic capability for composing applications from distributed services.

8.1 Introduction to SCA

The *Service Component Architecture* (SCA) is an initiative introduced in 2005 by a consortium of companies called the Open Service Oriented Architecture (OSOA) collaboration. SCA has since been adopted by the OASIS group, a standards organization responsible for notable standards such as Electronic Business using XML (ebXML) and Web Services Business Process Execution Language (WS-BPEL), among others. SCA is a set of specifications that provide a programming model for developing enterprise applications based on service-oriented architectural principles. Using SCA, software components supported by a variety of languages can be exposed as services, which can then be accessed using different connection mechanisms such

© Springer International Publishing AG 2017
H.-y. Paik et al., *Web Service Implementation and Composition Techniques*,
DOI 10.1007/978-3-319-55542-3_8

as SOAP, JMS and REST, and others. These fine-grained services can be further assembled to form a higher-level service or composite, where each composite creates a solution that addresses a specific business requirement. In the next section, we present an example to illustrate the challenges in architecting an SOA application followed by an overview of SCA, and we contrast how SCA helps resolve these challenges.

8.1.1   The SOA Integration Problem

To recap, SOA is based on the idea that a business application is broken down as a series of services, where a *service* encapsulates a reusable piece of business function and has a well-defined interface that identifies how the service may be invoked to provide that function. Figure 8.1 demonstrates an example made up of services that are developed in various technologies and accessed using different protocols. This mix of languages and connection mechanisms is typical of an enterprise application today. The danger with this scenario, involving *point-to-point* invocations of different services, is that the technology to handle the integration logic can become intermingled with the business logic, making the services hard to maintain and reuse. SCA addresses this complexity by defining a **consistent** way for the **assembly** and **access** of such services.

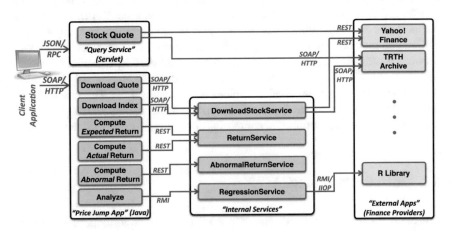

Fig. 8.1 SOA integration problem for a finance application

8.1.2   Overview of SCA

SCA provides a set of specifications that can be split into four main categories as shown in Fig. 8.2.

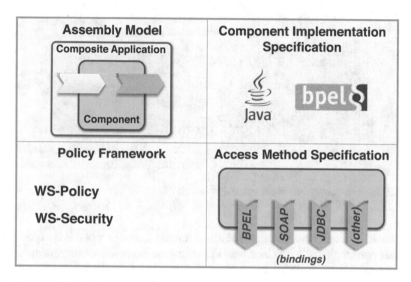

Fig. 8.2 The SCA specifications

SCA Assembly Model

The assembly model represents the core of the SCA specifications. It is an abstract component model that defines a series of artifacts to enable the assembly of distributed software components into a composite application. Figure 8.3 shows the main artifacts of the SCA assembly model. A *component* is the basic building block of an SCA application. An SCA component, like an SOA service, is a self-contained unit of functionality. However, unlike an SOA service, an SCA component is not necessarily available for external consumption. An SCA component advertises its capabilities to external applications by defining a *service*. Each *service* has a name and an interface that define the operations provided by the service. Each SCA component has a *concrete* implementation that describes the business logic of the component developed using a regular programming language such as Java or BPEL.

SCA components can call another service using a *reference*. The connection between the reference and the service is called a *wire*. A collection of SCA components is assembled together to form a *composite* application to serve a particular business need. The *composite* is described in simple XML constructs. The SCA assembly model is a recursive compositional model in that it allows fine-grained *components* to be composed into an SCA *composite* and these coarse-grained composites can in turn be used as components in higher-level composite applications.

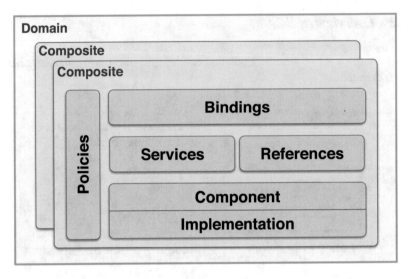

Fig. 8.3 High-level overview of the assembly model

Like an SCA component, a composite also becomes a *service* when it is exposed for external consumption. An SCA *domain* provides the execution environment for one or more composite applications. A service or reference specifies a *binding*, which is the mechanism or communication protocol by which an SCA component can be accessed. This is the high-level overview of SCA and an example of an SCA assembly consisting of an SCA domain with two composite applications deployed as shown in Fig. 8.4. Composite X has one component M which is implemented using Java. Composite Y is made up of two components A and B which are implemented by composites A and B respectively. Within the composite Y, the service exposed by component B is wired to the reference defined on component A. Finally, component M defines a reference to access the service exposed by component A. Section 8.3 elaborates in detail on each of the above SCA concepts.

SCA Component Implementation Specification

The SCA component specifications specify how each SCA component is actually built using a particular language or framework. The standard programming languages supported include Java, BPEL, C++ and COBOL. The supported frameworks include Spring, Enterprise Java Beans (EJB) and JAX-WS. Several containers implementing the SCA specification can support additional implementation types like .Net, OSGI bundles, etc. In theory, a component can be developed using any technology as long as it is defined with a common set of abstractions, e.g. services, references and bindings.

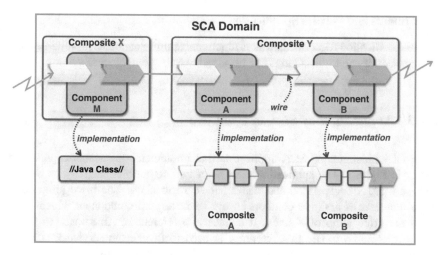

Fig. 8.4 An example of an SCA domain

SCA Binding Specification

The binding specification specifies how the services exposed by a component can be accessed using a particular communication protocol. SCA bindings encapsulate the complexities of transport protocols and enable components to be developed and wired without any direct dependency on the communication protocol(s) used. The technology used to join two components is unrelated to how the components are implemented. Therefore, an SCA component could be communicating with another component within the same process or on another process or even in another machine. The current binding types described by the SCA binding specification include SOAP-based, JMS, EJB and JCA bindings. Containers implementing the SCA specification can include support for additional bindings such as JSON-RPC, etc.

To understand why bindings are useful, think about how traditional applications communicated with distributed components. Distributed communication could use different protocols such as SOAP over HTTP, RMIIIOP, JMS, etc. Each protocol is provided by a distinct technology, and has its own API (Application Programming Interface). For example, a Web service interaction using SOAP over HTTP typically is based on JAX-WS, interaction with an EJB component could use IIOP, and a queued messaging protocol requires Java Message Service (JMS). In the past, application developers were required to intermingle communication logic with business functionality. However, with SCA through a binding, the details of a component's implementation are abstracted away from the other components that it is connected to. This completely decouples a component's business logic from its access logic, thereby freeing the developer from having to learn different APIs to focus on the component's business functionality. SCA components therefore encapsulate pure business logic and are not cluttered by details of transport mechanisms.

SCA Intents and Policies Specification

These specifications describe how non-functional requirements such as reliable messaging, security and transactions can be added to SCA components.

8.1.3   Application of SCA to Use Case

Figure 8.5 illustrates an SCA application that implements the scenario presented earlier in Fig. 8.1. The application consists of two composites, namely, as shown, `pricejump.composite` and `finance.composite`. The price jump composite consists of a single component, the `PriceJump` component which computes the price jump of a stock. It defines two references, `AbnormalReturn` and `Regression`. The first reference is used to invoke the service `DailyAR` defined by the finance composite through a Web service binding, while the second invokes an external non-SCA application (implemented as an R library) through an RMI binding. The finance composite consists of several other components such as `DailyAbnormalReturn`, `StockQuote` and `DailyMarketData`, together with `StockReturn`. Within the finance composite, components interact using an SCA binding. Finally, the `PriceJump` component exposes `PriceJumpService`, that can be invoked by client applications through a Web service binding.

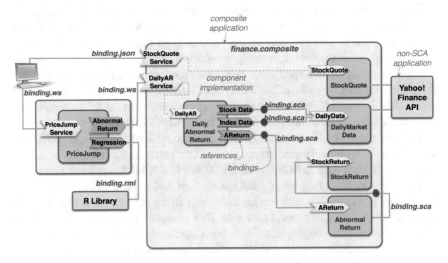

Fig. 8.5   Finance application implemented using SCA

8.1.4 SCA Runtime

Apache Tuscany developed by the Apache Software Foundation was the first open-source reference implementation of SCA. Tuscany was designed to provide a light-weight infrastructure for developing and running applications and it implements the Service Component Architecture (SCA), Service Data Objects (SDO) and Data Access Service (DAS) technologies and is designed to be embedded in a number of different host environments. The Tuscany software is freely available from the project website[1] under the Apache 2.0 license. As of this writing, Apache Tuscany has released its 2.0.1 version. Since its inception, several other open-source and commercial implementations have evolved. Another notable open-source implementation is Frascati 0.5.[2] Some of the notable commercial implementations include Oracle SOA Suite 12g[3] and IBM Websphere Process Server.[4] For the purposes of the examples in this book, we have decided to use Apache Tuscany as our SCA run-time environment.

8.1.5 Benefits of SCA

SCA addresses the challenges of developing a successful SOA solution by providing a single, uniform technology-neutral component model for assembling business solutions from new components or reusing existing components. SCA promotes *rapid application development* as developers implementing a service component focus purely on the application business logic rendered by the component without worrying about how the service component may be invoked or how the component might fit into the overall solution. A composite application invokes a Web service using SOAP over HTTP in the same way it invokes a POJO (Plain Old Java Object) component or an RMI service. An application developer only needs to know how to invoke an SCA component, and is not required to learn new programming interfaces or networking protocols. Decoupling component business logic from details of component composition ensures that SCA components are *loosely coupled* and can also be easily replaced by newer components.

SCA also offers enterprises *increased productivity* and a *return on investment* through reuse. By providing a standard approach to encapsulating components and by being able to bind to any communication protocol seamlessly, it allows enterprises to leverage investments in existing software resources such as legacy systems. SCA's *flexible* assembly model enables components to be wired and rewired in new and different ways to assemble different composite applications to address different

---

[1] http://tuscany.apache.org.

[2] http://frascati.ow2.org.

[3] http://www.oracle.com/technetwork/middleware/soasuite/overview/index.html.

[4] https://www-01.ibm.com/software/integration/wps/.

business requirements. Within an SCA composition, given that components can be easily replaced provided they share the same contract, this enables application builders to leverage newer and revised component implementations, without impacting the overall composite application. Similarly, references invoked by the composite application can also be easily replaced. For example, an application developer who perceives that better performance is achieved through an RMI service instead of a Web service accessed with SOAP over HTTP can make this switch with ease. Furthermore, no training overhead costs are incurred if the team lacks expertise in RMI technology, as an RMI service is invoked in the same manner as a Web service would be invoked using SOAP over HTTP.

8.2   The Stock Application

To demonstrate the concepts in SCA (using Apache Tuscany runtime), we construct a hypothetical stock application called *Tuscany Stock Application* that is intended to provide a financial researcher a range of services to be able to analyze financial stock data. The financial content provider used by our examples is **Yahoo! Finance**. This application will make use of the Tuscany SCA runtime. Figure 8.6 shows the high-level architecture of this composite and the relevant SCA components. In the next section, code snippets of this application will be provided to demonstrate the various concepts in SCA. The steps taken to build the complete application will be provided as a lab tutorial at the end of the section. The following are the requirements of our hypothetical stock application:

- The stock application must provide users with a set of useful functions to be able to analyse hypothetical stock data. These functions are listed below:

  - Conversion of currencies to compute real-time exchange rates.
  - Downloading of daily stock market data related to the stock symbol that a user entered.
  - Downloading of real-time intra-day stock quotes consisting of "ask" (best sell price) and "bid" (best buy price) for a given stock symbol.
  - Calculating the expected returns of the stock for a given period.
  - Calculating the abnormal returns of the stock for a given period.

- The stock application must expose the functionality to compute the stock abnormal return and intra-day stock quote as services. It should be implemented such that it can be invoked as a Web service using SOAP, which will enable the application to be embedded within many different applications.

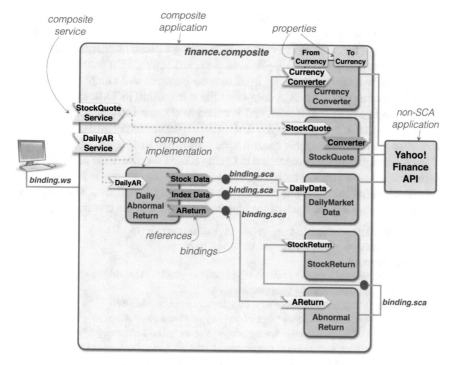

Fig. 8.6 An SCA composite diagram showing the high-level architecture of the stock application

8.3 The SCA Assembly Model

Section 8.1.2 provided a high-level overview of the SCA assembly model and its key artifacts. In this section, we examine each of these abstractions in more detail. We start with the top-level building blocks of SCA – *composite.*

8.3.1 SCA Composite

An SCA *composite* is an assembly of *components* and other related elements such as *services, references, properties* and *wiring* that describe how these components are configured and linked together. A composite often represents a logical grouping of functional components, e.g., all functional components related to inventory management for a retail store could be grouped together into a composite. The components that make up a single composite might all run in the same process, might be spread across different processes on the same machine, or might run on different machines

(Duggan). In all of these cases, SCA's assembly model defines how components in a composite relate to one another, specifying things like how those components should be wired together. In effect, it allows treating a group of possibly distributed components as a single unified application. As noted before, SCA facilitates a *recursive composition* as the *composite* itself may be included as a component within a higher-level composite. An SCA composite file is expressed in XML format in a file with a `*.composite` extension and is called as *Service Component Description Language* (SCDL). A snippet of the XML schema definition for an SCA composite as defined in the SCA assembly specification is shown in Listing 8.1; and an example of an SCA composite file is presented in Listing 8.2. At the root of the XML file is the element `<composite>`, which provides the name of the composite and associated namespace definitions and encloses all other assembly definitions. The following sections will elaborate on each of the elements described in the composite file.

```
1  <element name="composite" type="sca:Composite"/>
2    <complexType name="Composite">
3      <sequence>
4        <element name="include" type="anyURI" minOccurs="0"
5              maxOccurs="unbounded"/>
6        <choice minOccurs="0" maxOccurs="unbounded">
7          <element name="service" type="sca:Service"/>
8          <element name="property" type="sca:Property"/>
9          <element name="component" type="sca:Component"/>
10         <element name="reference" type="sca:Reference"/>
11         <element name="wire" type="sca:Wire"/>
12       </choice>
13       ... ...
14    </complexType>
15 <element>
```

Listing 8.1 XML definition for an SCA composite

```
1  <composite name="stockreturn" xmlns= ... >
2    <component name="StockReturnComponent">
3        <implementation.java
4            class="au.edu.unsw.soacourse.sca.components.
5                       impl.StockReturnImpl"/>
6    </component>
7  </composite>
```

Listing 8.2 An example of an SCA composite file

8.3.2 SCA Component

An SCA *component* represents the basic building block of an SCA application. Every SCA composite is built from one or more SCA components. Each SCA component implementation encapsulates a reusable piece of business logic. SCA components are assembled together to service a specific business need. In the next section, we examine how an SCA component is configured within a composite using a *component definition*.

SCA Component Definition

An SCA component is configured within a composite using a *component definition*. The component definition is specified with a `component` element, which is defined as a child element to the `composite`. The attribute name within the `component` element specifies the name of the component. This is used to refer to the component and qualify references to its constituent parts. A composite cannot contain more than one component with the same name. Every SCA component has a *component implementation* that provides the component's business logic and a *component implementation type* that identifies the implementation technology. Listing 8.3 shows the component definition for an SCA component, *StockReturnComponent*. This component has an *implementation type* of Java as identified by the element `implementation.java`. The class attribute identifies the *component implementation* specified by the fully qualified name of the implementation class, `au.edu.unsw.soacourse.sca.components.impl.Stock ReturnImpl`.

```
                    implementation
                        type

1  <?xml version="1.0" encoding="UTF-8" standalone="no"?>
2
3  <composite name="stockreturn" …>
4      <component name="RateOfReturnComponent">        component
5      <implementation.java                            implementation
6          class="au.edu.unsw.soacourse.sca.
7                  components.impl.RateOfReturnServiceImpl"/>
8      </component>
   </composite>

component
definition
```

Listing 8.3 Component definition for StockReturnComponent SCA component

An SCA component can thus be implemented using any programming language (e.g. Java, C++, etc.), or using BPEL, EJB, Spring, etc. The assembly approach allows SCA components implemented with different technologies to be connected to each other, whereby the component's implementation is abstracted from other components it is connected to. Components are not aware of each other's implementation type, e.g. a Java component is allowed to be wired to a BPEL component, or vice versa. The supported implementation types are governed by the SCA runtime environment. Apache Tuscany, the open-source SCA offering, supports the following implementation types as listed in Table 8.1.

Table 8.1 Apache tuscany implementation types (Davis)

TYPE
Java
Spring assemblies – invoke Java Code exposed through Spring
Scripting Languages – Ruby, Groovey, Javascript, Python and XSLT
BPEL – Only integrates with Apache ODE for BPEL process
XQuery – Supports Saxon XQuery
OSGi – Supports Apache Felix OSGi implementation

By convention, all implementation types are identified by the element denoted by `implementation.*`, where the `*` is replaced by the specific implementation type (e.g., `implementation.bpel` or `implementation.spring`, etc.). The SCA 1.0 specification defines standard implementation types for Java, BPEL, C++, C, and COBOL, as well as Spring, Web applications (.war files), EJBs, and Java EE archives (.ear files). SCA also provides an extension point for creating additional implementation types. For example, Oracle SOA Suite provides custom implementation types to include its Oracle Mediator, Oracle BPEL and Human Task. Similarly, Apache Tuscany includes additional implementation types to support popular technologies such as Python, JRuby, Groovy and Javascript. One implementation type anticipated to be supported by all SCA-compliant products is the composite implementation, `implementation.composite`, in support of its recursive assembly policy. This enables a composite of fine-grained components to be wrapped up as a coarse-grained component that can be included as part of a higher-level composite. This allows components that were originally designed for one purpose to be repurposed for another use. Another distinct feature of the SCA in contrast to other component technologies, such as EJB, Microsoft .NET and Spring, is that its container-specific dependencies are encapsulated in the implementation type, instead of being part of the component definitions as depicted in Fig. 8.7.

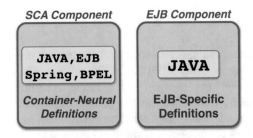

Fig. 8.7 Illustration of SCA vs. EJB component implementation

Defining Services

As described earlier, the SCA specification defines a *service* to enable a component's functionality to be exposed for external consumption through a number of communication protocols, such as SOAP and JMS. A *service* is an addressable interface to the component's implementation and is defined by a name and an interface. The name identifies the *service* and the *interface* defines the names, inputs and outputs of the operations provided by the service. The service consumer can be another SCA component or an external non-SCA client. Figure 8.8 shows an SCA component with one service. The service's *binding* method will specify the communication protocol by which the service can be invoked.

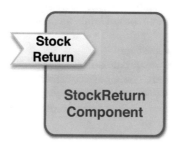

Fig. 8.8 Illustration of the StockReturn component with one service

Each binding has a binding type that identifies the communication technology used by it, such as Web Service or JMS. The code fragment in Listing 8.4 below shows the updated *component definition* for the StockReturnComponent that exposes a service, StockReturnService, accessed by Web service binding binding.ws. The <binding.ws> is the binding type, which specifies that the component is published as a SOAP Web service for external consumption. The URI attribute of the binding defines the WSDL endpoint as http://localhost: 9080/StockReturnService?wsdl. Bindings are discussed further in section "Defining Bindings for Services and References" in Sect. 8.3.2.

```
1  <composite name="stockreturn" ... >
2      <component name="StockReturnComponent">
3          <implementation.java
4              class="au.edu.unsw.soacourse.sca.
5                          components.StockReturnServiceImpl"/>
6          <service name="StockReturnService">
7              <binding.ws uri="http://localhost:9080/
8                          StockReturnService"/>
9          </service>
10     </component>
11 </composite>
```

Listing 8.4 Updated component definition for RateOfReturn component with a single service

Having configured the SCA component within the composite file, the next step is to build the *component implementation*. Listing 8.5 shows the concrete implementation for the component StockReturnComponent that is given by the Java class: au.edu.unsw.soacourse.sca.components.impl.Stock ReturnServiceImpl.

```
1  package soacourse.sca.components.impl;
2  import org.oasisopen.sca.annotation.Service;
3  ... ...
4  @Service(StockReturnService.class)
5  public class StockReturnServiceImpl
6                          implements StockReturnService {
7
8    public double computeROR(double currentStockPrice,
9        double previousStockPrice, ReturnTypes returnType) {
10
11     StockReturn stockReturn =
12       ReturnFactory.getReturnService(returnType);
13     return stockReturn.computeRateOfReturn(
14                        currentStockPrice,
15                        previousStockPrice);
16   }
17 }
```

Listing 8.5 Java component implement class

The *services* provided by a component are implemented by the component implementation. The details of how services are defined within a component implementation depend upon the component's implementation type. Components with implementation type as implementation.java make use of Java annotations within the Java class. For example, the annotation @Service identifies the services provided by the component. The annotation @Service also identifies one or more Java interfaces which represent the services provided by this component implementation. The component implementation StockReturnServiceImpl identifies a single service StockReturnService as seen in the code above. The code below in Listing 8.6 shows the Java interface definition for the service operations implemented by StockReturnServiceImpl.

```
1  import org.oasisopen.sca.annotation.Remotable;
2  import soacourse.model.components.ReturnTypes;
3
4  @Remotable
5  public interface StockReturnService {
6
7    public double computeRateOfReturn(
8                   double currentStockPrice,
9                   double previousStockPrice,
10                  ReturnTypes returnType);
11 }
```

Listing 8.6 Java component interface to define StockReturnService

The methods defined on this interface are exposed by the service for external consumption. In this example, the method `computeRateOfReturn` is exposed as a public operation. SCA supports *local* and *remotable* interfaces. A service with a local interface can be invoked by clients running within the same operating system process (local call). The annotation `@Remotable` on the interface denotes that the service is remotely accessible; that is, the service is accessible to clients running on an operating system different from that of the service (remote call).

As seen in the code in Listing 8.5, the component implementation class implements the Java interface `StockReturnService`. This is not strictly mandated by the SCA specification. If the implementation class does not implement the Java interface, SCA assumes that the implementation class implements all of the methods specified in the Java interface identified by the `@Service` annotation. If the component implementation Java class is not annotated with `@Service`, SCA assumes that the implementation class has services corresponding to all the implemented interfaces that are annotated with the `@Remotable` annotation.

A few points to consider about *remotable* interfaces...

- Method or operation overloading must not occur in a remotable interface. Overloading may occur in local interfaces.
- All data exchange, regardless of whether the client is local or remote, is performed using pass-by-value semantics.
- Pass-by-reference semantics for local clients of a service with a remotable interface can be enabled in Java, by using the `@AllowPassByReference` annotation.
- Method parameter types and return value types must be compatible with the marshalling technology used by the service binding.
- With bidirectional services, both interfaces must be either remotable or local. Local and remotable interfaces cannot be mixed.

Further note. SCA specifies that components which are implemented with *implementation.java* do not require the use of Java annotations such as the ones defined in the examples above. Instead, you can also use SCA's component definition type file to define the service as an alternative approach to defining a service. See next subsection for further details.

Previously, we have seen how the service element is embedded within the component definition. The SCA specification offers the flexibility to define the service outside the component definition as a direct child element to the composite. This is illustrated in Listing 8.7.

```
1  <composite name="stockreturn" ... >
2    <service name="StockReturnService"
3                         promote="StockReturnComponent">
```

```
4      <binding.ws
5           uri="http://localhost:8085/StockReturnService" />
6    </service>
7
8    <component name="StockReturnComponent">
9      <implementation.java
10             class="au.edu.unsw.soacourse.sca.components.
11                         impl.StockReturnServiceImpl"/>
12     </component>
13 </composite>
```

Listing 8.7 Service defined outside the component definition

The service element is defined as a direct child of the root node composite and is associated to the specific component implementation through the promote attribute within the service element. The functionality of the composite is identical whether the service is defined within the component or outside the component as a child element of the composite. We have thus seen how services are defined by components that have an implementation type of Java. Different implementation types have different ways of defining the services. For example, for components with an implementation type of BPEL (*implementation.bpel*), the BPEL process is introspected to find partner-links which are mapped to SCA services.

Interface Definitions in SCA

Every SCA service has an interface, as we have seen, that specifies the operations provided by the service and the input and output types of those operations. In SCA, different interface types can be used to define SCA interfaces. In our example previously (Listing 8.6), we have seen the use of a Java interface to define the service's interface. To recap, for this example, the SCA interface is defined by a Java interface whose fully qualified name is specified as au.edu.unsw.soacourse.sca.components.StockReturnService.

However, if a subset of the operations defined in the Java interface is to be exposed, in this case, a second Java interface can be defined which only lists the operations that are intended for the public. For example, if our Java interface had two operations, namely computeArithmeticReturn and computeLogReturn, and we decide that only one of the operations, computeLogReturn, is to be exposed, then we could define a second Java interface called StockReturnService2 that lists only the required operation; accordingly the *component definition* can be updated to reflect the use of this second interface as shown in Listing 8.8:

```
1 <component name="StockReturnComponent">
2      <implementation.java
3        class="au.edu.unsw.soacourse.sca.components.
4                       impl.StockReturnServiceImpl"/>
5      <service name="StockReturnService">
6          <interface.java
7               interface ="au.edu.unsw.soacourse.sca.
```

```
8                  components.StockReturnService2"/>
9             <binding.ws
10              uri="http://localhost:9080/StockReturnService"/>
11          </service>
12      </component>
13 </composite>
```

Listing 8.8 Component definition overriding the service interface

In the example above, the Java interface `StockReturnService2` (defined in the component definition) **overrides** the component implementation's service interfaces. The component definition cannot define additional services beyond those defined by the component implementation or remove services defined by the component implementation. If the component definition does not provide any configuration for the service (e.g. the interface) or does not define the service at all, these are determined by introspection from the component's implementation class as described before; and as the component implementation type is Java, this implies that the introspected interface type will be *interface.java*.

Another SCA interface type that is quite useful, particularly when the component implementation type is non-Java is the *WSDL interface* type. Listing 8.9 is an example of a component definition using a *WSDL interface* type, where an SCA interface is defined using a *WSDL 1.1 portType* named `StockReturnService`.

```
1 <composite name="stockreturn" ...>
2   <component name="StockReturnComponent">
3    <implementation.java
4     class="au.edu.unsw.soacourse.sca.
5                  components.impl.StockReturnImpl"/>
6     <service name="StockReturnService">
7      <interface.wsdl interface = "http://localhost/
8          #wsdl.interface(StockReturnService)"/>
9      <binding.ws
10         uri="http://localhost:9080/StockReturnService"/>
11     </service>
12    </component>
13 </composite>
```

Listing 8.9 Example of a component definition with a WSDL Interface

Defining Properties for Components

The SCA specification provides a convenient mechanism to facilitate the runtime configuration of components by defining *properties*. *Properties* provide a neat way to set environment-specific values or configure runtime behavior of the component without having to resort to using an external property file. More impressively, properties can be complex XML structures, which can be referenced via XPath[5] locations by the components using it.

---

[5]https://www.w3.org/TR/xpath/.

As with services and references, the way the properties are defined depends upon the implementation type. For Java implementations, the `@property` annotation is used to define an SCA property. To demonstrate how properties are injected into an SCA component, we will develop a currency converter component. Listing 8.10 shows the component definition for this new component, which defines two properties, `fromCurrency` and `toCurrency`.

```
1  <composite
2     xmlns="http://docs.oasis-open.org/ns/opencsa/sca/200912"
3     xmlns:tuscany="http://tuscany.apache.org/xmlns/sca/1.1"
4     targetNamespace="http://soacourse.scaexamples"
5     name="currencyconverter">
6
7     <component name="CurrencyConverterComponent">
8
9          <implementation.java
10            class="au.edu.unsw.soacourse.sca.
11                        components.CurrencyConverterImpl"/>
12
13         <property name="fromCurrency">AUD</property>
14         <property name="toCurrency">USD</property>
15
16     </component>
17  </composite>
```

Listing 8.10 Component that defines properties

The two properties, `fromCurrency` and `toCurrency`, are defined in the above example within the component. Alternatively, they can also be defined as *global* properties and referenced within the component using the `@source` attribute of the embedded property element as shown in Listing 8.11 below.

```
1  <composite
2     xmlns="http://docs.oasis-open.org/ns/opencsa/sca/200912"
3     name="currencyconverter" ... />
4
5     <property name="fromCurrency">AUD</property>
6     <property name="toCurrency">USD</property>
7
8     <component name="CurrencyConverterComponent">
9       <implementation.java
10        class="au.edu.unsw.soacourse.sca.
11                    components.CurrencyConverterImpl"/>
12        <property name="fromCurrency" source="$fromCurrency"/>
13        <property name="toCurrency" source="$toCurrency"/>
14     </component>
15  </composite>
```

Listing 8.11 Updated composite definition with global properties

Regardless of the approach used to define the properties within the composite file, the next step is to define the component interface and component implementation. Listing 8.12 illustrates the component interface `CurrencyConverter` and component implementation `CurrencyConverterImpl` for the currency converter component. Within the component implementation class, the injected properties are captured through the use of the Java annotation `@Property`. Two member variables, `fromCurrency` and `toCurrency`, are defined within the implementation class and annotated with the `@Property` annotation. When the Tuscany runtime creates an instance of `CurrencyConverterImpl`, the property values are injected into these fields.

```
1  package au.edu.unsw.soacourse.sca.components;
2
3  public interface CurrencyConverter {
4      float convertCurrency(Float amount);
5  }
6
7  package au.edu.unsw.soacourse.sca.components;
8  import org.oasisopen.sca.annotation.Property;
9
10 public class CurrencyConverterImpl
11                     implements CurrencyConverter {
12
13   @Property String fromCurrency;
14   @Property String toCurrency;
15
16   public float convertCurrency(float amount) {
17     float rate = getRate(fromCurrency,toCurrency);
18     return amount * rate;
19   }
20
21   public float getRate(String fromCurrency,
22                        String toCurrency) {
23     // ... code to get the exchange rate goes here
24     return rate;
25   }
26 }
```

Listing 8.12 Component interface and associated implementation

In the above example, if properties are injected into member variables, they must be defined with a *public* or *protected* access modifier. If a non-private access modifier is used, then properties can be injected using *setter* methods, in the more traditional JavaBean style. Properties can also be injected into constructor parameters. The different styles of property injection are shown in Table 8.2 below.

Table 8.2 Different styles of property injection

Field injection	//A *public* or *protected field*
	@property
	protected float brokerFee;
Injection through setter methods	//A *public* or *protected field*
	@property
	public void setBrokerFee(float fee){
	this.brokerFee = brokerFee;
	. . .
	}
Injection through constructor	//A parameter on the class constructor
	@Constructor({"brokerFee",...})
	public BuyStockImpl(
	@Property float brokerFee, ...){
	. . .
	}

Using Complex Types for Properties. We have seen how scalar string values can be specified in the contents of the property element in the component definition. Properties can also use more complex data structures that are defined using an XML schema complex type. Listing 8.13 shows an example of an XML schema global element representing a set of credentials.

```
1  <schema xmlns="http://www.w3.org/2001/XMLSchema"
2       targetNamespace="http://soacourse/scaexamples"
3       elementFormDefault="qualified">
4  <element name="credentials">
5    <complexType>
6      <sequence>
7      <element name="username" type="string" />
8      <element name="password" type="string" />
9      </sequence>
10    </complexType>
11  </element>
12  </schema>
```

Listing 8.13 XML schema definition for an SCA property

Within the component implementation class, the type Credentials can be used to specify the type of the property as shown in Listing 8.14. First, a Java class Credentials is generated from the XML schema using an appropriate JAXB[6] binding implementation, and this is then used to define the type of the property in the component implementation.

---

[6]https://jaxb.java.net/.

```
 1 package au.edu.unsw.soacourse.sca.components;
 2 import org.oasisopen.sca.annotation.Property;
 3 import soacourse.model.domain.Credentials;
 4     // Generated JAXB Implementation
 5
 6 public class CurrencyConverterImpl implements CurrencyConverter {
 7     ...
 8         @Property Credentials credentials;
 9     ...
10 }
```

Listing 8.14 Generated JAXB implementation imported into the component implementation class

In the following, we show the component definition of the currency converter component with a configured value for the credentials property, as illustrated in Listing 8.15.

```
 1 <composite
 2    xmlns="http://docs.oasis-open.org/ns/opencsa/sca/200912"
 3    xmlns:tuscany="http://tuscany.apache.org/xmlns/sca/1.1"
 4    name="currencyconverter"
 5    xmlns:t="http://soacourse/scaexamples"
 6        targetNamespace="http://soacourse.scaexamples">
 7
 8    <component name="CurrencyConverterComponent">
 9        <implementation.java .....
10
11        <property name="credentials" element="t:credentials">
12            <t:credentials xmlns="">
13                <t:username>tom</t:username>
14                <t:password>jones</t:password>
15            </t:credentials>
16        </property>
17
18    </component>
19 </composite>
```

Listing 8.15 Component definition with configured credentials property

In the above example, we have shown how property values can be specified within component definitions using XML. It is also possible to set the value of the property from the contents of a file. The full scope of properties is described in the SCA Assembly Model specification.[7]

---

[7]http://docs.oasis-open.org/opencsa/sca-assembly/sca-assembly-spec/v1.2/sca-assembly-spec-v1.2.html.

Defining References

Just as a component can provide services, it might also need to use other services. The dependent services are identified by defining *references*. The SCA *reference* will insert the dependent class instance into the implementation class using a form of *dependency injection*, an approach that was popularized by Spring with its innovative *inversion of control* features, similarly to how *properties* are used to insert static data into an implementation class. To understand references, we build a hypothetical example, where we require the current price of a stock quoted in the local currency. For this, we will create a new SCA component `StockQuoteComponent` that uses the *Yahoo Finance API* to derive the current stock price for a quote, and use the `CurrencyConverter` component that we built in the last section (Listing 8.12) to return the price in the local currency (see Fig. 8.9). The component definition for this `StockQuoteComponent` is shown below in Listing 8.16.

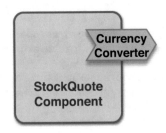

Fig. 8.9   Illustration of the `StockQuoteComponent` with one reference

```
1  <composite ...>
2
3  <component name="StockQuoteComponent">
4    <implementation.java
5      class="au.edu.unsw.soacourse.sca.components.
6                        impl.StockQuoteImpl"/>
7      <reference name="currencyConverter"
8                        <! Injects Reference >
9              target="CurrencyConverterComponent"/>
10                       <! Reference Component >
11 </component>
12
13 <component name="CurrencyConverterComponent">
14    <implementation.java
15      class="au.edu.unsw.soacourse.sca.components.
16                        impl.CurrencyConverterImpl"/>
17        <property name="fromCurrency" source="$fromCurrency"/>
18        <property name="toCurrency" source="$toCurrency"/>
19 </component>
20
21 </composite>
```

Listing 8.16   `StockQuoteComponent` specifying one reference

The component definition above illustrates how the component implementation class, StockQuoteImpl, defines an associated dependency through the child *reference* element, currencyConverter. Listing 8.17 shows how the *references* are injected into the implementation class. The details of how the *references* are injected into the component depend upon the component's implementation type. For Java implementation types, similarly to *services*, Java annotations are used to define the references. The @Reference annotation is used to inject the dependencies into the component implementation as shown below.

```
1 public class StockQuoteImpl implements StockQuote {
2    @Reference
3    protected CurrencyConverter currencyConverter;
4    @Override
5    public double getStockQuote(String stockSymbol) {
6              // ... code to getStockQuote
7          return currencyConverter.convertCurrency(stockPrice);
8       }
9 }
```

Listing 8.17 Component implementation with injected reference

The dependency is defined in the class through the field currencyConverter, which is annotated with @Reference. The name of the reference defaults to the name of this field. This default name can be overridden by specifying a name attribute to the @Reference annotation. When an SCA runtime environment such as *Apache Tuscany* instantiates the implementation class CurrencyConverter, it injects a proxy for the dependency class CurrencyConverter into the member variable. The injected proxy implements the same interface as the service that it calls. Within the implementation class, the proxy could be invoked as shown in the code below to invoke the operations on the dependent service:

```
currencyConverter.convertCurrency(...);
```

Similarly to properties, component implementation can define references in a number of ways. In the example above, the reference is injected using fields. References can also be injected into the Java implementation class using construction parameters or setter methods. The following table shows the different ways a reference can be injected into the implementation class (Table 8.3).

Table 8.3 Methods for defining references within a component implementation

Field injection	Reference
	protected currencyConverter
	currencyConverter;
Injection through setter methods	Reference
	public void setCurrencyConverter
	(CurrencyConverter converter){
	this.currencyConverter = converter;
	...
	}

Injection through constructor	```public CurrencyConverterImpl`` ``(@Reference(name="currencyConverter")`` ``CurrencyConverter converter) {`` ``this.currencyConverter = converter;`` ``...`` ``}```

So far, we have described how an SCA component can define services, references and properties. Next, we will show how to use SCA *component definitions* to configure implementations in different ways.

SCA Component – A Configured Implementation

An SCA component as defined within a composite by a *component definition* is a *configured* SCA implementation. What this means is that the same component implementation can be configured in various ways in different components, allowing the same component implementation to be reused – thus providing a high degree of flexibility and customizability. The component *services*, the *references* to other services, and the *properties* constitute the *configurable* aspects of an implementation. These elements are collectively described as the *component type* of the implementation and are configured within the component definition. At runtime, an SCA component instance is a *configured instance*, which is done by setting values for the properties and promoting components to services and wiring components to references. An example is provided at Listing 8.18, showing the definition of two components. In this example, a user may want to gather raw *trades* and *quotes* from Yahoo! Finance. They may want to compute both *daily* and *monthly* time series, where the raw stock data is aggregated over intervals of 24 hours and one month respectively for the requested time period.

```
1  <composite name="finance" ... >
2
3    <!- Component Definitions >
4    <component name="DailyTimeSeriesComponent">
5      <implementation.java class="com.sca.components.
6         impl.TimeSericesServiceImpl"/>
7        <property name="interval_unit"> hour </property>
8        <property name="interval_period"> 24 </property>
9    </component>
10
11   <component name="MonthlyTimeSeriesComponent">
12     <implementation.java class="com.sca.components.
13        impl.TimeSericesServiceImpl"/>
```

```
14        <property name="interval_unit"> month </property>
15        <property name="interval_period"> 1 </property>
16    </component>
17
18 </composite>
```

Listing 8.18 SCA components for *Daily* and *Monthly* time series

In this case, two configured components would be generated: namely this is the DailyTimeSeriesComponent and MonthlyTimeSeriesComponent – corresponding to the two definitions as shown. Each component would also contain the non-configurable business logic, in this example represented by the Java class com.sca.components.impl.TimeSeriesImpl. However, this same time series implementation can be configured to produce a component for both the *daily* and *monthly* time series, by *configuring* each differently (e.g. setting different values for the properties interval_unit and interval_period). It should also be noted that the *implementation type* (section "SCA Component Definition" in Sect. 8.3.2) of a component is different from the *component type*. While the former defines the technology with which the component is implemented, the latter shapes the behavior of the component as specified by its *services*, *references* and *properties*.

Two different approaches are available in SCA for discovering or configuring the component type of an implementation. SCA Java annotations can be used to configure the component type when the implementation type is Java. These annotations are metadata used to configure dependencies at runtime, such as *properties* and *references*. If the option for annotations is either not available (e.g. non-Java languages) or not desirable (as annotations are defined inside the code and constrain the runtime configurability), then a separate **component type file** is defined using the convention <component-implementation-class>.componentType. The StockQuoteImpl component in the previous example (Listing 8.17) used the @Property and @Reference annotations to define the configurable aspects of the implementation. Instead, the component implementation class can be created without the use of annotations as described in Listing 8.19 and a component type file used in lieu of the annotations as shown in Listing 8.20.

```
1 public class StockQuoteImpl implements StockQuote {
2     @Override
3     public double getStockQuote(String stockSymbol) {
4         // ... code to getStockQuote
5         return currencyConverter.convertCurrency(stockPrice);
6     }
7 }
```

Listing 8.19 StockQuoteImpl defined without Java annotations

```
1 <componentType xmlns=http://www.osoa.org/xmlns/sca/1.0
2                 xmlns:xsd="http://www.w3.org/2001/XMLSchema">
3
4     <service name="StockQuoteService">
```

```
5          <interface.java=
6            interface="au.edu.unsw.soacourse.
7                         sca.components.StockQuote"/>
8     </service>
9
10      <reference name="currencyConverter"
11        <interface.java=
12            interface="au.edu.unsw.soacourse.sca.
13                        components.CurrencyConverter"/>
14     </reference>
15
16      <property name="fromCurrency" source="$fromCurrency"/>
17      <property name="toCurrency" source="$toCurrency"/>
18 </componentType>
```

Listing 8.20   A *component-type* file used instead of the annotations

As can be seen, using a component type file allows you to declaratively define your configuration in a way that appears more flexible – though arguably less convenient than using annotations.

Defining Bindings for Services and References

As described earlier, the SCA *binding* is a mechanism by which a component service or reference can be accessed using an appropriate transport mechanism. Binding is declared for an SCA service or reference within the composite file. SCA bindings can be added to a composite application on either a component service or a composite service element. Examples of both these approaches are specified below in Listings 8.21 and 8.22.

```
1 <?xml version="1.0" encoding="UTF-8" standalone="no"?>
2 <composite xmlns=...>
3   <component name="StockReturnComponent">
4     <implementation.java
5        class="au.edu.unsw.soacourse.sca.
6                    components.impl.StockReturnImpl"/>
7
8     <service name="StockReturnService"
9        <interface.java
10            interface="au.edu.unsw.soacourse.
11                        sca.components.StockReturn"/>
12        <binding.ws uri="http://localhost:8085/
13                        StockReturnService"/>
14     </service>
15
16    </component>
17 </composite>
```

Listing 8.21   Using SCA bindings on a *Component* service element

```
1  <?xml version="1.0" encoding="UTF-8" standalone="no"?>
2  <composite name= ?stockreturn? xmlns=?...>
3      <!-- This is a composite service element that
4          promotes an existing service and declares
5          a binding for the service in question. -->
6
7      <service name="StockReturnService"
8              promote="StockReturnComponent/StockService">
9          <binding.ws requires="SOAP.1\_2"
10             uri="http://localhost:8080/
11                     StockReturnService"/>
12     </service>
13
14     <component name="StockReturnComponent">
15         <implementation.java
16             class="au.edu.unsw.soacourse.sca.
17                     components.impl.StockReturnImpl"/>
18         <service name="StockReturnService">
19             <interface.java
20                 interface="au.edu.unsw.soacourse.
21                     sca.components.StockReturn"/>
22         </service>
23     </component>
24 </composite>
```

Listing 8.22 Using SCA bindings on a *Composite* service element

> **Note:** The current version of Apache Tuscany (2.0.1) fails to honour binding settings in a `<service>` element that is external to the `<component>` element of the component that is seeks to expose. Consequently, an external service is sometimes not exposed at all. This has been raised as an issue in the Tuscany mailing list. Thus the example presented in Listing 8.22 may not work, albeit it is nonetheless presented here for the purpose of theoretical discussion on the preferred way of doing things.

Practical Exercise VI

8.4   Lab Exercise 06: SCA

Finally, we provide two exercises: The first looks at building a simple Hello World SCA composite to enable students to get started with SCA. The second provides a complete tutorial to build the Stock Application that was discussed earlier. Both these examples are implemented using Apache Tuscany, build 2.0.1.

8.4.1 Activity 1: Building the First SCA Composite – Hello World Service

In this tutorial, we will build a simple Hello World service that greets a person and an accompanying client to demonstrate the basics of SCA.

Setting Up the Development Environment

This lab assumes you have completed the setup necessary to carry out this exercise from the instructions provided earlier in the chapter. Additionally, we use soapUI (http://www.soapui.org), which is the same tool used in our earlier labs. These examples have been tested on Eclipse Luna, using Apache Tuscany 2.0.1.

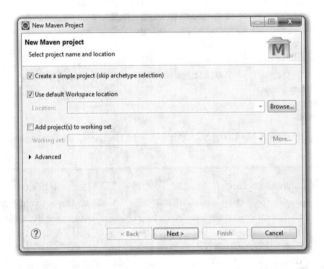

Fig. 8.10 New SCA project

Setting Up an SCA Project

1. Open Eclipse. Create a new Maven project by choosing File → New → Maven Project.
2. Configure the new project by not using any archetype, as shown in the picture below (Fig. 8.10).
3. Enter the group ID and artifact ID of the project. The SCA examples in this chapter used the group ID com.edu.unsw.soacourse.scaexamples. The artifact ID is specific to each project. Here the artifact ID is called scaHelloWorld. Click the Finish button to complete creating the Maven project (Fig. 8.11).

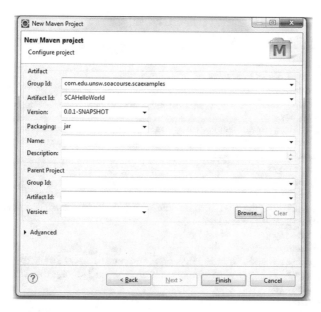

Fig. 8.11 New SCA project – Maven details

4. Ensure that the Java compiler compliance level is at least 1.6. The compliance level is set as follows: Right click on the project name and select Properties (we use Java 1.7). Select Java Compiler from the left-hand-side menu and choose 1.7 as the Compiler Compliance level. Next, make sure that the appropriate JRE system library is included on the project class path. If your compiler compliance level is 1.7, use JRE 7 library and so on. Click OK to complete the configuration.

5. (e) The next step is to declare the dependencies of this project and this is done using the pom.xml file. The pom.xml file declared with the Apache Tuscany 2.0.1M dependencies looks like this (Listing 8.23):

```
1  <project xmlns="http://maven.apache.org/POM/4.0.0"
2  xmlns:xsi="http://www.w3.org/2001/XMLSchema-instance"
3  xsi:schemaLocation="http://maven.apache.org/POM/4.0.0
4  http://maven.apache.org/xsd/maven-4.0.0.xsd">
5    <modelVersion>4.0.0</modelVersion>
6    <groupId>com.edu.unsw.soacourse.scaexamples</groupId>
7    <artifactId>SCAHelloWorld</artifactId>
8    <version>0.0.1-SNAPSHOT</version>
9    <repositories>
10     <repository>
11       <id>java.net2</id>
12       <name>java.net Maven 2.x Repository</name>
13       <url>http://download.java.net/maven/2</url>
14     </repository>
15   </repositories>
16
17 <dependencies>
18 <!--  module jars for modules directory  -->
```

```
19 <dependency>
20 <groupId>org.apache.tuscany.sca</groupId>
21 <artifactId>tuscany-feature-all</artifactId>
22 <type>pom</type>
23 <version>2.0.1</version>
24 </dependency>
25 <!-- aggregation jars for lib directory -->
26 <dependency>
27 <groupId>org.apache.tuscany.sca.aggregation</groupId>
28 <artifactId>tuscany-base-runtime-aggregation</artifactId>
29 <version>2.0.1</version>
30 </dependency>
31 <dependency>
32 <groupId>org.apache.tuscany.sca.aggregation</groupId>
33 <artifactId>tuscany-binding-rmi-runtime-aggregation</artifactId>
34 <version>2.0.1</version>
35 </dependency>
36 <dependency>
37 <groupId>org.apache.tuscany.sca.aggregation</groupId>
38 <artifactId>tuscany-binding-ws-runtime-axis2-aggregation
39 </artifactId>
40 <version>2.0.1</version>
41 </dependency>
42 </dependencies>
43 </project>
```

Listing 8.23   pom.xml for an SCA project

Building the Hello World Service

In this section, we build the Hello World service to demonstrate the basics of SCA using Apache Tuscany. Detailed explanations of the SCA concepts are provided following the example.

(1) Defining the Service Interface

The service interface defines what operations are available to clients invoking the service. Under the folder src/main/java, create a Java package and name it unsw.soacourse.sca.components. Under this package, create a new Java interface called HelloWorldService. The listing below shows the code for this service (Listing 8.24).

```
1 package com.sca.components;
2 import org.oasisopen.sca.annotation.Remotable;
3 @Remotable
4 public interface HelloWorldService
5 {
6   /**
7    * Extends a greeting to the person with the supplied name.
8    * The greeting will contain the date and time when the greeting
9    *    was issued.
10   *
11   * @param name Name of person to greet.
12   * @return Greeting.
13   */
14 String sayHello(final String name);
15 }
```

Listing 8.24 HelloWorld service interface

(2) Defining the Service Implementation

An implementation is provided for the service defined in the previous step through the service implementation class. Under the folder src/main/java/ create a Java package called unsw.soacourse.sca.components.impl. Under this package, create a new Java class called HelloWorldServiceImpl. The listing below shows the code for this class.

```
1 package soacourse.sca.components.impl;
2 import java.util.Date;
3 import org.oasisopen.sca.annotation.Service;
4 import soacourse.sca.components.HelloWorldService;
5 /**
6  * This class provides the implementation of the
7    Hello World service.
8  *
9  * @see HelloWorldService
10 */
11 @Service(HelloWorldService.class)
12 public class HelloWorldServiceImpl implements HelloWorldService {
13
14     public String sayHello(String name) {
15         Date currentDate = new Date();
16         return "Hello " + name + ", Today is: " + currentDate;
17     }
18 }
```

Listing 8.25 Service implementation for HelloWorldService

(3) Configure the SCA Composite

An SCA composite is a container used to assemble SCA artifacts into logical group-ings of components and is defined as an XML file with a .composite extension. In this example, the SCA composite has a single service, the Hello World service.

Under the folder src/main/resources, create a new XML file and name it helloworld.composite, and paste the contents below into the file. This is the assembly definition for the Hello World composite application.

```
1  <?xml version="1.0" encoding="UTF-8" standalone="no"?>
2  <composite
        xmlns="http://docs.oasis-open.org/ns/opencsa/sca/200912"
3       xmlns:tuscany="http://tuscany.apache.org/xmlns/sca/1.1"
4       name="helloworld"
5       targetNamespace="http://soacourse.scaexamples">
6    <component name="HelloWorldComponent">
7      <implementation.java
8         class=
9            "soacourse.sca.components.impl.HelloWorldServiceImpl"/>
10     <service name="HelloWorldService">
11       <binding.ws uri="http://localhost:9084/HelloWorld"/>
12     </service>
13   </component>
14 </composite>
```

Listing 8.26 SCA composite for the Hello World application

(4) Creating the SCA Contributions Metadata Document

In our SCA application, in order for the SCA runtime to find our Hello World composite, we create an SCA contribution metadata document that is used to define the runnable components of the SCA application, imported and exported definitions.

In our project, create a new folder META-INF under src/main/resources and create a new file called sca-contribution.xml under this folder, and populate the file with the xml listing shown below.

```
1  <?xml version="1.0" encoding="UTF-8"?>
2  <!-- SCA Contribution Metadata document -->
3  <contribution
4      xmlns="http://docs.oasis-open.org/ns/opencsa/sca/200912"
5      xmlns:sample="http://soacourse.scaexamples">
6      <deployable composite="sample:helloworld" />
7  </contribution>
```

Listing 8.27 SCA contributions meta data document for Hello World service

The deployable element identifies the composite being deployed by referencing the composite name, which is defined in the composite assembly. The composite name is namespace-aware, so the namespace sample must match the one used in the composite file. With the above steps completed, the project should look like this in the Eclipse Package browser (Fig. 8.12):

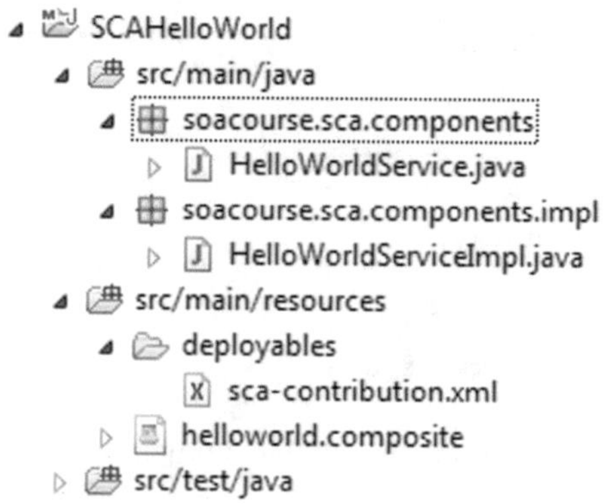

Fig. 8.12   Project structure in Eclipse

Creating the Client Class

We build a client class to start the SCA node containing the `Hello World` service and invoking the service (Figs. 8.13 and 8.14).

- Under the folder `src/main/java`, create a Java new package and name it `soacourse.sca.client`.
- In this package, create a Java class named `HelloWorldClient` and populate the class with the code shown in the listing below.

```
1  package soacourse.sca.client;
2
3  import soacourse.sca.components.HelloWorldService;
4  import org.apache.tuscany.sca.node.Node;
5  import org.apache.tuscany.sca.node.NodeFactory;
6
7  /**
8   * This class creates and starts the SCA node containing the
9   * Hello World service, retrieves the service and invokes it.
10  */
11 public class HelloWorldClient {
12
13    public static void main(String[] args) throws Exception
14    {
15      System.out.println("Starting ...");
16      Node node = NodeFactory.newInstance().createNode();
```

```
17      node.start();
18
19      HelloWorldService helloService =
20          node.getService(HelloWorldService.class,
21          "HelloWorldComponent");
22
23      System.out.println(helloService.sayHello("sam"));
24
25      System.in.read();
26      System.out.println("Stopping ...");
27      node.stop();
28      System.out.println();
29   }
30 }
```

Listing 8.28   Client class

With the client class in place, the complete project should look like this in the Eclipse Package browser:

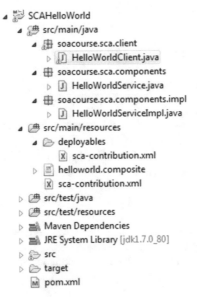

Fig. 8.13   Project structure (with the client class)

Running the Example

To run the example, right click on the `HelloWorldClient` class and choose Run As → Java Application. The following output is produced on the console output.

```
Starting ....
Aug 31, 2015 3:58:14 PM org.apache.tuscany.sca.node.impl.NodeImpl start
INFO: Starting node: http://tuscany.apache.org/sca/1.1/nodes/default0 domain: default
Aug 31, 2015 3:58:14 PM org.apache.tuscany.sca.node.impl.NodeFactoryImpl loadContributions
INFO: Loading contribution: file: IC: /source/eclipse/test_wkspace/SCAilelloWorld/target/classes/
Aug 31, 2015 3:58:16 PM org.mortbay.log.Slf4jLog info
INFO: Logging to org.slf4j.implADK14LoggerAdapter(org.mortbay.log) via org.mortbay.log.Slf4jLog
Aug 31, 2015 3:58:16 PM org.apache.tuscany.sca.http.jetty.Jettylogger info
INFO: jetty-6.1.26
Aug 31, 2015 3:58:16 PM org.apache.tuscany.sca.http.jetty.Jettylogger info
INFO: Started SelectChannelConnector@localhost:9080
Aug 31, 2015 3:58:16 PM org.apache.tuscany.sca.http.jetty.JettyServer addServletMapping
INFO: Added Servlet mapping: http://localhost:9080/HelloWorld
Aug 31, 2015 3:58:16 PM org.apache.tuscany.sca.core.assembly.impl.DomainRegistryImpl addEndpoint
INFO: Add endpoint - binding.ws - http://localhost:9080/HelloWorld
Calling HelloworldComponent.sayHello()
Hello sam, Today is: Mon Aug 31 15:58:17 AEST 2015
```

Fig. 8.14 Console output

8.4.2   Activity 2: Building the Stock Application

In this exercise, we will build the Tuscany Stock Application. A diagram showing the Tuscany Stock Composite is shown below (Fig. 8.15).

From the diagram above we may learn the following:

- There is a single composite called finance composite (i.e. `finance. composite`).
- The finance composite has the following components: Currency Converter, Stock Quote, Daily Market Data, Stock Return, Abnormal Return and Daily Abnormal Return.
- The Daily Abnormal component computes the daily abnormal return and makes use of the services of the Daily Market Data, Stock Return and Abnormal Return components.
- The Daily Abnormal component publishes a service that is promoted to become a service offered by the composite
- The Daily Market Data component is used to download data using the Yahoo Finance API.
- The Currency Converter component calculates real-time foreign exchange rates.
- The Stock Quote component uses the service of the Currency Converter component to report the stock quote in the requested currency. The Stock Quote component publishes a service that is promoted to become a service offered by the composite.
- The Stock Return component computes two types of stock returns: arithmetic stock and logarithmic stock returns.

In preparation for this example, create a new Maven project `TuscanyStockApp` with the Maven artifact ID being the same as the project name as described in the previous exercise section.

Creating SCA Components

(1) Implementing the Stock Quote Service

First, we create the `CurrencyConverter` and `StockQuote` components with a Java implementation and by making use of Java annotations. The currency converter component exposes a service only available to other services in the same composite, which are accessed using an *SCA Binding*. The stock quote component makes use of the currency converter component to return the stock price in the nominated currency. The stock quote component publishes a service which is promoted as a service on the composite, accessed using a *Web service binding*. The component service interface and corresponding implementations for the two components are shown below. The service's interface is created under the directory `src/main/java` in the package `au.edu.unsw.soacourse.sca.components`, and service implementations are under `au.edu.unsw.soacourse.sca.components.impl`.

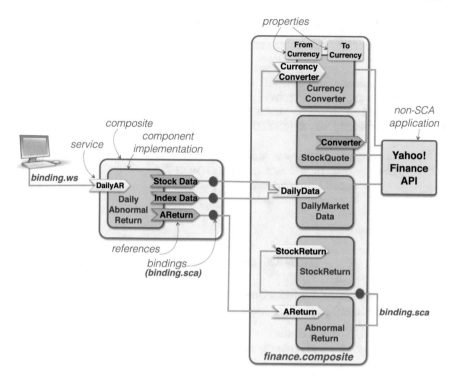

Fig. 8.15 Stock application (in Tuscany)

```
1  public interface CurrencyConverter {
2      double convertCurrency(double stkreturn);
3      void printCredentials();
4  }
```

Listing 8.29 Currency converter service interface

```
1  @Service(CurrencyConverter.class)
2  public class CurrencyConverterImpl implements CurrencyConverter {
3
4    @Property String fromCurrency;
5    @Property String toCurrency;
6
7    public double convertCurrency(double amount) {
8      double rate = getRate(fromCurrency,toCurrency);
9      return amount * rate;
10   }
11
12   public double getRate(String fromCurrency, String toCurrency) {
13   String uri = "http://quote.yahoo.com/d/quotes.csv?s="
14      + fromCurrency + toCurrency + "=X&f=l1&e=.csv";
15   HttpClient httpClient = new HttpClient();
```

```
16    HttpMethod getMethod = new GetMethod(uri);
17    double rate = 0;
18    try
19    {
20        int response = httpClient.executeMethod(getMethod);
21        if (response != 200) {
22          String error = "HTTP problem, httpcode: " + response;
23          // Build error-handling to log error.
24        }
25        String responseText = getMethod.getResponseBodyAsString();
26        rate = Double.valueOf(responseText);
27            } catch (IOException e) {
28              e.printStackTrace();
29            }
30    return rate;     }
31 }
```

Listing 8.30 Currency converter service implementation

Next, we implement the StockQuote component in a similar manner. The component service interface and Java implementation are shown below.

```
1 @Service(StockQuote.class)
2 public class StockQuoteImpl implements StockQuote {
3
4    @Reference
5    protected CurrencyConverter currencyConverter;
6
7    @Override
8    public double getStockQuote(String stockSymbol) {
9        String uri = "http://finance.yahoo.com/d/
10       quotes.csv?s=AAPL&f=s1l1d1t1";
11     HttpClient httpClient = new HttpClient();
12     HttpMethod getMethod = new GetMethod(uri);
13     double stockPrice = 0;
14     try {
15       int response = httpClient.executeMethod(getMethod);
16         if (response == 200) {
17         String responseText =
18               getMethod.getResponseBodyAsString();
19         String[] stockInfo = responseText.split(",");
20         stockPrice=Double.valueOf(stockInfo[1]);
21       }
22     }
23     catch(Exception e){
24             e.printStackTrace();
25     }
26
```

```
27        return currencyConverter.convertCurrency(stockPrice);
28     }
29  }
```

Listing 8.31 Stock quote service implementation

In order to declare the above components in the composite, first create a composite file, `finance.composite`, under the `src/main/resource` directory. Paste the following contents into that file:

```
1  <?xml version="1.0" encoding="UTF-8" standalone="no"?>
2  <composite
3      xmlns="http://docs.oasis-open.org/ns/opencsa/sca/200912"
4      xmlns:tuscany="http://tuscany.apache.org/xmlns/sca/1.1"
5      name="finance"
6      targetNamespace="http://au.edu.unsw.soacourse.scaexamples">
7
8      <property name="fromCurrency">AUD</property>
9      <property name="toCurrency">USD</property>
10
11     <component name="StockQuoteComponent">
12     <implementation.java
13             class= "au.edu.unsw.soacourse.sca.
14             components.impl.StockQuoteImpl"/>
15     <reference name="currencyConverter"
16             target=" CurrencyConverterComponent"/>
17     <service name="StockQuote">
18             <interface.java
19                     interface= "au.edu.unsw.soacourse.
20                         sca.components.StockQuote"/>
21             <binding.ws uri="http://localhost:8085/
22                         StockQuoteService"/>
23     </service>
24     </component>
25
26     <component name="CurrencyConverterComponent">
27         <implementation.java
28             class= "au.edu.unsw.soacourse.sca.components.
29                 impl.CurrencyConverterImpl"/>
30         <property name="fromCurrency" source="$fromCurrency"/>
31         <property name="toCurrency" source="$toCurrency"/>
32     </component>
33  </composite>
```

Listing 8.32 Declaring the components in the finance composite file

(2) Implementing the Abnormal Return Service

Several components are required for the implementation of this service. The steps required to implement this service along with some background information on key financial concepts are presented below:

Background Information:

There are several mathematical techniques to compute the abnormal return of an asset. Our examples employ the Market Adjusted Returns benchmark model, where the abnormal return U_j of an asset j is determined by computing the difference between its *actual return*, R_j, and its *expected return*, E_j.

$$U_j = A_j - E_j \tag{8.1}$$

Abnormal returns are triggered by "events" such as corporate actions or global news. Let us first define the notion of a return. A return is a measure of the performance of an investment. In order to calculate the rate of return, we will use the following variables:

- P_i: the initial value of an investment
- P_f: the final value of an investment

Two principle ways of calculation are used.

- Arithmetic return:

$$\text{Arithmetic return} = \frac{p_f - p_i}{p_i} \tag{8.2}$$

This return has the following characteristics:

– Rate of return $= +1.00 = +100\%$ when the final value is twice than the initial one
– Rate of return > 0 when this is a profitable investment
– Rate of return < 0 when the investment is not payable
– Rate of return $= -1.00 = -100\%$ when the investment is not retrievable

- Logarithmic return:

$$\text{Logarithmic return} = \ln(p_f/p_i) \tag{8.3}$$

This return has the following characteristics:

– Rate of return > 0 means a profit
– Rate of return < 0 means a loss
– The investment is doubled when rate of return $= \ln(2) = 69.3\%$
– The investment is lost when rate of return $\rightarrow -\infty$

The logarithmic return and the arithmetic return are not equal, but approximately the same for small returns. Now, either of the above techniques can be used to compute the expected and actual return of a stock, which are required in order to determine the abnormal return of an asset. Expected return for any asset in a period is equal to the expected market return for the same period.

Workflow to Compute the Daily Abnormal Return:

The workflow to compute the daily abnormal return and the associated SCA components are described below:

1. Download the "daily data" for a particular asset for a specific period.
2. Download the "market data" for an appropriate index such as the S&P 500 or AORD index for the same period. (This data is required to compute the expected return of an asset. The expected return for an asset is equal to the expected market return for the same period.) The download tasks are carried out by the DailyMarketData component, which accesses the Yahoo Finance API to import the relevant data.
3. Compute the actual return and expected return of the asset using the downloaded "daily data" and "index data" respectively. Computation of both the returns is accomplished by the StockReturn component, which will be used to compute both returns. This component will be configured with an SCA property to specify the type of return that is required to be computed, an arithmetic return or logarithmic return.
4. Compute the daily abnormal return by calculating the difference between the actual return and expected return. This task is performed by the third component AbnormalReturn.
5. Finally, a fourth component, DailyAbnormalReturn, captures the above workflow and makes use of the components DailyMarketData, StockReturn and DailyAbnormalReturn to compute the daily abnormal return for an asset for a defined period.

Implementing the Components:

Daily Market Data component First, we define the DailyMarketData component to import daily data for any asset. The corresponding service interface and implementation, along with the addition to the composite file to define the new component, are shown below:

```
1 @Remotable
2 public interface DailyMarketData {
3
4    public InputStream getDailyData(String stockSymbol,
5          DateRange startDate,   DateRange endData);
6 }
```

Listing 8.33 Component interface for DailyMarketData

```
1  @Service(DailyMarketData.class)
2  public class DailyMarketDataImpl implements DailyMarketData {
3    private static final String NEW_LINE_SEPARATOR = "\n";
4
5    @Override
6    public InputStream getDailyData(String stockSymbol,
7              DateRange startDate,     DateRange endDate) {
8
9    String uri = buildUrl(stockSymbol, startDate, endDate);
10
11   System.out.println(uri);
12   InputStream is = null;
13   try {
14      is = invokeUri(uri);
15   } catch (IOException e) {
16       e.printStackTrace();
17   }
18   return is;
19
20 }
21 // private helper classes
22 private InputStream invokeUri(String uri) throws IOException {
23
24   HttpClient httpClient = new HttpClient();
25   HttpMethod getMethod = new GetMethod(uri);
26
27   InputStream stream = null;
28       int response = httpClient.executeMethod(getMethod);
29   System.out.println(response);
30   if (response == 200) {
31          stream = getMethod.getResponseBodyAsStream();
32       }
33   return stream;
34 }
35 private String buildUri(String stockSymbol,
36                      DateRange startDate, DateRange endDate)
37 {
38   StringBuffer uri = new
39   StringBuffer("http://ichart.finance.yahoo.com/table.csv?s=");
40   uri.append(stockSymbol);
41   uri.append("&a="+startDate.getMonth());
42   uri.append("&b="+startDate.getDay());
43   uri.append("&c="+startDate.getYear());
44   uri.append("&d="+endDate.getMonth());
45   uri.append("&e="+endDate.getDay());
46   uri.append("&f="+endDate.getYear());
47   uri.append("&g=d");
48
49   return new String(uri);
```

```
50   }
51 }
```

Listing 8.34 Component implementation for daily market data

```
1 <?xml version="1.0" encoding="UTF-8" standalone="no"?>
2 <composite name="finance"
3
      xmlns="http://docs.oasis-open.org/ns/opencsa/sca/200912"
4           xmlns:t="http://soacourse/scaexamples"
5        xmlns:tuscany="http://tuscany.apache.org/xmlns/sca/1.1"
6            targetNamespace="http://soacourse.scaexamples">
7
8 ... snip ...
9 <component name="DailyMarketDataComponent">
10   <implementation.java class=
11 "au.edu.unsw.soacourse.sca.components.impl.DailyMarketDataImpl"/>
12 </component>
13 </composite>
```

Listing 8.35 Composite file updated to include the DailyMarketData component

Stock Return Component

Next, we define the StockReturn component that enables the computation of either an arithmetic return or a logarithmic return. The component service interface and Java implementation, along with the addition to the composite file, are shown below.

```
1 @Remotable
2 public interface StockReturn {
3   public double computeROR(double currentStockPrice,
4     double previousStockPrice, ReturnTypes returnType);
5 }
```

Listing 8.36 Component interface for stock return

```
1 @Service(StockReturn.class)
2 public class StockReturnImpl implements StockReturn {
3 public double computeROR(double currentStockPrice,
4         double previousStockPrice, ReturnTypes returnType) {
5
6   RateOfReturn stockReturn =
7   ReturnFactory.getReturnService(returnType);
8   double stkreturn =
9   stockReturn.computeROR(currentStockPrice, previousStockPrice);
10   return stkreturn;
11   }
12 }
```

Listing 8.37 Component implementation for stock return

The implementation above uses a factory class `ReturnFactory` to support the two types of computational methods for the stock return. The code for these helper classes is provided below:

```
1  //Other Helper classes to compute Stock Return
2  public class ReturnFactory {
3
4    private ReturnFactory() {}
5    public static RateOfReturn getReturnService(ReturnTypes
       criteria) {
6      if ( criteria.equals(ReturnTypes.ARITHMETIC_RETURN))
7            return new ArithmeticReturnImpl();
8      else if ( criteria.equals(ReturnTypes.BIDVOLUME))
9              return new LogReturnImpl();
10     return null;
11   }
12 }
13
14 public class ArithmeticReturnImpl implements RateOfReturn {
15   public double computeROR(double currentStockPrice,
16                      double previousStockPrice) {
17       return
        (currentStockPrice-previousStockPrice)/previousStockPrice;
18   }
19 }
20
21 public class LogReturnImpl implements RateOfReturn  {
22   public double computeROR(double currentStockPrice,
23                      double previousStockPrice) {
24          return (Math.log(currentStockPrice) -
25     Math.log(previousStockPrice))/Math.log(previousStockPrice);
26   }
27 }
```

Listing 8.38   Other Helper classes to compute stock return

```
1  <?xml version="1.0" encoding="UTF-8" standalone="no"?>
2  <composite ... >
3
4  <component name="StockReturnComponent">
5   <implementation.java class=
6   "au.edu.unsw.soacourse.sca.components.impl.StockReturnImpl"/>
7  </component>
8  </composite>
```

Listing 8.39   Updated composite to include the stock return component

Abnormal Return Component The third component that is required is the Abnormal-Return component. This component implements the simple Market Returns model to compute the abnormal return by calculating the difference between the expected return and the actual return. The service interface, Java implementation and changes to the composite file are presented below.

```
1 @Remotable
2 public interface AbnormalReturn {
3
4   public double computeAR(double currentReturn,
5     double expectedReturn,  ReturnTypes returnType);
6
7   public String computeARonStream(InputStream stockData,
8     InputStream     indexData, ReturnTypes returnType);
9 }
```

Listing 8.40 Component interface for abnormal return component

```
1 <?xml version="1.0" encoding="UTF-8" standalone="no"?>
2 <composite ...>
3   <component name="AbnormalReturnComponent">
4     <implementation.java class=
5 "au.edu.unsw.soacourse.sca.components.impl.AbnormalReturnImpl"/>
6   </component>
7 </composite>
```

Listing 8.41 Composite file updated to include the abnormal return component

Daily Abnormal Return Component Finally, we define the `DailyAbnormal` `Return` component that captures the workflow to compute the daily abnormal return. This makes use of other components such as `DailyMarketData`, `Stock` `Return` and `AbnormalReturn`. This component also publishes the functionality to compute the daily abnormal return for any asset as a service, which is promoted as a service on the composite, accessible through a Web service binding. The service interface and implementation are provided below.

```
1 @Remotable
2 public interface DailyAbnormalReturns {
3   public String computeDailyAbnormalReturns(String stockSymbol,
4     DateRange startDate, DateRange endData);
5 }
```

Listing 8.42 Component interface for daily abnormal return component

```
1 @Service(DailyAbnormalReturns.class)
2 public class DailyAbnormalReturnsImpl implements
      DailyAbnormalReturns {
3
4  @Reference
5  DailyMarketData dailyData;
6
7  @Reference
8  AbnormalReturn abnormalReturn;
```

```
9
10  @Override
11  public String computeDailyAbnormalReturns(String stockSymbol,
        DateRange startDate, DateRange endData) {
12
13  //Get Daily Stock Data
14  InputStream stockData =
15    dailyData.getDailyData(stockSymbol, startDate,    endData);
16
17  //Get Index Data
18  InputStream indexData =
19    dailyData.getDailyData("^AORD", startDate,    endData);
20
21  //Compute daily abnormal return
22  return abnormalReturn.computeARonStream(stockData, indexData,
        ReturnTypes.ARITHMETIC_RETURN);
23   }
24 }
```

Listing 8.43 Component implementation for daily abnormal return

```
1 <?xml version="1.0" encoding="UTF-8" standalone="no"?>
2 <composite ...>
3     ......//other component declarations
4   <component name="DailyAbnormalReturnComponent">
5     <implementation.java
6        class="au.edu.unsw.soacourse.sca.components.
7             impl.DailyAbnormalReturnImpl"/>
8   </component>
9 </composite>
```

Listing 8.44 Updated composite definition to include the daily abnormal return component

Creating the Complete SCA Composite

The completed finance.composite containing the DailyAbnormalReturn component along with other dependencies is defined below.

```
1 <?xml version="1.0" encoding="UTF-8" standalone="no"?>
2 <composite
       xmlns="http://docs.oasis-open.org/ns/opencsa/sca/200912"
3  xmlns:t="http://soacourse/scaexamples"
4  xmlns:tuscany="http://tuscany.apache.org/xmlns/sca/1.1"
5  name="finance"
6  targetNamespace="http://soacourse.scaexamples">
7
8 <property name="fromCurrency">AUD</property>
9 <property name="toCurrency">USD</property>
10
```

```
11 <service name="DailyAbnormalReturnService"
12      promote="DailyAbnormalReturnsComponent/DefaultService">
13   <interface.java
14      interface="au.edu.unsw.soacourse.sca.components.
15                                      DailyAbnormalReturn"/>
16   <binding.ws uri="http://localhost:8086/DailyAbnormalReturn"/>
17 </service>
18
19 <service name="StockQuoteService"
20          promote="StockQuoteComponent/StockQuote">
21   <interface.java
22      interface="au.edu.unsw.soacourse.sca.components.StockQuote"/>
23   <binding.ws uri="http://localhost:8085/StockQuoteService"/>
24 </service>
25
26 <component name="DailyAbnormalReturnsComponent">
27   <implementation.java
28      class="au.edu.unsw.soacourse.sca.components.impl.
29                                      DailyAbnormalReturnsImpl"/>
30     <service name="DefaultService"/>
31   <reference name="dailyData"
32                          target="DailyMarketDataComponent"/>
33   <reference name="abnormalReturn"
34                          target="AbnormalReturnComponent"/>
35 </component>
36
37 <component name="AbnormalReturnComponent">
38   <implementation.java
39      class="au.edu.unsw.soacourse.sca.components.impl.
40                                      AbnormalReturnImpl"/>
41 </component>
42
43 <component name="DailyMarketDataComponent">
44   <implementation.java
45      class="au.edu.unsw.soacourse.sca.components.impl.
46                                      DailyMarketDataImpl"/>
47 </component>
48
49 <component name="StockQuoteComponent">
50   <implementation.java
51      class="au.edu.unsw.soacourse.sca.components.impl.
52                                      StockQuoteImpl"/>
53   <service name="StockQuote"/>
54   <reference name="currencyConverter"
55                  target="CurrencyConverterComponent "/>
56 </component>
57
58 <component name="CurrencyConverterComponent">
59   <implementation.java
```

```
60        class="au.edu.unsw.soacourse.sca.components.impl.
61                                        CurrencyConverterImpl"/>
62    <property name="fromCurrency" source="$fromCurrency"/>
63    <property name="toCurrency" source="$toCurrency"/>
64    <service name="CurrencyConverter">
65       <binding.sca/>
66    </service>
67  </component>
68  </composite>
```

Listing 8.45 Creating the complete SCA composite

Chapter 9
Conclusion

As with many Web technologies, there is a plethora of online resources available on the topics discussed in this book. However, we felt that much of the information available seemed disjointed or focused on a particular context or technology such as an implementation language. There are also well-established textbooks that discuss the academic views on Web services as well, but many of them could be conceptual and abstract. When we decided to write this book, we wanted to provide a unique value to the readers in that we would present the topics with a good overview of the concepts, but also link them with practical exercises for hands-on learning.

In particular, we aimed to achieve two goals: First of all, we wanted to introduce the topic of "Web services and compositions" from a broader viewpoint than that of just writing a BPEL program. Based on the years of experience in designing and delivering tertiary-level courses on this topic, we believe we have developed a well-informed view on how to synthesize the concepts in the conventional Web services and "newer" breeds of Web services, what the differences and commonalities are, and where they should be placed in building modern software systems.

Web services should be understood as an abstract design concept that promotes the core idea that when we design a piece of software, we should always have in mind the fact that its main function is to provide "services" to the users, which are likely to be other software systems. This mindset allows the designer to approach the whole software building process as that of "building various access paths" into the functionality of the software, rather than as that of "building a self-contained, enclosed system hidden behind a user interface". This "API" view of the services in a piece of software then can be applied to exposing the functionality at any logical layer of a software system, which could take the form of WS-based implementation, or REST-based implementation, or purely data provision service implementation.

Secondly, we combined the concept overviews in each chapter with practical exercises. These exercises are designed to be self-guided and would provide a good starting point for many Web service building projects. Our aim is to use these practical components of the book and the website as a springboard for creating a suite of various online materials to further support learning activities on the topics.

© Springer International Publishing AG 2017
H.-y. Paik et al., *Web Service Implementation and Composition Techniques*,
DOI 10.1007/978-3-319-55542-3_9

References

1. Allen, P., Frost, S.: Component-Based Development for Enterprise Systems: Applying the SELECT Perspective. Cambridge University Press, Cambridge (1998)
2. Alonso, G., Casati, F., Kuno, H., Machiraju, V.: Web Services. Springer, Berlin (2004)
3. Benatallah, B., Motahari Nezhad, H.R.: Service oriented architecture: overview and directions. In: Börger, E., Cisternino, A. (eds.) Advances in Software Engineering, pp. 116–130. Springer, Berlin (2008)
4. Berardi, D.: Automatic composition services: models, techniques and tools. Ph.D. thesis, Universita degli Studi di Roma-La Sapienza (2005)
5. Boyaci, O., Beltran, V., Schulzrinne, H.: Bridging communications and the physical world: sense everything, control everything. In: 2010 IEEE GLOBECOM Workshops (GC Wkshps), pp. 1735–1740. IEEE (2010)
6. Statistic Brain. Facebook statistics. http://www.statisticbrain.com/facebook-statistics/
7. Burbeck, S.: The tao of e-business services: the evolution of web applications into service-oriented components with web services. Online document, IBM Software Group (2000)
8. Chatterjee, S., Webber, J.: Developing Enterprise Web Services: An Architect's Guide. Prentice Hall, Englewood Cliffs (2006)
9. Curbera, F., Duftler, M., Khalaf, R., Lovell, D.: Bite: Workflow Composition for the Web. Springer, Berlin (2007)
10. Daniel, F., Matera, M.: Mashups - Concepts. Models and Architectures. Data-Centric Systems and Applications. Springer, Berlin (2014)
11. Daniel, F., Matera, M., Yu, J., Benatallah, B., Saint-Paul, R., Casati, F.: Understanding UI integration: a survey of problems, technologies, and opportunities. IEEE Internet Comput. 11(3), 59–66 (2007)
12. Duggan, D.: Service Oriented Architecture: Entities, Services, and Resources. Wiley, New York (2012)
13. Dustdar, S., Schreiner, W.: A survey on web services composition. Int. J. Web Grid Serv. 1(1), 1–30 (2005)
14. Endrei, M., Ang, J., Arsanjani, A., Chua, S., Comte, P., Krogdahl, P., Luo, M., Newling, T.: Patterns: service-oriented architecture and web services. IBM Corporation, International Technical Support Organization (2004)
15. Erl, T.: SOA: Principles of Service Design. Prentice Hall, Englewood Cliffs (2005)
16. Andrews, T., et al.: Business Process Execution Language for Web Services 1.1 (BPEL4WS). Technical Report TUV-1841-2004-16, BEA, IBM, Microsoft, SAP, Siebel (2003)
17. Fielding, R.T.: Architectural styles and the design of network-based software architectures. Ph.D. thesis, University of California (2000)

© Springer International Publishing AG 2017

H.-y. Paik et al., *Web Service Implementation and Composition Techniques*,
DOI 10.1007/978-3-319-55542-3

18. Giza, M.: SOA trends: From microservices to appdev, what to expect in 2015
19. IFTTT. IFTTT – Put the internet to work for you. https://ifttt.com
20. Marconi, A., Pistore, M., Traverso, P.: Implicit vs. explicit data-flow requirements in web service composition goals. In: Dan, A., Lamersdorf, W. (eds.) Service-Oriented Computing– ICSOC 2006, pp. 459–464. Springer, Berlin (2006)
21. Michael Maximilien, E., Ranabahu, A., Gomadam, K.: An online platform for web APIs and service mashups. IEEE Internet Comput. **12**(5), 32–43 (2008)
22. McLarty, M.: A business perspective on APIs. http://www.infoq.com/articles/web-apis-business-perspective
23. Medjahed, B., Benatallah, B., Bouguettaya, A., Ngu, A.H.H., Elmagarmid, A.K.: Business-to-business interactions: issues and enabling technologies. VLDB J. Int. J. Very Large Data Bases **12**(1), 59–85 (2003)
24. Papazoglou, M.: Services: Principles and Technology. Prentice Hall, Englewood Cliffs (2007)
25. Papazoglou, M.P., van den Heuvel, W.-J.: Web services management: a survey. IEEE Internet Comput. **9**(6), 58–64 (2005)
26. Papazoglou, M.P., van den Heuvel, W.-J.: Service oriented architectures: approaches, technologies and research issues. VLDB J. **16**(3), 389–415 (2007)
27. Richardson, L., Ruby, S.: RESTful Web Services. O'Reilly Media Inc, Sebastopol (2008)
28. Silberstein, A., Machanavajjhala, A., Ramakrishnan, R.: Feed following: the big data challenge in social applications. In: Databases and Social Networks, pp. 1–6. ACM (2011)
29. Stamplay. Stamplay | Connect. Automate. Invent. https://stamplay.com
30. BEA Inc. Systems. Domain Model for SOA: Realising the Business Benefit of Service-Oriented Architecture. BEA Inc Systems (2005)
31. TechCrunch. APIs fuel the software that's eating the world. http://techcrunch.com/2015/05/06/apis-fuel-the-software-thats-eating-the-world/
32. van der Aalst, W.M.P.: Business process management demystified: a tutorial on models, systems and standards for workflow management. In: Desel, J., Reisig, W., Rozenberg, G. (eds.) Lectures on Concurrency and Petri Nets, pp. 1–65. Springer, Berlin (2004)
33. van der Aalst, W.M.P., ter Hofstedte, A., Weske, M.: Business process management: a survey. In: van der Aalst, W.M.P., Weske, M. (eds.) Business Process Management, pp. 1–12. Springer, Berlin (2003)
34. Webber, J., Parastatidis, S., Robinson, I.: REST in Practice: Hypermedia and Systems Architecture. O'Reilly Media Inc., Sebastopol (2010)
35. White, B.: The implications of Web 2.0 on Web information systems. In: Filipe, J., Cordeiro, J., Pedrosa, V. (eds.) Web Information Systems and Technologies, pp. 3–7. Springer, Berlin (2007)
36. Ziegler, P., Dittrich, K.R.: Three decades of data integration - all problems solved? In: Jacquart, R. (ed.) Building the Information Society, pp. 3–12. Springer, Berlin (2004)

Index

B

BPEL Data Flow, 194
Business Process Execution Language
   (BPEL), 159, 203
   activities, 161
   language model, 160
   partner link types, 163
   partners, 163
Business Process Model and Notation
   (BPMN), 166
   artifacts, 174
   connecting objects, 172
   flow objects, 171
   language model, 171
   swimlanes, 173

D

Data Access Service, 209
Data as Services, 95, 140
Data flow paradigms, 12, 193
   blackboard, 12, 193
   explicit data flow, 13, 196
Data services, 93

E

EbXML, 203
Enterprise Application Integration (EAI), 6

F

Feed/Stream Services, 11
FLWOR expressions, 133
   conditions, 134
   for and let, 133
   joins, 135

sorting, 134
text match, 138

H

HATEOAS, 75
HTTP content negotiation, 71
HTTP operations, 72, 73
   DELETE, 72
   GET, 72
   POST, 72
   PUT, 72

I

Interoperability, 2

J

JAX-RS specification, 84

M

Mashups Data Flow, 196

R

REST, 10, 67, 93
   addressability, 69
   content negotiation, 71
   HATEOAS, 75
   representations, 71, 75
   resource identification, 68
   resources, 68
   statelessness, 70
   uniform interface, 72
   URI, 69